STUDY GUIDE

for

MACIONIS / GERBER

SOCIOLOGY

SIXTH CANADIAN EDITION

Prepared by

GERALD V. BOOTH
University of Windsor

HEATHER METCALFE
University of Windsor

HENRY BORNE

ABIGAIL E. BORNE

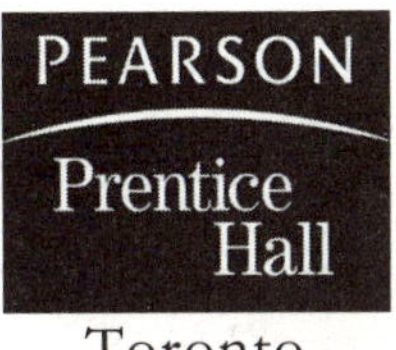

Toronto

Original edition published by Pearson Prentice Hall, a division of Pearson Education, Inc. Upper Saddle River, New Jersey. Copyright © 2008, 2005, 2002, 1999, 1997, 1995. This edition is authorized for sale only in Canada.

ISBN-13: 978-0-13-156358-2
ISBN-10: 0-13-156358-0

Senior Acquisitions Editor: Laura Forbes
Development Editor: Charlotte Morrison-Reed
Executive Marketing Manager: Judith Allen
Production Editor: Richard di Santo
Production Coordinator: Janis Raisen

1 2 3 4 5 2007

CONTENTS

CHAPTER 1

The Sociological Perspective

CHAPTER OUTLINE

I. **The Sociological Perspective**
   - A. Seeing the General in the Particular
   - B. Seeing the Strange in the Familiar
   - C. Seeing Personal Choice in Social Context
   - D. Seeing Sociologically: Marginality and Crisis

II. **The Importance of a Global Perspective**

III. **Applying the Sociological Perspective**
   - A. Sociology and Public Policy
   - B. Sociology and Personal Growth
   - C. Careers: The "Sociology Advantage"

IV. **The Origins of Sociology**
   - A. Social Change and Sociology
     1. A New Industrial Economy
     2. The Growth of Cities
     3. Political Change
     4. A New Awareness of Society
   - B. Science and Sociology
   - C. Canadian Sociology: Distinctive Touches

V. **Sociological Theory**
   - A. The Structural-Functional Approach
   - B. The Social-Conflict Approach
     1. Feminism and the Gender-Conflict Approach
     2. The Race-Conflict Approach
   - C. The Symbolic-Interaction Approach
   - D. The Postmodern Paradigm
   - E. Applying the Approaches: The Sociology of Sports
     1. The Functions of Sports
     2. Sports and Conflict
     3. Sports as Interaction

VI. **Making the Grade**

VII. **Key Points**

VIII. **Key Concepts**

IX. **Applications and Exercises**

X. **MySocLab**

LEARNING OBJECTIVES

- To understand how perspective is shaped and becomes the basis for "reality"
- To be able to define sociology and understand the basic components of the sociological perspective
- To be able to provide examples of the way in which social forces affect our everyday lives
- To understand the significance of the research on suicide done by Emile Durkheim, showing the impact of social forces on individual behaviour
- To comprehend how personal problems can be viewed as social issues
- To recognize more about ourselves as Canadians through global comparisons and to see how Canada fits into the rest of the world
- To understand how the socially marginal and those undergoing social change experience sociological vision
- To recognize how sociological thinking can have an impact upon our daily lives
- To recognize how sociological thinking affects social policy decisions
- To understand how sociological study can be linked to careers
- To be able to identify important historical factors in the development of sociology
- To be able to identify and understand the differences between the three major theoretical approaches used by sociologists
- To understand the challenge of newer approaches to traditional sociological thinking
- To be able to provide illustrative questions raised about society using each of the theoretical approaches
- To be able to differentiate between sociological observations and stereotypical statements
- To be able to apply sociological thinking to areas of everyday activity

CHAPTER REVIEW

Much of the behaviour that people exhibit in society is highly predictable. For the most part people conform to a set of social expectations, whether they are explicitly identified or not. The scenario outlined to begin this chapter illustrates how something as simple as males and females holding hands appears to operate according to a set of unwritten rules. Sociology helps us to comprehend the social forces that influence behaviour patterns.

THE SOCIOLOGICAL PERSPECTIVE

Sociology is defined as the systematic study of human society. Sociology as a discipline is guided by a distinctive perspective. The qualities of this perspective are outlined, with illustrations for each being presented.

Seeing the General in the Particular

Sociologist Peter Berger refers to the fact that sociologists see general social patterns in the behaviour of particular individuals. In fact, each chapter in the text will illustrate how social forces shape our lives. Age, gender, and social class, for example, are seen to have a remarkable impact upon behaviour and life chances. While not erasing our uniqueness as individuals, social forces touch our lives in many unseen, yet significant ways, such as the behaviour of Canadian "peacekeepers" in Somalia who responded to cultural imperatives in the commission of atrocities.

Seeing the Strange in the Familiar

This is the process of detaching oneself from "familiar" individualistic interpretations of human behaviour and the acceptance of the initially "strange" notion that behaviour is a product of social forces.

Students will typically respond to a question about their own attendance at a university in a personal way while, in social reality, factors such as family income, age, and race influence the choice.

Seeing Personal Choice in Social Context

In a society that emphasizes individuality we are often reluctant to admit that our lives are predictable and patterned. The **Window on the World Global Map 1-1** (p. 4 titled "Women's Childbearing in Global Perspective," indicates that the decision to bear children is clearly shaped by social conditions. Even suicide, a seemingly very personal act, can be seen to be affected by social forces. The research by Emile Durkheim on suicide clearly shows how impersonal social forces affect personal behaviour. Records of suicide in central Europe during the last part of the nineteenth century were found by Durkheim to show certain social categories as having higher suicide rates than others. It was found that the degree of ***social integration***, or how strongly a person is bound to others by social ties, had a significant influence on the patterns of suicide rates. **Figure 1-1** (p. 5) provides rates of suicide over time in Canada for males and females, and

Figure 1-2 (p. 5) demonstrates that the rates of suicide also vary by age in Canada.

Seeing Sociologically: Marginality and Crisis

Social marginality or being an "outsider" enhances sociological thinking. Women, gay people, visible minorities, and the very old are aware of social patterns others rarely think about. As well, social crisis can lead to a "sociological imagination." C. Wright Mills shows how people experiencing the Great Depression in the 1930s came to understand their loss of job as less a personal problem than a public issue. The **Thinking Critically Box** (p. 7) explores his thinking.

THE IMPORTANCE OF A GLOBAL PERSPECTIVE

Although many academic disciplines have incorporated a global perspective, such an inclusion is especially important to the sociological perspective because our basic understanding is that where we are placed within some social construct (including global constraints) shapes our experiences as people. Comparative data indicate that Canada is a very wealthy nation where most people enjoy material abundance. In fact, **Table 1-1** (p. 10) shows Canada as one of the best places to live in the world, according to the United Nations' Human Development Index. Although many of our citizens experience relative poverty, it is not the abject poverty felt by most of the globe's peoples. The **Thinking Globally Box,** "The Global Village: A Social Snapshot of Our World" (p. 9), indicates the nature of international distribution of income, food, and education. Quite clearly, globalization has led to increasing interconnectedness, which has enabled us to see ourselves and examine ourselves and perhaps learn more about ourselves in the light of other nation's experiences.

APPLYING THE SOCIOLOGICAL PERSPECTIVE

Sociology is useful for guiding public policy and expanding social awareness.

Sociology and Public Policy

Much of Canadian social policy in such areas as medicare, bilingualism, the status of women, and Aboriginal peoples has been influenced by sociological thinking.

Sociology and Personal Growth

Four general benefits of using the sociological perspective are identified. They include the following:

1. It challenges familiar understandings about ourselves and others, so that we can critically assess the truth of commonly held assumptions.
2. It allows us to recognize both opportunities we have and the constraints that circumscribe our lives.

3. It empowers us as active members of our world through the grasp of our "sociological imagination," thc capacity to comprehend the interplay between personal life and societal forces.
4. It helps us to recognize human diversity and to begin to understand the challenges of living in a diverse world.

Careers: The "Sociology Advantage"

Many jobs in the public and private sectors require thinking that identifies how various categories of people will respond to a variety of circumstances. The physician, the police officer, or the lawyer, for example, will be helped to make good decisions by a sociological perspective.

THE ORIGINS OF SOCIOLOGY

Powerful social forces led to the development of sociology.

Social Change and Sociology

Four key factors are identified as reshaping society during the seventeenth and eighteenth centuries. These include the following:

➢A New Industrial Economy

Rapid technological changes of the eighteenth century brought people in great numbers to work in factories, thus breaking down established patterns of social life.

➢The Growth of Cities

As factories spread across Europe, drawing people out of the countryside seeking employment due to the changing nature of the economy, this massive influx of people into cities created many social problems. The crises that emerged stimulated the development of the sociological perspective.

➢Political Change

The rapid economic and urban growth created a context for change in political thinking. Traditional notions of divine law were being replaced by ideas of individual liberty and freedom. Such rights are now enshrined in the Canadian Charter of Rights and Freedoms.

➢A New Awareness of Society

The huge changes in economic, social, and political life led to a new awareness of the importance of social forces and sociology is born.

Science and Sociology

This new way of looking at society was coined "sociology" by the French social thinker Auguste Comte in 1838. While Comte certainly wasn't the first person to think about society, he was among the first to be concerned about the reality of society rather than the ideal. The key to achieving this understanding was to use the scientific approach. He divided the history of society into three distinct eras, which he labelled the ***theological,*** the ***metaphysical***, and the ***scientific***. The latter he called ***positivism***, a way of understanding the world based on science. Even today, most sociologists in North America accept the importance of the scientific perspective, but there is a recognition that human behaviour may never conform to the rigid "laws of society" and many contemporary sociologists think, like Karl Marx, that the discipline should be used to improve social conditions in society.

Canadian Sociology: Distinctive Touches

Sociology began in Canada and the United States in the early part of the twentieth century, but the traditions differ because of Canada's two major cultures and linguistic communities. A European influence was historically obvious in both French Canadian sociology and the University of Toronto, where the focus was on political and economic issues, while at McGill the American approach to social problems and community studies was in evidence. The works of Harold Innis on Canadian economic development, Marshall McLuhan on the impact of electronic communications, and John Porter on inequality are noted for their influence on Canadian sociology. The **Media Perspectives Box** (p. 16) visits McLuhan's observation that content is often less important than the medium that delivers it: "The medium is the message."

SOCIOLOGICAL THEORY

While the sociological perspective provides us with a unique vantage point from which to observe our social world, theory helps us to meaningfully organize and explain the linkages among the specific observations we make. A ***theory*** is a statement of how and why specific facts are related. There are a number of research methods available to researchers that are used to evaluate whether a theory is supported by facts. The basis upon which sociologists choose to study particular issues is a "road map" or ***theoretical approach,*** *"a basic image of society that guides thinking and research."*

There are three major theoretical approaches used by sociologists. Each theory focuses the researcher's attention on particular types of questions about how society is organized, and each provides a different explanation about why certain patterns are found in society.

The Structural-Functional Approach

This approach is a framework for building theory guided by the assumption that society is a complex system whose parts work together to promote stability. The two basic components of this approach are ***social structure***, or relatively stable patterns of behaviour, and ***social functions,*** which refer to consequences for the operation of society as a whole. Structural functionalists often liken society to the human body, with different parts of society being interdependent, much like the various organs of the body. Early structural-functionalists included Herbert Spencer, Durkheim, and Comte. As sociology developed in the United States during the twentieth century, researcher Robert K. Merton further applied and developed the thinking of these early social scientists. Merton differentiated between what he called ***manifest functions***, or consequences of social structure recognized by people within a society, and ***latent functions***, which are unrecognized or unintended consequences of social structure. Merton further points out that elements of social structure may be functional for one aspect of society and not for others. There may be undesirable effects on the operation of society, or ***social dysfunctions***. In critically evaluating this approach, it is pointed out that it is a conservative approach to the study of society that tends to ignore tension and conflict in social systems often brought about by inequalities based upon social class, race, ethnicity, and gender.

The Social-Conflict Approach

This approach is a framework for building theory based on the assumption that society is a complex system characterized by inequality and conflict that generate social change. Power and privilege are distributed unequally by social class, race, gender, sexual orientation, and age and often these inequalities are reinforced in various societal institutions such as education. "Streaming" (the placement of students in academic and non-academic programs), for example, often has less to do with talent than social background.

Karl Marx, the major proponent of this approach, sought not only to understand society but also to change it for the better.

➢Feminism and the Gender-Conflict Approach

The gender-conflict approach is a point of view that focuses on inequality and conflict between women and men. This approach is linked to "feminism," which demonstrates the multiple ways in which men are in positions of power over women.

This approach also illuminates the contributions of women to the development of sociology through the works of Harriet Martineau in England and Jane Addams in the United States. Feminist sociology has also critiques the theories and methodologies developed by males.

➢The Race-Conflict Approach

This approach focuses upon inequality and conflict among people of different racial and ethnic categories. White people are found to have extensive advantages over visible minority people. The work of W.E.B. Dubois is notable in the United States for its efforts to improve the lot of the Black Community, and Canadian sociology is characterized by extensive work on the position of visible minority people in Canadian society.

Critics of the social-conflict approach suggest it ignores evidence of social unity and compromises objectivity in its pursuit of political goals.

The Symbolic-Interaction Approach

The first two approaches discussed focus on a ***macro-level*** orientation, meaning a concern with large-scale patterns that characterize society as a whole. An alternative approach is to take a ***micro-level orientation***, meaning a concern with small- scale patterns of social interaction in specific settings. This third approach, ***symbolic interactionism***, is a theoretical framework based on the assumption that society is continuously recreated as human beings construct reality through interaction. The symbolic-interactionist approach was greatly influenced by the work of Max Weber, a German sociologist of the late nineteenth and early twentieth centuries. In the United States, during the twentieth century, the work of George Herbert Mead, Erving Goffman, George Homans, and Peter Blau were instrumental in the development of this approach. Mead's work on socialization, Goffman's work on ***dramaturgical analysis*** and Homans's and Blau's development of ***social-exchange analysis*** are discussed in later chapters.

In critically analyzing this view, it must be stressed that the focus is on how individuals personally experience society. This approach does not allow us to examine the impact of larger social structures on people's lives.

The Postmodern Paradigm

Postmodernism rejects the usual theories and methods of social science because objective truth cannot be discovered due to human subjectivity. Postmodernists attempt to uncover the assumptions and ideological motivations of the social scientists through deconstruction of existing text. Michel Foucault, perhaps the most influential postmodernist, suggests that power permeates all of society.

Each of the approaches provides a unique perspective for the development of greater understanding of society. The **Applying Theory Box** (p. 21) reviews the level of analysis, image of society, and illustrative questions representative of each of the three classical theoretical approaches and the two recent ones.

Applying the Perspectives: The Sociology of Sports

Sports in North America are discussed as a large and important part of social life. The question becomes what insights can the sociological perspective provide us concerning sports?

➢The Functions of Sports

The structural-functional approach reveals many functional and dysfunctional consequences that sports have for society. Sports, for example, promote the pursuit of success, but university student athletes are often primarily athletes and secondarily students.

➢Sports and Conflict

The social-conflict approach provides an analysis of sports focusing upon the social inequalities within sports at all levels of competition. Male and female inequalities are addressed, as well as racial inequalities in professional sports. **Figure 1–3** (p. 22) reveals that professional football players are allocated positions based on race. It is observed, however, that more and more minority athletes are achieving immense success.

➢**Sports as Interaction**

The symbolic-interactionists view sports as ongoing processes and not merely as a "system." The individual perceptions of specific participants concerning the reality, as each experiences it, become the focus.

No one approach is better than another in analyzing sports, or any other aspect of society. The sociological perspective is enriched by the controversy and debate brought about through the application in research of these different approaches.

Reining in the Cowboys in Outer Space

The **Applying Sociology Box** (p. 12) discusses the problematic relationships between people of divergent cultures in a 110-day simulated space mission. In the absence of naturally emergent norms, planners for space stations will be required to devise workable codes of conduct.

Sociology: Nothing More Than Stereotypes?

The **Thinking It Through Box** (p. 23) indicates that while sociology employs generalizations, these are more than simple stereotypes applied unfairly to whole categories of people. Sociological statements are not applied indiscriminately to all individuals in a category; they are supported by facts, and they are stated within a framework of fair-minded pursuit of the truth.

KEY CONCEPTS

Define each of the following concepts on a separate sheet of paper. Check the accuracy of your answers by referring to the key concepts in the text, as well as by referring to italicized definitions located throughout the chapter.

gender-conflict approach
global perspective
feminist approach
high-income countries
latent functions
low-income countries
macro-level orientation
manifest functions
metaphysical stage
micro-level orientation
middle-income countries
positivism
postmodernism
race-conflict approach
scientific stage
seeing personal choice in social context
seeing the general in the particular
seeing the strange in the familiar
social-conflict approach
social dysfunctions
social functions
social structure

sociological imagination
sociology
stereotype
structural-functional approach
symbolic-interaction approach
theological stage
theoretical approach
theory

STUDY QUESTIONS

 **True-False**

1. T F Knowledge of social forces allows sociologists to understand and predict the behaviour of individuals, groups, or categories of people.

2. T F In general, people from rich countries have more children than people from poor countries.

3. T F Durkheim suggested that categories of people with weak social ties will have high suicide rates.

4. T F C. Wright Mills's concept of "sociological imagination" focuses upon individuals recognizing their own contribution to life's failures.

5. T F Although sociology promotes intellectual growth, it has had little impact on social policy in Canada.

6. T F Sociology flowered in societies where change was greatest.

7. T F Marx wanted the new discipline of sociology to change society, not simply understand it.

8. T F Manifest functions are consequences that are largely unrecognized and unintended.

9. T F Placement of students into academic streams is based solely on their academic abilities.

10. T F Racial and ethnic diversity have never been dominant themes in Canadian sociology.

✎ Multiple Choice

1. While we usually think of postsecondary education as a personal choice, which of the following are social factors that influence that choice?

   (a) age
   (b) family income
   (c) race
   (d) all of the above
   (e) none of the above

2. Which of the following are accurate representations of suicide rates in Canada?

   (a) Male rates are higher than female rates.
   (b) Female rates are higher than male rates.
   (c) Male rates are highest at age 20-24.
   (d) Female rates are highest at age 55-59.
   (e) None of the above is accurate.

3. According to the United Nations' Human Development Index, what country in 2005 was judged to be the best country in the world to live?

   (a) Canada
   (b) United States
   (c) Netherlands
   (d) Belgium
   (e) Norway

4. Because of the current cost-conscious political climate, many sociologists find work in _______________.

   (a) banking
   (b) evaluation research
   (c) teaching
   (d) the criminal justice system
   (e) journalism

5. Which of the following was (were) important to the development of sociology?

   (a) large rural populations
   (b) a large agricultural sector
   (c) new political ideas
   (d) all of the above
   (e) none of the above

6. The Canadian sociologist best known for his work on inequality and elites was __________________.

   (a) John Porter
   (b) Harold Innis
   (c) Marshall McLuhan
   (d) Erving Goffman
   (e) Peter Berger

7. __________ are the unrecognized and unintended consequences of any social pattern.

   (a) Manifest functions
   (b) Latent functions
   (c) Social dysfunctions
   (d) Conflict functions
   (e) (none of the above)

8. Which of the following people is regarded as the first woman sociologist?

   (a) Jane Addams
   (b) W.E.B. Dubois
   (c) Harriet Martineau
   (d) Metta Spencer
   (e) Madeline Smith

9. Sociologists who view society as a mosaic of subjective meanings and variable responses are guided by the __________________________.

   (a) conflict approach
   (b) symbolic-interaction approach
   (c) social Darwinism
   (d) structural-functional approach
   (e) (none of the above)

10. The approach that suggests that the social sciences cannot be scientific is the __________ approach.

    (a) symbolic-interaction
    (b) structural-functional
    (c) postmodernist
    (d) feminist
    (e) social conflict

Fill in the Blank

1. The systematic study of human society is the general definition for ____________ .

2. We begin to think sociologically, according to Berger, when we see the _______________ in the _____________.

3. C. Wright Mills suggested that times of ___________ foster widespread sociological thinking.

4. In the global village of 1000 people, ______________ are citizens of China.

5. The development of sociology as an academic discipline was shaped within the context of three revolutionary changes in Europe during the seventeenth and eighteenth centuries. These included ________________ , __________________ , and ____________ .

6. Auguste Comte asserted that scientific sociology was a result of a progression throughout history of thought and understanding in three stages, the ____________ , ______________, and _________________.

7. The first person of colour to receive a doctorate from Harvard was ______________.

8. The symbolic-interaction approach has its roots in the thinking of __________.

9. "Our society encourages men to be athletes and women to be cheerleaders." This statement represents a __________approach to the analysis of sports.

10. An exaggerated generalization that one applies to all people in a given category is called a ___________________.

Definition and Short Answer

1. Using the perspective of a sociologist, explain how individuals come to study at universities.

2. Discuss Emile Durkheim's explanation of how suicide rates vary between different categories of people. Explain how this research demonstrates the application of the sociological perspective.

3. Of what value is global awareness to sociological thinking?

4. What three key societal changes during the seventeenth and eighteenth centuries were significant for the emergence of sociology as a scientific discipline?

5. How is Canadian sociology distinct from American sociology?

6. What are the four basic benefits of using the sociological perspective?

7. What are the three major theoretical approaches used by sociologists? Identify the key questions raised by each.

8. Discuss the advantages and disadvantages of adopting a micro-level orientation rather than a macro-level orientation.

9. Discuss the contributions to sociology made by the following theorists: Robert K. Merton, Karl Marx, and Emile Durkheim.

10. Discuss how the various sociological theoretical approaches apply to an analysis of sports.

Answers to Study Questions

True-False

1. T (p. 2)
2. F (p. 3)
3. T (p. 5)
4. F (p. 7)
5. F (p. 9)
6. T (p. 13)
7. T (p. 13)
8. F (p. 15)
9. F (p. 17)
10. F (p. 18)

Multiple Choice

1. d (p. 4)
2. a (p. 5)
3. e (p. 10)
4. b (p. 10)
5. c (p. 12)
6. a (p. 14)
7. b (p. 15)
8. c (p. 17)
9. b (pp. 18-19)
10. c (p. 19)

Fill in the Blank

1. sociology (p. 2)
2. general, particular (p. 2)
3. social crisis (p. 6)
4. 200 (p. 9)
5. rise of the industrial economy, growth of cities, and new ideas about democracy and politics (p. 11)
6. theological, metaphysical, and scientific (p.13)
7. W.E.B. Dubois (p. 18)
8. Max Weber (p. 19)
9. social conflict (p. 20)
10. stereotype (p. 23)

ANALYSIS AND COMMENT

Go back through the chapter and write down in the spaces below key points from each of the following boxes.

THINKING CRITICALLY

"The Sociological Imagination: Turning Personal Problems into Public Issues"
Key points:

THINKING GLOBALLY

"The Global Village: A Social Snapshot of Our World"
Key points:

APPLYING SOCIOLOGY

"Reining in the Cowboys in Outer Space"
Key Points:

MEDIA PERSPECTIVES

"Marshall McLuhan: Media Theorist"
Key points:

____
____
____
____
____
____

THINKING IT THROUGH

"Is Sociology Nothing More Than Stereotypes?"
Key Points:

____
____
____
____
____
____

SUGGESTED READINGS

Classic Sources

C. Wright Mills. 1959. *The Sociological Imagination*. New York: Oxford University Press.
This classic elaborates on the benefits of learning to think sociologically and links this perspective to the possibilities for social activism.

Peter Berger. 1963. *An Invitation to Sociology*. Garden City, NY: Anchor Books.
Berger's classic account of the sociological perspective highlights its value for enhancing human freedom.

Contemporary Sources

Lynn McDonald. 1994a. *The Early Origins of the Social Sciences*. Montreal: McGill-Queen's University Press;
Lynn McDonald. 1994b. *The Women Founders of the Social Sciences*. Ottawa: Carleton University Press.
These books discuss the history of sociology.

Janet Mancini Billson and Bettina J. Huber. 1993. *Embarking Upon a Career with an Undergraduate Degree in Sociology*. 2nd ed. Washington, DC: American Sociological Association.
This publication is available for.$8.50 (U.S.) from the American Sociological Association, 1722 N Street N.W., Washington, D.C. 20036; (202) 833-3410.

Mary O'Brien. 1981. *The Politics of Reproduction*. London: Routledge and Kegan Paul.
Meg Luxton. 1981. *More Than a Labour of Love*. Toronto: Women's Press.
Dorothy Smith. 1987. *The Everyday World as Problematic*. Toronto: University of Toronto Press.
All written by three Canadian feminist sociologists.

Canadian Sources

Ann Hall, *et al*. 1991. *Sport in Canadian Society*. Toronto: McClelland and Stewart.
Helen Lenskyj. 1986. *Out of Bounds: Women, Sport, and Sexuality*. Toronto: Women's Press.
Barry D. McPherson, *et al*. 1989. *The Social Significance of Sport: An Introduction to the Sociology of Sport*. Champaign, IL: Human Kinetics Books.
These books provide a sociological analysis of sports.

Everett Hughes. 1943. *French Canada in Transition*. Chicago: University of Chicago Press.
S.D. Clark. 1966. *The Suburban Society*. Toronto: University of Toronto Press.
These books examine aspects of Canadian society from a structural-functional perspective.

John Porter. 1968. *The Vertical Mosaic: An Analysis of Class and Power in Canada*. Toronto: University of Toronto Press.
This classic book looks at Canada from a social-conflict or political economy perspective.

Marlene Shore. 1987. *The Science of Social Redemption: McGill, the Chicago School, and the Origins of Social Research in Canada*. Toronto: University of Toronto Press.
Robert J. Brym and Bonnie J. Fox. 1989. *From Culture to Power: The Sociology of English Canada*. Don Mills, ON: Oxford University Press.
Harry H. Hiller. 1987. *Society and Change: S.D. Clark and the Development of Canadian Sociology*. Toronto: University of Toronto Press.
These three books provide an introductory overview of the history of sociology in Canada.

Rex Lucas. 1971. *Minetown, Milltown, Railtown: Life in Canadian Communities of Single Industry*. Toronto: University of Toronto Press.
W. Shaffir. 1974. *Life in a Religious Community: The Lubavitcher Chassidim in Montreal*. Toronto: Holt, Rinehart, and Winston.
These books provide some examples of sociology done from a symbolic-interaction perspective.

Roy Turner, ed. 1974. *Ethnomethodology: Selected Readings*. Harmondsworth, UK: Penguin.
This book is a good introduction to ethnomethodology.

Elliott Layton. 1986. *Hunting Humans: The Rise of the Modern Multiple Murderer*. Toronto: McClelland and Stewart.
An analysis of multiple murderers.

Global Sources

Mike Featherstone. 1991. *Global Culture: Nationalism, Globalization, and Modernity*. Newbury Park, CA: Sage.
Roland Robertson. 1992. *Globalization: Social Theory and Global Culture*. Newbury Park, CA: Sage.
These two books provide a sophisticated overview of the process of globalization. The first, a collection of two dozen essays, explains the importance of global thinking to members of our society. The second offers one analyst's reflections on the meanings of globalization for our society as well as for sociology.

CHAPTER 2

Sociological Investigation

CHAPTER OUTLINE

I. **Basics of Sociological Investigation**
   A. Science as One Form of Truth
   B. Common Sense versus Scientific Evidence
II. **Three Ways To Do Sociology**
   A. Scientific Sociology
      1. Concepts, Variables, and Measurement
      2. The Ideal of Objectivity
      3. Some Limitations of Scientific Sociology
   B. Interpretive Sociology
   C. Critical Sociology
      1. The Importance of Change   2. Sociology as Politics
   D. Methods and Theory
   E. Gender and Research
   F. Women as Methodologists
   G. Research Ethics
III. **Methods of Sociological Research**
   A. Testing a Hypothesis: The Experiment
      1. The Hawthorne Effect
      2. An Illustration: The Stanford County Prison
   B. Asking Questions: Survey Research
      1. Population and Sample
      2. Using Questionnaires
      3. Conducting Interviews
      4. Illustration of Survey Research: The Case of Anti-Semitism in Quebec
   C. In the Field: Participant Observation
      1. Illustration of Participant Observation: *Street Corner Society*
   D. Using Available Data: Secondary and Historical Analysis
      1. Content Analysis
   E. Technology and Research
   F. The Interplay of Theory and Method
IV. **Putting It All Together: Ten Steps in Sociological Investigation**
V. **Making the Grade**
VI **Key Points**
VI. **Key Concepts**
VII. **Applications And Exercises**
VIII. **MySocLab**

LEARNING OBJECTIVES

- To understand the requirements fundamental to using sociological investigation
- To understand how the different ways of knowing facts affect what is considered "true"
- To become familiar with the basic elements of science and how they are used in sociological investigation namely concepts, variables, measurement, and relationships between variables
- To understand the three ways to do sociology
- To understand scientific sociology or positivism
- To recognize the importance of interpretive sociology, which focuses on the meanings people attach to their social world
- To understand critical sociology where the focus is on the need to change society, not simply to study it
- To recognize the advantages and limitations in the three ways to do sociology
- To understand the origins of special efforts to investigate the lives of women and the perspectives that have been used in those efforts
- To begin to view ethical considerations involved when studying people
- To become familiar with the major research methods used by sociologists, and to be able to compare and contrast the various procedures involved in each
- To be able to discuss the relative advantages and disadvantages for each of the different research methods
- To be able to correctly read a table
- To be able to discuss each of the examples of sociological research provided in the text, including research design used, variables identified and studied, findings, and interpretations
- To be able to recognize how technology has had an impact on research methodology
- To be able to relate theory and method
- To be able to identify and describe each of the ten steps in carrying out a research project using sociological investigation.

CHAPTER REVIEW

In the opening scenario, students gather data from federal ridings in order to comprehend voting behaviour in Canada. But this is only one example of the process of sociological investigation that can vary from information gathered from questionnaires, to participation in groups one wishes to understand. Research can strive to be "objective" or offer a prescription for change. **Table 2-1** (p. 29) shows the usefulness of questionnaire data for evaluating the impact of body piercing and tattoos on teenagers' self-image and behavioural values.

BASICS OF SOCIOLOGICAL INVESTIGATION

There are two basic requirements identified as underlying sociological investigation:

1. Look at the world using the sociological perspective.
2. Be curious and ask questions.

A fundamental issue being raised in this chapter concerns how we recognize information as being true. The requirements identified above are only the beginning of learning about the process of studying society using sociology. The focus now is on how sociologists find answers to questions about society.

Science as One Form of Truth

How do we come to know something to be true? Four ways of knowing are identified. These include faith, recognition of expertise, agreement through consensus, and science. ***Science*** is the basis of most sociological investigation, and is defined as a logical system that bases knowledge on direct, systematic observation. Science is based on ***empirical evidence***, meaning evidence that we can verify using our senses.

Common Sense versus Scientific Evidence

Six common sense statements considered to be true by many Canadians are identified in the text, but scientific evidence is presented that contradicts these "truths." The accuracy of the statement that most poor people do not want to work is seriously questioned by empirical evidence, for example. The majority of the poor in Canada are children, single-parent mothers, or the aged.

As a scientific discipline, sociology can provide us with a framework to critically evaluate the many kinds of information we are exposed to, and enable us to more systematically consider the assumptions we are making about social life.

THREE WAYS TO DO SOCIOLOGY

All sociology attempts to learn more about the social world but there are three different methodological orientations: scientific sociology, interpretive sociology, and critical sociology.

Scientific Sociology

Scientific sociology is the study of society based on systematic observation of social behaviour and is referred to as positivism, which assumes that an objective reality exists.

➢Concepts, Variables, and Measurement

Sociologists use concepts to identify elements of society. A ***concept*** is a mental construct that represents a part of the world, inevitably in a somewhat simplified form. For example, terms like family, society, and social class are concepts sociologists use to help orient us to our social world. A ***variable*** is a concept whose value changes from case to case. For example, social class varies with some people being identified as middle class and others as working class, etc. ***Measurement*** is the process of determining the value of a variable in a specific case. Sociological variables, however, can be measured in many different ways, leaving the measurement developed somewhat arbitrary. Social class, for example, might be measured by income, education, occupation, or all three, and in a multicultural society like Canada, the measurement of race and ethnicity is complex.

Since sociologists collect data on thousands or even millions of people, they make use of statistical measures such as averages to simplify the description.

Operationalzing a variable means to specify exactly what is to be measured in assigning a value to a variable. As mentioned earlier, social class can be measured using education, income, occupation, or any combination.

Careful and specific operationalization is critical, but there are two other important issues concerning the measurement of variables to be considered. First, there is the issue of ***reliability***, or the quality of consistency in measurement. For example, does a person taking several different math achievement tests score equivalently on each? If not, one or more of the tests are not reliable. The second issue is that of ***validity***, or the quality of measuring precisely what one intends to measure. The question here is, is the measurement device really measuring what it purports to measure? For example, are math tests truly measuring math skills and knowledge, or are they possibly measuring some other quality in a person, like obedience to rules?

Sociological investigation enables researchers to identify ***cause-and-effect*** relationships among variables. In cause-and-effect relationships we are saying one variable ***(independent)*** causes a change or effect in another variable ***(dependent)***. Determining real cause and effect is a difficult and complex process. While variables may be ***correlated***, meaning that two or more variables are related or change together in some way, it does not necessarily mean that one causes the change in the other(s). The concept ***spurious correlation*** refers to an apparent, although false, association between two (or more) variables caused by some other variable. **Figure 2-1** (p. 32) outlines an example using the variables population density, income level, and juvenile delinquency.

Using scientific ***control***, the ability to neutralize the effect of one variable in order to assess the relationships among other variables, researchers can check for spuriousness.

To conclude that a cause-and-effect relationship exists, at least three conditions must be established:

1. A correlation exists between the variables.
2. The independent variable precedes the dependent variable in time.

3. No evidence exists that a third variable is responsible for a spurious correlation between the two variables.

➢The Ideal of Objectivity

Scientific researchers make every effort to neutralize their personal biases and values. Complete neutrality ***(objectivity)*** is seen as an ideal rather than as a reality in science, and is defined as a state of personal neutrality in conducting research. Max Weber argued that research may be ***value-relevant,*** or of personal interest to the researcher, but the actual process of doing the research must be ***value-free***. One way biases are controlled is through ***replication***, or repetition of research by others in order to assess its accuracy. Although there are no guarantees of objectivity, the process of research does offer the probability of self-correction of bias.

➢Some Limitations of Scientific Sociology

In the application of the logic of science to our social world several important limitations must be recognized:

1. Sociologists can rarely make precise determinations of cause and effect because of the complexity of human behaviour.
2. The presence of the researcher can affect the behaviour of the people being studied.
3. Social patterns are constantly changing over place and time.
4. Objectivity is very difficult because sociologists are themselves part of the social world they are studying.

Interpretive Sociology

Interpretive sociology doesn't just record behaviour, it attempts to determine the meanings actors attach to their behaviour and the behaviour of others. Weber's concept of ***verstehen*** or "understanding" provides the foundation for interpretive sociology where reality is seen as something constructed by people and where qualitative information gathered in interaction with people allows us to best understand how they make sense of their everyday world.

Critical Sociology

Critical sociology rejects the notion of value freedom and suggests that all research is value-driven or political. Like Karl Marx, the founder of critical theory, contemporary critical theorists attempt to change the social world in the direction of democracy and social justice.

Methods and Theory

The **Summing Up Table** (p. 36) describes how the scientific, interpretive, and critical ways of doing sociology are attached to the major theoretical approaches.

Gender and Research

Values associated with gender influence research. Dangers to sound research that involve gender include androcentricity, overgeneralizing, gender blindness, double-standards, and interference.

Women as Methodologists

Feminist scholars suggest that special efforts must be made to study women's condition in society, recognizing explicitly their usual position of subordination to men. They reject Weber's value-free orientation and suggest that mainstream methodology is simply supportive of patriarchy. Some even argue that mainstream methodology is "malestream" methodology that must be transformed to allow a more sympathetic understanding of subjects' behaviour. Feminists are concerned to allow the subjects of research to participate in agenda establishment.

Such an approach is seen by conventional sociologists as more politics than science and Lynn McDonald, in a recent analysis of the role of women in the early development of sociology, suggests that feminists are missing much of what women have contributed to research methodology. Harriet Martineau and Florence Nightingale were conducting sophisticated research in the 1800s, a time when few men, except Durkheim, were actually gathering empirical data.

The **Applying Sociology Box** (p. 38) examines the works of Dorothy Smith, Meg Luxton, and Susan Wendell as critical and interpretive examples of how women's lives are ordered within a capitalist and patriarchal society. Smith illustrates how farm women's lives changed as the farm moved to cash production and their labours only benefitted their husband-owners, especially at the time of divorce, when they were unable to claim any portion of the farm property. Luxton's research demonstrates how women's and children's lives in a single industry town revolve around the needs of the husband/father in relation to his employment. Wendell shows how disabled women are marginalized in a society that idealizes strong bodies and personal independence. None of these studies is concerned with objective operationalization of concepts, but rather with subjective interpretation of exploitation and injustice with a view towards equitable change.

Research Ethics

Yet another issue concerns how research affects the people being studied. The American Sociological Association and various Canadian funding agencies have a set of formal guidelines for the conduct of social research, including technical competence, fair-mindedness, disclosure of findings, safety and privacy for subjects, accurate presentation, and disclosure of the sources of support. Generally speaking, researchers will obtain informal consent and carefully think through their responsibility to protect subjects from harm. The **Thinking About Diversity Box** (p. 40) indicates the guidelines for research established for the Royal Commission on Aboriginal Peoples whose mandate was to do extensive research and establish baseline data on Aboriginal life in Canada. The guidelines are concerned primarily with the protection of community interests.

METHODS OF SOCIOLOGICAL RESEARCH

A ***research method*** is defined as a systematic plan for conducting research. Four of the most commonly used methods are introduced, each with particular strengths and weaknesses for the study of social life.

Testing a Hypothesis: The Experiment

Experiments study cause-and-effect relationships under highly controlled conditions. This type of research tends to be explanatory. Experiments are typically designed to test a specific ***hypothesis***, or an unverified statement of a relationship between variables. The ideal experiment involves four steps leading to the acceptance or rejection of the hypothesis. The four steps are specification of the independent and dependent variables, measurement of the dependent variable, exposure of the dependent variable to the independent variable, and re-measurement of the dependent variable. The separation of subjects into ***control*** and ***experimental*** groups is a powerful technique of control.

➢The Hawthorne Effect

The issue of the awareness of subjects being studied and how this affects their behaviour is important. Distortion in research caused by such awareness is called the ***Hawthorne effect***, so labelled after a company in which an experiment was done on work productivity, and behaviour changed simply because of experimenter attention rather than the introduction of the experimental variable.

➢Illustration of an Experiment: The Stanford County Prison

Philip Zimbardo's classic study focuses on the structural conditions in prisons. The hypothesis being tested was that the character of prison itself, and not the personalities of the prisoners or guards, is the cause of prison violence. Twenty-four volunteers, deemed to be physically and emotionally healthy, were divided into two groups, prisoners and guards, and participated in this mock prison experiment that was scheduled to run for two weeks. Because of the stress created and the inhumane behaviour produced, the experiment had to be cancelled within a week.

Asking Questions: Survey Research

A ***survey*** is a research method in which subjects respond to a series of statements or questions in a questionnaire or interview. It is the most widely used of the research methods. Surveys can be used to do explanatory research, but are most useful for descriptive research, or research focusing on subjects' descriptions of themselves or some social setting.

➢Population and Sample

A ***population*** is defined as the people who are the focus of research. Generally, contacting all members of a population is impossible, so samples are taken from the population to be studied. ***Samples*** are a part of a population selected to represent the whole.

The most critical issue concerns how a researcher knows the sample truly is representative of the population, meaning, does the sample reflect the qualities present in the population? ***Random selection*** techniques are used to help ensure the probability that inferences made from the results of the sample actually do reflect the nature of the population as a whole.

➢Using Questionnaires

Selection of the subjects is only one step in a survey. Another step requires the researcher to develop a specific plan for asking questions and recording answers.

A ***questionnaire*** is a series of questions presented to subjects. Two basic types of questions are ***open-ended*** and ***closed-ended*** formats. Generally, surveys are mailed to subjects who are asked to complete a form and return it. This technique is called a self-administered survey. A low response rate renders this technique problematic.

➢Conducting Interviews

An ***interview*** is a series of questions administered personally by a researcher to respondents. This strategy has advantages, including more depth and high rates of completion, but also involves the disadvantages of extra time and expense, and the influence of the researcher's presence on the subjects' responses.

For both questionnaires and interviews, how the questions are asked is extremely important; poor questions will lead to poor research results and conclusions.

➢Illustration of Survey Research: The Case of Anti-Semitism in Quebec

Paul Sniderman, *et al.* used an existing survey to test the hypothesis that French Canadians are more anti-Semitic than English Canadians. The authors find evidence to support the hypothesis but note that most Québéecois, as is the case with other Canadians, are not anti-Semitic.

In the Field: Participant Observation

Participant observation is a method in which researchers systematically observe people while joining in their routine activities. The approach is very common among cultural anthropologists who use ***fieldwork*** as the principal method to gather data in the form of ***ethnographies***. Sociologists refer to the same activities as the ***case-study*** approach when doing exploratory research. This is a very valuable approach when there is not a well-defined understanding of the social patterns being investigated.

Participant observation has two sides, the participant and observer, sometimes referred to as the insider-outsider roles and these can come into conflict with one another. Field notes, or the daily record kept by researchers, will reveal not only the conclusions of the researcher, but also the experience of the research itself. Such participant observation is classified as a form of ***qualitative research***, or research based heavily on researcher impressions.

➢Illustration of Participant Observation: *Street Corner Society*

In the 1930s, William F. Whyte conducted what was to become one of the classic participant observation studies. He sought to study a poor, Italian, urban neighbourhood of Boston (which he called Cornerville) to determine the true social fabric of the community. His work reveals the conflict between the roles of participant and observer, involvement and detachment. The role of a ***key informant*** is highlighted as part of this research process indicating the strengths of assistance and the weakness of the introduction of bias.

Using Available Data: Secondary and Historical Analysis

Secondary analysis is a research method in which researchers utilize data collected by others. Advantages of this approach are the considerable saving of time and money, and the typically high quality of data available from agencies such as Statistics Canada. Problems, however, are also involved, including the possibility that data were not systematically gathered, or not directly focused on the interests of the researcher. Durkheims research on suicide is an example of secondary analysis with possible classification problems. The **Thinking Critically** and **Media Perspective Boxes** (pp. 47 and 48) are based upon secondary analysis of existing data.

➢Content Analysis

Content analysis entails the counting or coding of the content of written, aural, or visual materials, such as television programming or newspapers. This method has a long history in sociology including the renowned ***Polish Peasant in Europe and America*** where Thomas and Znaniecki used diaries and letters, written to and from Polish immigrants to the United States, to describe their adjustment processes.

Technology and Research

Personal computers and the internet have transformed the research process giving researchers remarkable technical competence and a rapidly expanding source of information. Soon the internet will provide faculty and students with instant access to current information that, in the past, would have taken years to reach libraries.

The **Media Perspectives Box** (p. 48) elaborates on the changes to research function accompanying computer development. From constant re-entry of computer cards to mainframes and the tedious re-typing of journal papers, we have moved to sophisticated, continuous analysis of data on personal computers and the production of journal articles by electronic transfer of information.

The Interplay of Theory and Method

The obtaining of facts is not the final goal of science. Beyond facts is the issue of the development of theory, or combining facts into meaning. Scientists use two processes of logical thought. ***Deductive logical thought*** is reasoning that transforms general ideas into specific hypotheses suitable for scientific testing. Zimbardo's prison research is a good example of this type of thinking. ***Inductive logical thought*** involves reasoning that builds specific observations into general theory. **Figure 2–2** (p. 49) illustrates both kinds of reasoning.

The **Summing Up Table** (p. 50) provides a quick review of the four major methods of sociological investigation.

PUTTING IT ALL TOGETHER: TEN STEPS IN SOCIOLOGICAL INVESTIGATION

The general guidelines for conducting sociological research follow these steps:

1. What is your topic?
2. What is known already?
3. What, exactly, are your questions?
4. What will you need to carry out the research?
5. Are there ethical concerns?
6. What method(s) will you use?
7. How will you record your data?
8. What do the data tell you?
9. What are your conclusions?
10. How can you share what you have learned?

Can People Lie with Statistics

The **Thinking It Through Box** (p. 51) warns us of the possibility of being misled by researchers. The choice of which data to use, how to interpret it, and how to present that data rests with the researcher. The possibility always exists that the researcher will make sure that the data "fit" with his or her hypothesis.

KEY CONCEPTS

Define each of the following concepts on a separate sheet of paper. Check the accuracy of your answers by referring to the text as well, as referring to italicized definitions located throughout the chapter.

cause and effect
concept
content analysis
control
control group
correlation

critical sociology
deductive logical thought
dependent variable
empirical evidence
experiment
experimental group
gender
Hawthorne effect
hypothesis
independent variable
inductive logical thought
interpretive sociology
interview
measurement
objectivity
operationalizing a variable
participant observation
population
qualitative research
quantitative research
questionnaire
reliability
replication
research method
sample
science
scientific sociology
secondary analysis
spurious correlation
survey
validity
variable

STUDY QUESTIONS

True-False

1. T F Reginald Bibby has found that teenagers who have body piercing or tattoos are much more likely to engage in sex than teenagers who do not.

2. T F In the year 2000, 16% of Canadians were living below the poverty line.

3. T F Reliable measurement means getting the same result time after time.

4. T F When two variables are correlated they are said to demonstrate a cause-and-effect relationship.

5. T F Max Weber was the first sociologist to argue that researchers must adopt value positions favouring the disadvantaged in society.

6. T F Because researchers are known to be objective, their presence ordinarily does not affect the behaviour patterns of the people they are studying.

7. T F Interpretive sociology differs from scientific sociology in that it tends to rely on qualitative data.

8. T F Scientific sociology is generally linked to the symbolic interaction approach.

9. T F In William F. Whyte's "Cornerville," Doc was what is called a secret informant.

10. T F The first step in the scientific research process should be the determination of the research design to be used to obtain the data.

Multiple Choice

1. Bibby has found that teenagers who have body piercing or tattoos are more likely to _____________.

(a) think they are bad persons
(b) lack confidence
(c) have a lack of concern for others
d) (all of the above)
(e) (none of the above)

2. Science, as a way of knowing, relies on _______________________.

(a) the wisdom of experts
(b) faith
(c) empirical evidence
(d) general consensus
(e) common sense

3. Specifying exactly what one intends to measure in assigning a value to a variable is called ___________________.

(a) measurement
(b) reliability
(c) operationalizing a variable
(d) validity
(e) correlation

4. Measuring what one intends to measure is the quality of measurement known as ____________________.

(a) reliability
(b) operationalization
(c) validity
(d) control
(e) objectivity

5. When two variables are related to each other but only through the existence of another variable, the relationship is said to be ___________________.

(a) a reliable measure
(b) a valid measure
(c) spurious correlation
(d) empirically sound
(e) average

6. Interpretive sociology ____________________.

   (a) focuses upon the meanings people attach to their behaviour
   (b) sees an objective reality "out there" in society
   (c) makes use of quantitative data
   (d) takes careful measurement of people's behaviour
   (e) (none of the above)

7. What theoretical approach is most clearly linked with the critical methodological approach?

   (a) Social-conflict
   (b) Structural-functional
   (c) Social-exchange
   (d) Symbolic-interaction
   (e) None of the above

8. Dorothy Smith notes that the condition of approximate equality between men and women in the farming community changed as the economic unit moved to _____________.

   (a) share-cropping
   (b) proximate justice
   (c) cash production
   (d) (all of the above)
   (e) (a and b above)

9. The change in a subject's behaviour caused simply by the awareness of being studied is called ____________________.

   (a) the Western Electric effect
   (b) the "placebo effect"
   (c) the experimental effect
   (d) the control variable effect
   (e) the Hawthorne effect

10. In the study by Paul Sniderman, anti-Semitism in Quebec was found to be culturally supported by _________________.

   (a) a history of discrimination in France
   (b) normative prejudice
   (c) nationalism
   (d) normative conformity
   (e) authoritarian personality types

11. *The Polish Peasant in Europe and America* by Thomas and Znaniecki was produced by the methodological technique called ____________________.

   (a) participant observation
   (b) case study
   (c) content analysis
   (d) survey
   (e) (none of the above)

12. If a researcher begins a sociological investigation with general ideas about the world that then are used to produce specific hypotheses suited for scientific testing, the process is known as ______________________.

    (a) inductive logical thought
    (b) qualitative methodology
    (c) empirical analysis
    (d) deductive logical thought
    (e) speculative reasoning

Fill in the Blank

1. ________________ is a logical system that bases knowledge on direct, systematic observation.

2. The scientific orientation to knowing is called _______________.

3. In a cause-and-effect relationship, the variable that causes the change in the ______variable is called the _____________ variable.

4. The state of personal neutrality in conducting research is referred to as ________.

5. In the mid 1800s, _______________ noted that crime, suicide, mortality, accident, marriage, and poverty levels could be predicted with exact precision.

6. The ______________ group is the group that typically receives a "placebo."

7. A ______________ is a part of a population that represents the whole.

8. Most _____________ is exploratory and descriptive.

9. In _______________ analysis, a researcher utilizes data collected by others.

10. By choosing particular data from their study and interpreting it in a particular way, researchers can be said to ______________ with statistics.

Definition and Short Answer

1. What are the two requirements that underlie the process of sociological investigation?

2. What are the three ways to do sociology?

3. What are the three factors that must be determined to conclude that a cause-and-effect relationship between two variables may exist?

4. What must the sociological researcher do to be ethically sound?

5. Review Max Weber's points concerning objectivity in science.

6. Margaret Eichler points out five dangers to sound research that involve gender. Please identify and define each.

7. Define the concept "hypothesis." Further, write your own hypothesis and operationalize the variables that you identify.

8. What are the twin roles of the research involved in participant observation?

9. What are the basic steps of the sociological research process? Please briefly describe each step in the process.

10. Discuss the impact of the Information Revolution on Canadian society and Canadian sociology.

Answers to Study Questions

True-False

1. T (p. 29)
2. T (p. 30)
3. T (p. 31)
4. F (p. 32)
5. F (p. 33)
6. F (p. 34)
7. T (p. 35)
8. T (p. 36)
9. F (p. 46)
10. F (p. 50)

Multiple Choice

1. e (p. 29)
2. c (p. 30)
3. c (p. 31)
4. c (p. 31)
5. c (p. 32)
6. a (p. 35)
7. a (p. 36)
8. c (p. 38)
9. e (p. 41)
10. d (p. 44)
11. c (p. 46)
12. d (p. 49)

Fill in the Blank

1. science (p. 30)
2. positivism (p. 30)
3. independent (p. 32)
4. objectivity (p. 33)
5. Florence Nightingale (p.39)
6. control (p. 41)
7. sample (p. 42)
8. field research. (45)
9. secondary (p. 46)
10. lie (p. 51)

ANALYSIS AND COMMENT

Go back through the chapter and write down in the spaces below key points from each of the following boxes.

APPLYING SOCIOLOGY

"Feminist Research: Critical and Interpretive Examples"
Key Points:

THINKING ABOUT DIVERSITY: RACE, CLASS, AND GENDER

"Conducting Research with Aboriginal Peoples"
Key Points:

THINKING CRITICALLY

"Reading Tables: An Important Skill"
Key Points

MEDIA PERSPECTIVES

"From Card Punching to Cyberspace: Evolution in the Media of Research"
Key Points:

THINKING IT THROUGH

"Can People Lie With Statistics?"
Key Points:

SUGGESTED READING

Classic Sources

Alvin Gouldner. 1970. *The Coming Crisis in Western Sociology.* New York: Aveon Books.
In this volume, Alvin Gouldner provided one of the earliest and best efforts to evaluate the place of values and politics in sociological research.

Feminist Research

Dorothy Smith. 1974. "The Social Construction of Documentary Reality." *Sociological Inquiry*, Vol. 44, No. 4: 257–68.
Dorothy Smith. 1987. *The Everyday World as Problematic: A Feminist Sociology.* Toronto: University of Toronto Press.
Winnie Tomm, ed. 1989. *The Effects of Feminist Approaches on Research Methodologies.* Calgary: Calgary Institute for the Humanities.
Lynn McDonald. 1994b. *The Women Founders of the Social Sciences.* Ottawa: Carleton University Press.
These books provide an historical and feminist antidote to the concerns of contemporary feminists about traditional, positivist social science research

Floyd J. Fowler, Jr. 1993. *Survey Research Methods.* Newbury Park, Calif.: Sage.
This book is filled with technical detail about implementing sociology's most widely used method of investigation.

Harriet Zuckerman, Jonathan R. Cole, and John T. Bruer, eds. 1991. *The Outer Circle: Women in the Scientific Community.* New York: Norton.
There is a widespread notion that sex discrimination in the scientific community has all but disappeared: However, the articles in this edited volume tell a different story.

Global Sources

Gerardo Marín and Barbara VanOss Marín. 1991. *Research with Hispanic Populations.* Newbury Park, Calif.: Sage.
This book explores the meaning of Hispanic ethnicity and its implications for sociological research.

Melvin L. Kohn. 1989. *Cross-National Research in Sociology.* Newbury Park, Calif.: Sage.
Global research offers valuable insights into other societies as well as our own way of life. This provocative paperback includes seventeen essays on global research.

CHAPTER 3 Culture

CHAPTER OUTLINE

I. **What is Culture?**
- A. Culture and Human Intelligence
- B. Culture, Nation State, and Society
- C. How Many Cultures?

II. **The Elements of Culture**
- A. Symbols
- B. Language
  - 1. Does Language Shape Reality?
- C. Values and Beliefs
  - 1. Values: Inconsistency and Conflict
  - 2. Values: A Global Perspective
- D. Norms
  - 1. Mores and Folkways
  - 2. Social Control
- E. Ideal and Real Culture
- F. Material Culture and Technology
- G. New Information Technology and Culture

III. **Cultural Diversity in Canada**
- A. High Culture and Popular Culture
- B. Subculture
- C. Multiculturalism
- D. Counterculture
- E. Cultural Change
  - 1. Causes of Cultural Change
- F. Ethnocentrism and Cultural Relativism
- G. A Global Culture?

IV. **Theoretical Analysis of Culture**
- A. The Functions of Culture: Structural-Functional Analysis
- B. Inequality and Culture: Social Conflict Analysis
- C. Evolution and Culture: Sociobiology

V. **Culture and Human Freedom**

VI. **Making the Grade**

VII. **Key Points**

VIII. **Key Concepts**

IX **Applications And Exercises**

IX. **MySocLab**

LEARNING OBJECTIVES

- To understand the sociological meaning of the concept culture
- To understand the experience of culture shock
- To understand the relationship between human intelligence and culture
- To understand the relationship between culture, society, nation, and state
- To know the elements of culture and to be able to provide examples of each
- To understand how symbolic meanings can change over time
- To understand how cultural differences can lead to misunderstandings
- To understand that Aboriginal languages in Canada are in danger of extinction
- To understand the Sapir-Whorf hypothesis
- To be able to identify the major Canadian values and to recognize their interrelationships with one another and with other aspects of our culture
- To comprehend the differences between American and Canadian values
- To know that values are affected by stages of economic development
- To be able to provide examples of the different types of norms operative in a culture
- To understand the impact of technology on culture
- To understand the cultural diversity of Canada
- To explain how subcultures and countercultures contribute to cultural diversity
- To be able to explore the nature of multiculturalism in Canada
- To understand that not all elements of a culture change together
- To be able to differentiate between ethnocentrism and cultural relativism
- To be able to compare and contrast analyses of culture using structural-functional, social-conflict, and sociobiological approaches
- To comprehend that culture can both constrain and enhance human freedom

CHAPTER REVIEW

WHAT IS CULTURE?

Culture is defined as the values, beliefs, behaviour, and material objects that form a people's way of life. The scenario addressed at the beginning of the chapter suggests some common Canadian cultural values, but enormous differences as well. Indeed when people travel between societies or even within their own, they can experience ***culture shock***, a personal disorientation that can come from encountering an unfamiliar way of life.

Sociologists differentiate between ***non-material culture***, the intangible creations of human society, and ***material culture***, the tangible products of human society.

Sociologically, culture is viewed in the broadest possible sense, referring to everything that is part of a people's way of life. Our lives become meaningful to us through culture. Our lifestyles are not determined by ***instincts***, or biological forces, as is true in large degree for other species. We are the only species whose survival depends on what we learn through culture, rather than by what we are naturally given through biology.

Culture and Human Intelligence

The primates emerged on Earth about 65 million years ago. Humans diverged from our closest primate relatives some 12 million years ago and the first creatures with clearly human characteristics (who walked upright, made use of fire, tools, and weapons, built shelters, and fashioned clothing) emerged about 3 million years ago. Our species, ***homo sapiens,*** (meaning thinking person) evolved 250 000 years ago and creatures that look very much like us, a mere 40 000 years ago. Civilization, based on permanent settlements, has existed for only the last 12 000 years.

Instincts have largely been replaced by a capacity to fashion the material environment to suit human needs, which has permitted a fascinating array of human diversity to develop.

Culture, Nation, State, and Society

While ***culture*** is shared values, ideas, and artifacts, a ***nation*** is a people who share a culture, usually within a ***state***, a political entity with designated borders. ***Society*** is the organized activities of people within that nation or state. Multicultural Canada may be said to contain many nations. The continuing challenge is to build a federal nation that supersedes the others.

How Many Cultures?

Although there are many cultures and nations globally, distinctions have declined with increased global contact.

THE ELEMENTS OF CULTURE

Even though considerable cultural variation exists, all cultures share four components: symbols, language, values and beliefs, and norms.

Symbols

A ***symbol*** is anything that carries a particular meaning recognized by people who share a culture. Symbols, often taken for granted, are the means by which we make sense of our lives. Symbols vary widely globally and even within a given society, and societies create new symbols regularly. The **Applying Sociology Box** (p. 61) describes cyber-symbols in the world of computer communication.

Language

The significance of language for human communication is vividly illustrated by the story of Helen Keller recounting the moment she acquired language and a symbolic understanding of the world, through the help of her teacher Ann Sullivan. ***Language*** is a system of symbols that allows people to communicate with one another. Humans have created many different language symbols as **Figure 3–1** (p. 62) indicates. **Global Map 3–1** (p. 63) indicates the location of the three major world languages. The process by which culture is passed, through language, from one generation to the next, is our most important form of ***cultural transmission***. As the **Thinking About Diversity Box** (p.59) makes clear, the loss of Aboriginal languages means a serious loss to world culture. We are very familiar with the link between language and culture in Canadian society as the debate over Bill 101 in Quebec makes amply clear. Language is rooted in oral cultural tradition. Only in the last 5000 years did humans invent writing and even in countries like Canada, many people have limited literacy skills. Language is our linkage to cultural pasts and the generation of ideas for the future.

➢Does Language Shape Reality?

Two anthropologists, Edward Sapir and Benjamin Whorf, have argued that language is more than simply attaching labels to the "real world." They reject the view that language merely describes a single reality. The ***Sapir-Whorf hypothesis*** holds that we know the world only in terms of our language. Language, according to them, determines our cultural reality. More recently, scholars have suggested that people can conceptualize an idea, before actually naming it.

Values and Beliefs

Values are defined as the standards by which people assess desirability, goodness, and beauty; they are broad principles that underlie ***beliefs,*** specific statements that people hold to be true. They are learned through socialization and help shape how we perceive our surroundings and how our personality develops. Indeed they provide the cultural capital by which we evaluate our future possibilities.

Although in our diverse society few cultural values are shared by everyone, there are several central values that are widely accepted in Canadian society. As Martin Lipset has suggested in the **Thinking It Through Box** (p. 66), while Americans value freedom and individual initiative, Canadians stress conformity and obedience to the law. The Canadian tendency to emphasize the good of the collectivity over the good of the individual has resulted in social programs such as universal medicare. Futurist Roger Sauvé has recently identified substantial value differences between the U.S. and Canada as have Bricker and Wright. Robertson Davies suggests that Canada is "a country you worry about."

➢Values: Inconsistency and Conflict

In a society characterized by cultural diversity and rapid social change, cultural values can be inconsistent and even contradictory. On the one hand, Canadians espouse equality and, on the other, they degrade people because of their race, gender, or sexual orientation. Even hockey is transformed from a cultural point of view as women win more medals than men in the international arena.

➢Values: A Global Perspective

While thousands of cultures have different values, in general, low-income societies espouse traditional, security-laden values, while high-income societies espouse values of individualism and self-expression in secular-oriented circumstances. **Figure 3–2** (p. 68) compares selected countries in terms of their cultural values.

Norms

Norms are defined as rules that guide behaviour. They can be ***proscriptive***, mandating what we should not do, or ***prescriptive***, stating what we should do. They can change over time, as illustrated by norms regarding sexual behaviour. Some are meant to apply to all situations and all people, while others apply to only certain people and vary situation to situation.

➢Mores and Folkways

Norms vary in their degree of importance. ***Mores*** distinguish between right and wrong while ***folkways*** distinguish between right and rude.

➢Social Control

Norms provide for conformity. ***Sanctions*** are positive and negative responses to the behaviour of people that reward conformity and punish deviance. They are an important part of our cultural system of ***social control***, or the various means by which members of society encourage conformity to cultural norms. Through socialization we internalize cultural norms and impose constraints on our own behaviour. The "breaking" of an internalized norm results in ***guilt*** and ***shame***.

Ideal and Real Culture

Values and norms are not descriptions of actual behaviour, but rather reflect how we believe members of a culture should behave. Therefore, we distinguish between ***ideal culture,*** or social patterns mandated by cultural values and norms, and ***real culture,*** or social patterns that only approximate cultural expectations.

Material Culture and Technology

Material and nonmaterial culture are very closely related. ***Artifacts***, or physical human creations, express the values of a culture. For instance, the Yąnomamö value militaristic skill and devote great care to making weapons, while Canadians value independence and build highways for our automobiles.

Material culture also reflects a culture's ***technology***, which is the application of cultural knowledge to the task of living in a physical environment. While we, in Canada, attempt to manipulate our natural environment, most technologically "simple" cultures attempt to adapt to their natural worlds. Also, advances in technology can create both positive and negative effects for the quality of life. The Old Order Mennonites in Ontario, for example, shun modern technological conveniences and their communities flourish.

New Information Technology and Culture

The industrial society is giving way to the information society, where the focus is on the creation, processing, and application of information. Symbolic skills replace mechanical skills and people generate new cultural ideas and products.

CULTURAL DIVERSITY IN CANADA

Cultural variety in Canada is described as a "patchwork quilt" or mosaic. We are a land of many peoples. **Figure 3-3** (p. 70) gives some indication of Canada's cultural diversity.

High Culture and Popular Culture

High culture refers to patterns associated with a society's elite, while popular culture refers to patterns widespread among a society's entire population. Sociologists tend to be uncomfortable with the implicit ranking of patterns of culture since the evaluation is more often a product of power and prestige than of inherent superiority or inferiority.

Subculture

Sociologists define ***subculture*** as cultural patterns that set apart some segment of a society's population. Subcultures can be based upon age, ethnicity, residence, sexual orientation, occupation, and many other factors. Ethnicity is perhaps the most recognized dimension with which to identify cultural diversity. While ethnicity is often a source of pleasant diversity, the conflict that has erupted in the former Yugoslavia illustrates it as a source of tension and outright violence. Cultural diversity in Canada is not without disadvantages, as subcultural groups are distinguished by hierarchy as well as variety.

Multiculturalism

Canadian society is officially multicultural, a society that encourages ethnic or cultural heterogeneity. Historically, a European (primarily English) style of life was identified as ideal, but with massive immigration from non-European societies, Canada moved away from Eurocentrism to multiculturalism. A debate rages on, however, about the usefulness of this concept for Canadian society. Proponents suggest a multicultural perspective will help us develop a more meaningful understanding of our past, present, and global interdependence, while strengthening academic achievement of all our children. Those opposed suggest that multiculturalism promotes divisiveness rather than cohesiveness and denies children access to the knowledge that will enable them to compete. **Table 3-1** (p. 72) illustrates the mother tongues spoken in Canada.

Counterculture

A ***counterculture*** is defined as a cultural pattern that strongly opposes those that are widely accepted in a society. Members of countercultures are likely to question the morality of the majority group and engage in some form of protest activities. Although countercultures are not as predominant now as they were in the 1960s, we currently experience militaristic groups that reject the legitimacy of the political system and sometimes engage in violent acts, such as the torching of Hummer dealerships by the Earth Liberation Front.

Cultural Change

Cultural change is continuous, and change in one area is usually associated with change in others. Family life in Canada, for example, has changed as more women work, some delay entry into marriage, and more, once married, decide to divorce.

These system-wide connections are described in the concept of ***cultural integration,*** but it is also recognized that some cultural elements change faster than others, leaving an inconsistency called ***cultural lag***.

Cultural change is set in motion by three different causes: invention, discovery, and diffusion.

Ethnocentrism and Cultural Relativity

Ethnocentrism is the practice of judging another culture by the standards of one's own culture. It creates a biased evaluation of unfamiliar practices. The evaluation of cultural variations in the maintenance of personal space is an illustration of this concept. ***Cultural relativism*** is the practice of judging a culture by its own standards. The issue of cultural sensitivity related to international business ventures is amusing, but there are some cultural practices that are deeply disturbing, such as child labour in various parts of the world. This suggests that perhaps there are some universal standards we could identify as necessary, rather than accepting any behaviour within the context of cultural relativity.

A Global Culture?

The recent flow of goods, information, and people between societies seems to have led to similarities in various cultural patterns worldwide. However, rural areas remain largely unaffected, few citizens of poorer societies can afford the goods from elsewhere, and a question yet remains whether people everywhere attach the same meaning to cultural entities.

THEORETICAL ANALYSIS OF CULTURE

We attempt to understand culture using several theoretical approaches.

The Functions of Culture: Structural Functional Analysis

Drawing on the philosophical doctrine of ***idealism***, this approach holds that core values bind members of society together in an integrated system. While core values may differ among societies, there appears to be ***cultural universals*** found in every culture of the world. The limitations of this approach include an underestimation of culture conflict and a downplaying of the extent of cultural diversity and change in society.

Inequality and Culture: Social-Conflict Analysis

The focus of researchers using this paradigm is the social conflict generated by inequality among different categories of people in a culture. The question of why certain values are dominant in a culture rather than others is central to this view. Karl Marx, using the philosophical doctrine of ***materialism***, argued that the way we deal with the material world (i.e., through capitalism) powerfully affects all other dimensions of our culture. A limitation of this perspective is an underestimation of the extent of integration in society.

Evolution and Culture: Sociobiology

Sociobiology is a theoretical paradigm that seeks to explain cultural patterns as a product, at least in part, of biological causes. Sociobiologists argue that Charles Darwin's theory of natural selection applies to human evolution as it does to all other species.

Controversy exists concerning the application of Darwin's insights to humans. Sociobiologists focus on the existence of certain cultural universals as evidence that culture is determined to a significant degree by biology. For example the ***double standard*** in sexuality is found, according to Alfred Kinsey, in all peoples and makes sense as a biological imperative. The most efficient reproductive strategy for males is promiscuity, while the best strategy for females is the selection of one male who will contribute to their child's survival.

Sociobiology has been criticized as historically supporting racism and sexism, and certainly there is little in the way of definitive proof that biological characteristics explain the roots of human culture. Perhaps sociobiology will help us understand why some cultural patterns are more common than others; however, it appears that most human behaviour is learned within a system of culture. The **Applying Sociology Box** (p. 78) summarizes the main lessons of each theoretical approach about culture.

CULTURE AND HUMAN FREEDOM

Over the course of human evolution, culture has become our means of survival; however, it has also become the burden of limited choices and isolation from others in our pursuit of success. **The Media Perspective Box** (p. 79) describes the terrible consequences of a cultural appetite for information about celebrities that culminated in the death of Princess Diana.

While being dependent on culture and constrained by our particular way of life, the capacity for creating change, or shaping and reshaping our existence, appears limitless. Culture is a liberating force to the extent we develop an understanding of its diversity and the opportunities available within it for change and autonomy.

KEY CONCEPTS

Define each of the following concepts on a separate sheet of paper. Check the accuracy of your answers by referring to the key concepts section in the text, as well as referring to italicized definitions located throughout the chapter.

beliefs
counterculture
cultural integration
cultural lag
cultural materialism
cultural relativism
cultural transmission
cultural universals
culture
culture shock
diffusion
discovery
ethnocentrism
Eurocentrism
folkways
high culture

ideal culture
invention
language
material culture
mores
multiculturalism
nonmaterial culture
norms
popular culture
real culture
Sapir-Whorf hypothesis
social control
sociobiology
subculture
symbols
technology
values

STUDY QUESTIONS

True-False

1. T F Material culture refers to the physical things created by members of a society.

2. T F The personal disorientation a person feels when moving from one society to another is referred to as social shock.

3. T. F Bill 101 in Quebec is designed to protect the English language in that province.

4. T F The Sapir-Whorf hypothesis states that people perceive the world through the cultural lens of a language.

5. T F Societies in lower-income nations have cultures that value survival.

6. T F The enforcement of norms always depends directly on the reactions of others.

7. T F Popular culture refers to patterns of behaviour that distinguish a society's elite.

8. T F Critics of multiculturalism contend that it fuels the "politics of difference."

9. T F The practice of judging any culture by its own standards is referred to as ethnocentrism.

10. T F The concept of the "global village" was conceived by Marshall McLuhan.

11. T F The structural-functionalist perspective argues that values are shaped by a society's system of economic production.

12. T F Humans are the ***only*** creatures who experience alienation.

Multiple Choice

1. The personal disorientation that comes from encountering an unfamiliar way of life is called ___________________.

   (a) cultural relativism
   (b) ethnocentrism
   (c) non-material culture
   (d) cultural schizophrenia
   (e) culture shock

2. Primates appeared on earth about ____________ years ago.

   (a) 3 billion
   (b) 65 million
   (c) 12 million
   (d) 250 000
   (e) 40000

3. Symbols, a component of culture, can ___________________.

   (a) vary from culture to culture
   (b) allow people to make sense of their lives
   (c) change over time
   (d) give rise to conflict
   (e) (all of the above)

4. A system of symbols that allows members of a society to communicate with one another is the definition of ___________.

   (a) values
   (b) language
   (c) norms
   (d) cultural relativity
   (e) cultural transmission

5. Standards by which members of a culture distinguish the desirable from the undesirable, what is good from what is bad, the beautiful from the ugly, is the definition for _______.

   (a) norms
   (b) beliefs
   (c) values
   (d) mores
   (e) sanctions

6. Specific statements that people hold to be true are ___________________.

   (a) standards
   (b) values
   (c) beliefs
   (d) norms
   (e) sanctions

7. According to Lipset, the differences in value structure between Americans and Canadians are deeply rooted in the past. The key event that differentiates them is _______________.

(a) the French in North America
(b) the climate
(c) slavery
(d) the American War of Independence

8. Which of the following countries is most characterized by both self-expression values and secular-rational values?

(a) China
(b) Norway
(c) Ethiopia
(d) Canada
(e) Paraguay

9. __________ refer to norms that are widely observed and have great moral significance.

(a) Mores
(b) Ideal cultures
(c) Folkways
(d) Technologies
(e) Subcultures

10. The new Information Society is characterized by ____________________________.

(a) the creation, processing, storing, and application of information
(b) cultural symbols that are intentionally created
(c) workers with symbolic skills
(d) (all of the above)
(e) (a and b above)

11. Inconsistencies within a cultural system resulting from the unequal rates at which different cultural elements change are termed ______________________.

(a) cultural lag
(b) culturc shock
(d) counterculture
(e) cultural relativity

12. Which of the following are reasons given for the spread of a global culture?

(a) the flow of goods
(b) the flow of communication
(c) global migration
(d) a and b above
(e) all of the above

13. The theoretical approach that focuses upon universal cultural traits is ______________.

(a) cultural ecology
(b) cultural materialism
(c) structural functionalism
(d) social-conflict
(e) socio-biology

14. The philosophical doctrine of materialism is utilized in the analysis of culture by proponents of which theoretical approach?

    (a) sociobiology
    (b) structural-functionalism
    (c) symbolic-interaction
    (d) cultural ecology
    (e) social-conflict

15. Which theoretical approach suggests that cultural patterns are rooted in humanity's biological evolution?

    (a) structural-functional
    (b) social conflict
    (c) sociobiology
    (d) all of the above
    (e) none of the above

Fill in the Blank

1. The ideas created by members of a society are referred to as ________________.
2. The concept ____________________ is derived from the Latin meaning "thinking person."
3. Only ___________ of the sixty Aboriginal languages are not on the brink of extinction.
4. A ________________ is anything that carries a particular meaning recognized by members of a culture.
5. The Canadian tendency to emphasize the good of the ________________ has resulted in the creation of social programs such as universal medical care.
6. ____________ are norms for routine or casual interaction.
7. ___________ ___________ is defined as the various means by which members of society regulate people's thoughts and behaviours.
8. ________________________ is a social policy in Canada designed to encourage ethnic or cultural heterogeneity.
9. The spread of cultural traits from one society to another is called ______________________.
10. A theoretical approach that focuses on the link between culture and inequality is _________________________.

Definition and Short Answer

1. Discuss the concept of culture shock, with specific reference to how you have experienced it.

2. What is the Sapir-Whorf hypothesis? Provide an example.

3. How do value systems differ in Canada and the United States?

4. How are values affected by the level of income in a society?

5. How has the concept of multiculturalism had an impact on Canada?

6. Three causes of cultural change are identified in the text. Identify these and provide an illustration for each.

7. Discuss the dangers of both ethnocentrism and cultural relativity in a society or humankind.

8. Define the philosophical doctrine of "idealism."

9. Define the philosophical doctrine of "materialism." How does this doctrine fit into the conflict theory of society?

10. What are the basic premises of the sociobiological approach to understanding human behaviour and what are the most common critiques of the approach?

11. What is the relationship between culture and human freedom?

Answers to Study Questions

True-False

1. T (p. 56)
2. F (p. 57)
3. F (p. 62)
4. T (p. 64)
5. T (p. 67)
6. F (p. 68)
7. F (p. 70)
8. T (p. 72)
9. F (p. 73)
10. T (p. 75)
11. F (p. 76)
12. T (p. 78)

Multiple Choice

1. e (p. 57)
2. b (p. 58)
3. e (pp. 60-61)
4. b (p. 62)
5. c (p. 64)
6. c (p. 64)
7. d (p. 66)
8. b (p. 68)
9. a (p. 67)
10. d (p. 69)
11. a (p. 73)
12. e (pp. 74-75)
13. c (p. 76)
14. e (p. 76)
15. c (p. 78)

Fill in the Blank

1. non-material culture (p. 56)
2. homo sapiens (p. 58)
3. four (p. 59)
4. symbol (p. 60)
5. collectivity (p. 66)
6. folkways (p. 67)
7. social control (p. 68)
8. multiculturalism (p. 71)
9. diffusion (p. 73)
10. social conflict (p. 76)

ANALYSIS AND COMMENT

Go back through the chapter and write down in the spaces below key points from each of the following boxes.

THINKING ABOUT DIVERSITY: RACE, CLASS AND GENDER

"Aboriginal Languages in Danger of Extinction"
Key Points:

APPLYING SOCIOLOGY

"New Symbols in the World of Instant Messaging"
Key Points:

MEDIA PERSPECTIVES

"A Lesson in Values from Cyberspace"
Key Points:

THINKING IT THROUGH

"Canadians and Americans: What Makes Us Different?"
Key Points:

MEDIA PERSPECTIVES

"The Paparazzi: Villains or Our Eyes to the World?"
Key Points:

SUGGESTED READINGS

Classic Sources

Napoleon A. Chagnon. 1992. *Y̨anomamö: The Fierce People.* 4th ed. New York: Holt, Rinehart, and Winston.
Napoleon Chagnon's updated account of the Y̨anomamö offers fascinating insights into a culture very different from our own. It is also a compelling tale of carrying out fieldwork in an unfamiliar world.

Margaret Mead. 1928. *Coming of Age in Samoa: A Psychological Study of Primitive Youth for Western Civilization.* New York: Wm. Morrow.
Margaret Mead, perhaps the best-known student of culture, carried out this study of the Samoan Islands, which demonstrates the variability of cultural systems.

Contemporary Sources

Seymour Martin Lipset. 1990. *Continental Divide: The Values and Institutions of the United States and Canada.* New York: Routledge.
This book compares the cultures of Canada and the United States.

Anastasia M. Shkilnyk. *A Poison Stronger than Love: The Destruction of an Ojibwa Community.* New Haven, CN.: Yale University Press.
Shkilnyk's book offers a telling description of the devastating effect of the state on the Grassy Narrows band in northern Ontario. The band was forced to relocate from its reserve to a narrow strip of land in order to facilitate the provision of some modern amenities such as a school, electricity, improved housing, and social services.

S. Crean and M. Rioux. 1983. *Two Nations.* Toronto: James Lorimer.
S. Ramcharan. 1982. *Racism: Non-Whites in Canada.* Toronto: Butterworths.
P.S. Li and B.S. Bolaria., eds. 1984. *Racial Minorities in Multicultural Canada.* Toronto: Garamond Press.
Mel Watkins. 1977. *Dene Nation: The Colony Within.* Toronto: University of Toronto Press.
Pierre Vallières. 1971. *White Niggers of America.* Toronto: McClelland & Stewart.
W. Clement. 1975. *The Canadian Corporate Elite: An Analysis of Economic Power.* Toronto: McClelland and Stewart.
S.M. Crean. 1976. *Who's Afraid of Canadian Culture?* Don Mills, ON: General Publishing.
R. Mathews. 1983. *The Creation of Regional Dependancy.* Toronto: University of Toronto Press.
These books describe cultural, class, regional, and racial divisions within Canadian society.

M. Patricia Marchak. 1975. *Ideological Perspectives on Canada.* Toronto: McGraw-Hill Ryerson.
R. Breton, J.G. Reitz, and V.F. Valentine. 1980. *Cultural Boundaries and the Cohesion of Canada.* Montreal: Institute for Research in Public Policy.
G. Caldwell and E. Waddell. 1982. *The English of Quebec: From Majority to Minority Status.* Quebec: Institut québecois de recherche sur la culture.
R.J. Bryan and R.J. Sacouman. 1979. *Underdevelopment and Social Movements in Atlantic Canada.* Toronto: Hogtown Press.
These books give a description of Canadian ideology, culture, and values. See the following.

D.H. Clairmont and D.W. Magill. 1974. *Africville: The Life and Death of a Black Community.* Toronto: Canadian Scholars' Press.
See this book for a classic Canadian community study.

Global Sources

Mike Featherstone, ed. 1990. *Global Culture: Nationalism, Globalization, and Modernity.* London: Sage.
These two dozen essays explore various ways in which a global culture is emerging.

Joana McIntyre Varawa. 1990. *Changes in Latitude: An Uncommon Anthropology.* New York: Harper & Row.
This fascinating book describes how a woman from Hawaii past midlife travelled to Fiji on vacation only to find a new home, a new husband, and a host of new challenges.

Craig Storti. *The Art of Crossing Cultures.* Yarmouth, MN: Intercultural Press, 1990.
This brief book explores the excitement as well as the difficulties of cross-cultural experience.

CHAPTER 4

Society

CHAPTER OUTLINE

I. **Gerhard Lenski: Society and Technology**
   A. Hunter/Gatherer Societies
   B. Horticultural and Pastoral Societies
   C. Agrarian Societies
   D. Industrial Societies
   E. Post-industrial Societies
   F. The Limits of Technology

II. **Karl Marx: Society and Conflict**
   A. Society and Production
   B. Conflict and History
   C. Capitalism and Class Conflict
   D. Capitalism and Alienation
   E. Revolution

III. **Max Weber: The Rationalization of Society**
   A. Two World Views: Tradition and Rationality
   B. Is Capitalism Rational?
   C. Weber's Great Thesis: Protestantism and Capitalism
   D. Rational Social Organization
      1. Rationality, Bureaucracy, and Science
      2. Rationality and Alienation

IV. **Emile Durkheim: Society and Function**
   A. Structure: Society beyond Ourselves
   B. Function: Society as System
   C. Personality: Society in Ourselves
   D. Modernity and Anomie
   E. Evolving Societies: The Division of Labour

V. **Critical Review: Four Visions of Society**
   A. What Holds Societies Together?
   B. How Have Societies Changed?
   C. Why Do Societies Change?

VI. **Making the Grade**

VII. **Key Points**

VIII. **Key Concepts**

IX. **Applications and Exercises**

X. **MySocLab**

LEARNING OBJECTIVES

- To give answers to the following questions: "What forces divide a society or hold it together?" "How do societies differ?" and "How and why do societies change?"
- To be able to differentiate between the four "visions" of society discussed in this chapter
- To explain the sociocultural evolution from hunting and gathering societies to industrial societies, as developed by Gerhard Lenski
- To contrast the different types of societies described by Lenski on the basis of their historical period, productive technology, population size, settlement pattern, and social organization
- To explain the model of society based on conflict and change developed by Karl Marx
- To be able to discuss the perspective of Marx on the concepts of capitalism, communism, revolution, alienation, and materialism
- To explain the role of rationality in modern society developed by Max Weber
- To be able to identify Weber's qualities of rationality in modern society
- To describe Emile Durkheim's functional view of society, including his analyses of the influence of social facts and the role of the division of labour in society
- To imagine how the Lenskis, Marx, Weber, and Durkheim would comprehend societal changes wrought by the Information Revolution.

CHAPTER REVIEW

The preface to this chapter addresses the basic issues of what holds a society together and what are the forces that divide it. Canada is more than 130 years old, yet is still characterized by a fragile national unity.

The concept ***society*** refers to people who interact within a defined territory and who share a culture. In this chapter four separate visions of society are discussed; each addresses questions that concern forces that shape human life. The visions include (1) Gerhard and Jean Lenski's focus on the importance of technology, (2) Karl Marx's understanding of the key role social conflict plays in society, (3) Max Weber's illustration of the significance of human ideas, and (4) Emile Durkheim's notion of the different ways that traditional and modern societies hang together.

GERHARD LENSKI: SOCIETY AND TECHNOLOGY

Until about 12 000 years ago the hunting and gathering type of society was the only one in existence. Comparing present day hunting and gathering societies with modern technologically "advanced" societies raises many interesting questions. Lenski analyzes human society using the ***sociocultural evolution*** approach, which focuses on the process of social change that results from gaining new cultural information, particularly technology. The greater the amount of technological information a society has, the more it can manipulate the physical environment and the faster it can change. Five general types of society are distinguished by using Lenski's work.

Hunter/Gatherer Societies

Hunting and gathering societies are defined as those that use simple technology to hunt animals and gather vegetation. Only a very small number of such societies are still in existence today. Typical characteristics of people using this subsistence strategy include small bands of people, a nomadic lifestyle over large territories, specialization based only on age and sex, and only a few positions of leadership. Social organization tends to be simple and equal, organized around the family. Life expectancy at birth is relatively low, however in environments with ample food supplies, the quality of life is good, with some leisure time.

Horticultural and Pastoral Societies

Approximately 10 000 to 12 000 years ago plants began to be cultivated. ***Horticultural*** societies are those that use hand tools to cultivate crops. This strategy first appeared in the Middle East and later, Latin America and Asia, and through diffusion spread throughout the rest of the world. Some societies combine horticulture with hunting and gathering strategies.

In regions where horticulture was impractical, societies based on ***pastoralism*** emerged. These societies' livelihood was based on the domestication of animals. Both horticultural and pastoral societies tend to have a more complex social organization and have increased specialization. ***Material surpluses*** become possible with these lifestyles, and this is often linked to greater social inequality. These societies, given their increased technological development, are more productive than hunting and gathering societies. Instead of the many gods of hunter/gatherers, they tend to think of one God as Creator.

Agrarian Societies

Agrarian societies emerged about 5000 years ago and are based on ***agriculture***, or the technology of large-scale farming using ploughs powered by animals or more powerful sources of energy. Technological change during this period was so dramatic that Lenski has argued it was the era of the "dawn of civilization." The use of the plough increased soil fertility as well as made agriculture more efficient. This also greatly increased the surplus of food available. Increased task specialization made the barter system obsolete and money was developed as a standard of exchange. The power of the elite greatly increased, supported by religious beliefs and the expanding political power structure. Men gained dominance over women, unlike the previous horticultural period where women were primary providers of food.

Industrial Societies

Industrialism is the technology that powers sophisticated machinery with advanced sources of energy. The muscle power of humans and animals are no longer the basis of production and tools and machinery become more complex and efficient. A major shift occurred that moved production within families to production within factories. Occupational specialization became even more pronounced and cultural values became more heterogeneous.

In the twentieth century the automobile, the airplane, and electronic communications have made a large world seem small, while the computer has ushered in the Information Revolution, which threatens to change the way we relate to one another. Industrialism, in time, leads to prosperity and a decrease in political, social, and economic inequality.

Post-Industrial Societies

An extension of Lenski's analysis can be applied to post-industrialism, where technology supports an information-based economy. Industrial work declines and workers who process information increase. The **Summing Up Table** (pp. 88-89) summarizes how changes in technology have had an impact on population size, settlement patterns, and social organization.

The Limits of Technology

While technology has relieved many human problems, it has created others. Our sense of community has diminished while the fear of nuclear war has increased. As well, our appetite for resources and the way we use them is endangering the environment. The **Thinking It Through Box** (p. 91) shows one author's attempt to demonstrate how social science might improve society.

KARL MARX: SOCIETY AND CONFLICT

Marx's thinking focused on a fundamental contradiction of industrial society. How could vast social inequality exist given the new industrial technology with its phenomenal productive capability? The central focus of Marx's work was on the idea of ***social conflict***, which means a struggle between segments of society over valued resources. For Marx, the most significant type of social conflict results from the manner in which society produces material goods.

Society and Production

Marx designated a very small part of the population as ***capitalists***, or those who owned factories and other productive enterprises. Their goal was profit. The vast majority of people, however, were termed the ***proletariat***, meaning those who provided the labour necessary for the operation of factories and other productive enterprises. Labour is exchanged by these people for wages. Fundamental conflict exists between the competing needs of these two groups who draw wages and profits from the same pool of funds.

Marx's analysis of society followed the philosophical doctrine of ***materialism*** in asserting that the system of producing material goods can shape all of society. He labelled the economic system the ***infrastructure*** and all other social institutions as the ***superstructure***. **Figure 4-1** (p. 92) illustrates this philosophical viewpoint.

Marx believed capitalism promoted ***false consciousness***, or the belief that the shortcomings of individuals, rather than society, are responsible for many of the personal problems people have.

Conflict and History

Marx understood historical change in society as operating in both gradual evolutionary and rapid revolutionary processes. He believed early hunting and gathering societies to be represented by communism, or the equal production of food and other material as a common effort shared more or less equally by everyone. He saw horticultural, pastoral, agrarian, and industrial societies as based on systems of inequality and exploitation. The concept ***bourgeoisie*** (French, meaning "of the town") is discussed further within the framework of social history during the period of industrialization. Industrialization also produced the proletariat who he thought might form a unified class across national boundaries, setting the stage for confrontation.

Capitalism and Class Conflict

Marx viewed all social history as one of ***class conflict***, or the struggle between social classes over the distribution of wealth and power in society. Social change involved workers first becoming aware of their shared oppression and then organizing and acting to address their problems. The process involved replacing false consciousness with ***class consciousness***, or the recognition by workers of their unity as a class in opposition to capitalists and, ultimately, to capitalism itself.

Capitalism and Alienation

For Marx, ***alienation*** meant the experience of isolation resulting from powerlessness. Workers themselves are a mere commodity. Four ways industrial capitalism alienates workers are identified: (1) alienation from the act of working, (2) alienation from the products of work, (3) alienation from other workers, and (4) alienation from human potential. These act as a barrier to social class unity.

Revolution

Marx viewed revolution as the only way to change the nature of society. The type of system he saw as replacing industrial capitalism was socialism, which he believed was a more humane and egalitarian type of productive system.

MAX WEBER: THE RATIONALIZATION OF SOCIETY

Weber made many contributions to sociology, perhaps more than any other sociologist. One of the most significant was his understanding about how our social world differs from societies of early times. His work reflects the philosophical approach of ***idealism,*** which emphasizes the importance of human ideas in shaping society. New ways of thinking, not merely technology and materialistic relationships, were the major force in social change. A conceptual tool used by Weber in his research was the concept ***ideal type***, defined as an abstract statement of the essential characteristics of any social phenomenon.

Two World Views: Tradition and Rationality

Weber differentiated between two types of societies in terms of how people thought. The first is characterized by ***tradition***, or sentiments and beliefs about the world that are passed from generation to generation. The other is characterized by ***rationality***, or deliberate, matter-of-fact calculation of the most efficient means to accomplish any particular goal. This process of change from tradition to rationality he termed the ***rationalization of society***, denoting the change in the type of thinking characteristic of members of society. Industrialization was an expression of this process. The **Window on the World Global Map** (p. 96) shows that personal computers are utilized intensively in the high-income countries and infrequently in low-income countries.

Is Capitalism Rational?

Weber saw industrial capitalism as the essence of rationality, while Marx did not, citing its failure to meet basic human needs.

Weber's Great Thesis: Protestantism and Capitalism

Weber points out that industrial capitalism developed where Calvinism was widespread. This is discussed as an example of how the power of ideas shapes human social development. A central doctrine of this religion was ***predestination***, creating visions of either damnation or salvation, but in the hands of God, not the people. Anxious to know their fate, people looked for signs of God's favour. Some reassurance was to be found in personal success and achievement. This success was accelerated through the acceptance of technological innovation. As religious fervour weakened, a "work" ethic replaced the "religious" ethic.

Rational Social Organization

Weber believed rationality shaped modern society in various ways. This included (1) creating distinctive *social institutions*, or major spheres of social life organized to meet basic human needs, (2) large-scale organizations, (3) specialized tasks, (4) personal discipline, (5) awareness of time, (6) technical competence, and (7) impersonality.

➢Rationality, Bureaucracy, and Science

While traditional societies had large-scale organizations, they were not based on rationality. Modern-day society becomes characterized by a type of social organization called ***bureaucracy***. Weber viewed this as the clearest expression of a rational world, especially within the capitalist market economy.

➢Rationality and Alienation

Weber, like Marx, was critical of modern society, but for different reasons. For Weber, economic inequality was not the major problem, rather dehumanization and alienation were what troubled society most. Weber saw individuality being constricted by modern rationality expressed through increasingly rigid rules.

EMILE DURKHEIM: SOCIETY AND FUNCTION

Durkheim suggests that society is both beyond us and a part of us.

Structure: Society beyond Ourselves

Central to the work of Durkheim is the concept of ***social fact***, any part of society that is argued to have an objective existence apart from the individual and is therefore able to influence individual behaviour. Examples are the cultural values and norms of a society. Society is something more than the sum of its parts and it has the power to shape our thoughts and tug at our conceptions of morality.

Function: Society as System

Function is another concept important in the understanding of Durkheim's view of society. The significance of social facts is to be discovered in the functional contribution to the general life of society, not in the experience of individuals. His perspective leads us to consider the functional consequences of any social phenomenon, even crime for example.

Personality: Society in Ourselves

According to Durkheim, society exists not only beyond us, having a life of its own, but also within us. Personalities are built through the internalization of social facts. Suicide, discussed in Chapter 1, illustrates this point. Individuals who are poorly regulated suffer the highest rates of suicide.

Modernity and Anomie

While modern society provides great personal freedom, the lack of regulation often leads to ***anomie***, where little moral guidance is provided.

Evolving Societies: The Division of Labour

Durkheim differentiated between two types of solidarity that have characterized societies over history. For most of history, human societies were dominated by a collective conscience, or moral consensus. Durkheim termed this ***mechanical solidarity***, meaning social bonds, common to pre-industrial societies, based on shared moral sentiments. Likeness was the rule in society. As this type declined it was replaced by ***organic solidarity***, or social bonds, common to industrialized societies, based on specialization. So Durkheim saw history in terms of a growing ***division of labour***, or specialized economic activity. Durkheim, like Weber and Marx, had concern about modern society and its effect on the individual. The dilemma for Durkheim was the fact that the positive benefits of modern society, such as technical advances and personal freedoms, were accompanied by diminishing morality and the danger of anomie.

CRITICAL REVIEW: FOUR VISIONS OF SOCIETY

The concluding section focuses on the questions raised at the beginning of this chapter using each of the four visions provided by Lenski, Marx, Weber, and Durkheim. These questions include the following:

What Holds Societies Together?

Lenski would answer by focusing on cultural patterns. Marx argued that only through co-operative productive enterprise could a united society develop. Weber saw unity created through a society's distinctive world view. Durkheim focused on the factor of social integration.

The **Thinking Critically Box** (p. 101) asks if our society is getting better? Despite the progress Canada has experienced in improved education, huge technological change, increase in average income, and increase in life expectancy in the last century, the level of optimism by Canadians has been declining for the last twenty-five years. Objectively, family incomes have recently increased only slightly, divorce rates have increased, while marriage rates have declined. There is also a perception that the crime rate is increasing, even though it isn't. Despite these concerns, most Canadians claim to be happy. Perhaps a Canadian economy that has outperformed the U.S. economy and a soaring "loonie" are partly responsible. A recent poll, however, found that Canadians worry about high taxes, debt, postsecondary education for their children, and health care costs. While most believe in God, few attend weekly religious services. The theorists who have been examined in this chapter may provide some answers. Lenski suggested that technology was no panacea and Marx, Weber, and Durkheim decried in various ways the increase in individualism at the cost of a sense of community. Perhaps that is what Canadians are experiencing now.

The **Applying Sociology Box** (p. 102) offers us the opportunity to imagine what Durkheim, Weber and Marx would think of the information society. Durkheim would probably note the increased specialization in the division of labour while Weber might celebrate the decline of rigid bureaucratic rules as factories become less important. Marx would likely identify a new elite, those who possess symbolic skills, and a new underclass, those with few.

How Have Societies Changed?

The sociocultural evolution model used by Lenski focuses on technology in answering this question. Marx's conflict approach focuses on historical differences in the productive system. And, while Weber focused on characteristics of human thought, Durkheim concentrated on how societies differ in terms of how they are bound together.

Why Do Societies Change?

Lenski sees change occurring through technological innovation. Marx saw class struggles as the "engine of history." Weber's idealist approach focused on how ideas contribute to social change. Finally, Durkheim believed the expanding division of labour was the main force behind the increasing complexity of society.

KEY CONCEPTS

Define each of the following concepts on a separate sheet of paper. Check the accuracy of your answers by referring to the key concepts section in the text, as well as referring to italicized definitions located throughout the chapter.

agriculture
alienation
anomie
capitalists
class consciousness
class conflict
division of labour
false consciousness
horticultural society
hunting and gathering society
ideal type
industrialism
mechanical solidarity
organic solidarity
pastoralism
post-industrialism
proletarians
rationalization of society
rationality
social conflict
social fact
social institutions
society
sociocultural evolution
tradition

STUDY QUESTIONS

True-False

1. T F As used sociologically, the concept of society refers to people who interact with one another within a defined territory and who share a culture.

2. T F The greater the amount of technological information a society has, the slower is the rate at which it changes.

3. T F Hunting and gathering societies disappeared from this planet in the middle of the twentieth century.

4. T F Horticultural societies use a technology based upon the domestication of animals.

5. T F Agrarian societies are often characterized as "the dawn of civilization."

6. T F Industrial societies transformed themselves more in a century than they had in thousands of years before.

7. T F The productive technology of post-industrial societies is mechanized through advanced sources of energy.

8. T F The most significant form of social conflict for Marx involved clashes between social classes that arise from the way a society produces material goods.

9. T F According to Weber, people in modern societies embrace rationality.

10. T F Organic solidarity characterizes pre-industrial societies.

11. T F Unlike Marx and Weber, Durkheim was relatively optimistic about industrialization and the development of modern society.

12. T F A recent Ipsos-Reid poll found that 84% of Canadians believe in God but only 75% attend weekly services.

Multiple Choice

1. Gerhard Lenski focuses on which factor as a major determinate of social change?

(a) human ideas
(b) technology
(c) social conflict
(d) social solidarity
(e) religious doctrine

2. Hunting and gathering societies have few formal leaders but most recognize a _____, a spiritual leader.

(a) hunter
(b) kaska
(c) shaman
(d) venerate
(e) (none of the above)

3. The first type of society to be characterized by economic inequality was __________.

(a) hunter/gatherer society
(b) horticultural society
(c) agrarian
(d) industrial
(e) post-industrial

4. Industrialism engenders ______________________.

(a) more prosperity
(b) a reduction in family importance
(c) a decline in inequality
(d) (all of the above)
(e) (a and b above)

5. Technology that supports an information-based economy is called ________.

(a) hunting and gathering
(b) agrarian
(c) horticultural
(d) industrial
(e) post-industrial

6. Although technology has generally improved life, the twenty-first century will likely still be dealing with the technologically produced problems of ______________.

(a) a lack of sense of community
(b) a damaged environment
(c) establishing peace
(d) (all of the above)
(e) (none of the above)

7. Marx contends that one institution dominates all others when it comes to steering the direction of a society. It is the ____________________.

(a) educational institution
(b) political institution
(c) mass media
(d) economic institution
(e) family institution

8. According to Marx, workers would become aware of their oppression and see capitalism as its true cause through the development of ______________________.

(a) false consciousness
(b) anomie
(c) class consciousness
(d) alienation
(e) a bourgeois attitude

9. Marx called the experience of isolation and misery resulting from powerlessness _______________.

   (a) alienation
   (b) false consciousness
   (c) anomie
   (d) communism
   (e) class conflict

10. Max Weber's analysis of society reflects the philosophical approach known as ____________.

   (a) materialism
   (b) idealism
   (c) cultural ecology
   (d) egalitarianism
   (e) radicalism

11. Weber contended that industrial capitalism was the legacy of _______________.

   (a) social conflict
   (b) technology
   (c) organic solidarity
   (d) false consciousness
   (e) Calvinism

12. If the classical scholars were alive to evaluate the impact of the Information Revolution on Canadian society, which one would likely identify a new elite who possessed symbolic skills?

   (a) Emile Durkheim
   (b) Max Weber
   (c) Leo Tolstoy
   (d) Karl Marx
   (e) Gerhard Lenski

Fill in the Blank

1. Hunting and gathering societies rarely form ______________ settlements.

2. When a society produces a _________________, not everyone has to work at providing food.

3. Marx referred to those who own the means of production as the _______________, and those who provide the labour for its operation as the _________________.

4. As a result of powerlessness, workers experience ___________________ in Marx's theory of social conflict.

5. Max Weber demonstrated the importance of _______________ in shaping social change and development.

6. According to Weber, an abstract description of a social phenomenon on the basis of its essential characteristics a(n) ____________.

7. Durkheim called any part of society that is argued to have an objective existence apart from the individual a ___________ ___________.

8. ____________ refers to a condition in which society provides individuals with little moral guidance.

9. According to Durkheim, social bonds common in industrial society, based on specialization, are called ___________ ______________.

10. Durkheim pointed to an expanding _____________ ____________ ___________as the key dimension of social change.

Definition and Short Answer

1. How does Lenski define sociocultural evolution?

2. What are the basic types of societies identified by Lenski? What are the basic characteristics of each?

3. What do our authors mean by the "limits of technology"?

4. What is the meaning of the philosophy of materialism?

5. How does Marx understand the role of social conflict through history?

6. According to Marx, what are the four ways in which industrial capitalism alienates workers?

7. According to Weber, what are the roots of rationality in modern society?

8. For Weber, what are the components of rational social organization?

9. What is the meaning of the term "social fact" as discussed by Durkheim?

10. Define the two types of solidarity according to Durkheim?

11. Compare the four visions of society as conceptualized by Lenski, Marx, Weber, and Durkheim.

Answers to Study Questions

True-False

1. T (p. 84)
2. F (p. 85)
3. F (p. 85)
4. F (p. 86)
5. T (p. 86)
6. T (p. 87)
7. F (p. 88)
8. T (p. 90)
9. T (p. 94)
10. F (p. 99)
11. T (p. 99
12. F (p. 101)

Multiple Choice

1. b (p. 84)
2. c (p. 85)
3. b (p. 86)
4. d (pp. 87-88)
5. e (p. 88)
6. d (p. 89)
7. d (p. 90)
8. c (p. 92)
9. a (p. 93)
10. b (p. 94)
11. e (p. 95)
12. d (p. 102)

Fill in the Blank

1. permanent (p. 85)
2. material surplus (p. 86)
3. capitalists; proletarians (p. 90)
4. alienation (p. 93)
5. ideas (p. 94)
6. ideal type (p. 94)
7. social fact (p. 98)
8. anomie (p. 99)
9. organic solidarity (p. 99)
10. division of labour (p. 102)

ANALYSIS AND COMMENT

Go back through the chapter and write down in the spaces below key points from each of the following boxes.

THINKING IT THROUGH

"Can Sociology Help Us To Design a Better Society?"
Key Points:

THINKING CRITICALLY

"Is Our Society Getting Better or Worse?"
Key Points:

APPLYING SOCIOLOGY

"The Information Revolution: What Would Durkheim (and Others) Have Thought?"

Key Points:

SELECTED READINGS

Classic Sources

Robert C. Tucker, ed. 1978. *The Marx-Engels Reader.* 2nd. Ed. New York: W.W. Norton.
This is an excellent source of essays by Karl Marx and Friedrich Engels.

Max Weber. 1995; orig. 1904-05. *The Protestant Ethic and the Spirit of Capitalism.* Los Angeles: Roxbury Press.
Perhaps Max Weber's best-known study is his analysis of Protestantism and capitalism.

Emile Durkheim. 1964; orig. 1893. *The Division of Labour in Society.* New York: The Free Press.
This is Durkheim's major contribution to our understanding of modern societies.

Contemporary Sources

Gerhard Lenski, Patrick Nolan, and Jean Lenski. 1995. *Human Society: An Introduction to Macrosociology.* 7th ed. New York: McGraw-Hill. 1995.
A comprehensive account of Gerhard and Jean Lenski's analysis of human societies is found in this textbook.

Irving Louis Horowitz. 1993. *The Decomposition of Sociology.* New York: Oxford University Press.
A well-known sociologist argues that the discipline, fraught with political, theoretical, and methodological divisions, is on the decline.

Michael S. Serrill. 1995. "A Nation Blessed, A Nation Stressed." *Time*, November 20, 20-43.

Global Source

Uta Gerhardt, ed. 1993. *Talcott Parsons on National Socialism.* Hawthorne, NY: Aldine de Gruyter.
This book explains how an outstanding theorist applied his research to the Allied effort in World War II and the structuring of a democratic postwar Germany.

Canadian Sources

S. D. Clark. 1942. *The Social Development of Canada.* Toronto: University of Toronto Press.
Wallace Clement. 1974. *The Canadian Corporate Elite: An Analysis of Economic Power.* Toronto: McClelland & Stewart.
Dennis Forcese. 1980. *The Canadian Class Structure.* 2nd. Ed. Toronto: McGraw-Hill Ryerson.
John Porter. 1965. *The Vertical Mosaic.* Toronto: University of Toronto Press
This brief sampling of some classics in Canadian sociology focuses on the structure and development of Canadian society.

CHAPTER 5

Socialization

CHAPTER OUTLINE

I. Social Experience: The Key to Our Humanity
- A. Human Development: Nature and Nurture
  1. The Biological Sciences: The Role of Nature
  2. The Social Sciences: The Role of Nurture
- B. Social Isolation
  1. Studies of Nonhuman Primates
  2. Studies of Isolated Children

II. Understanding Socialization
- A. Sigmund Freud's Elements of Personality
  1. Basic Human Needs
  2. Freud's Model of Personality
  3. Personality Development
- B. Jean Piaget's Theory of Cognitive Development
  1. The Sensorimotor Stage
  2. The Pre-operational Stage
  3. The Concrete Operational Stage
  4. The Formal Operational Stage
- C. Lawrence Kohlberg's Theory of Moral Development
- D. Carol Gilligan's Theory of Gender and Moral Development
- E. George Herbert Mead's Theory of the Social Self
  1. The Self
  2. The Looking-Glass Self
  3. The I and the Me
  4. Development of the Self
- F. Erik H. Erikson's Eight Stages of Development

III. Agents of Socialization
- A. The Family
- B. The School
- C. Gender
  1. What Children Learn
- D. The Peer Group
- E. The Mass Media
  1. Television and Bias
  2. Television and Violence

IV. Socialization and the Life Course
- A. Childhood
- B. Adolescence
- C. Adulthood
- D. Old Age
- E. Death and Dying
- F. The Life Course: Patterns and Variations

V. Resocialization: Total Institutions

VI. Making the Grade

VII Key Points

VIII. Key Concepts

IX. Applications and Exercises

X. MySocLab

LEARNING OBJECTIVES

- To understand the "nature versus nurture" debate regarding socialization
- To explain the effects of social isolation on humans and other primates
- To identify the key components in Sigmund Freud's model of personality
- To identify and describe the four stages of cognitive development in the theory of Jean Piaget.
- To understand both Lawrence Kohlberg's theory of moral development and Carol Gilligan's critique
- To comprehend whether males and females are different with respect to aggressive behaviour
- To explain the contributions of George Herbert Mead to the understanding of the process of socialization
- To understand Erik Erikson's eight stages of development
- To be able to compare and contrast the theories of Freud, Piaget, Mead, Kohlberg, Gilligan, and Erikson concerning socialization and human development
- To compare and contrast the agents of socialization (family, schooling, etc.) in terms of their effects on an individual's socialization experiences
- To understand the complexity of race and ethnicity and its impact upon socialization
- To compare and contrast the modes of socialization in childhood, adolescence, adulthood, and old age
- To understand the power of the mass media in shaping our understanding of the social world
- To describe the social experience of life within a total institution

CHAPTER REVIEW

SOCIAL EXPERIENCE: THE KEY TO OUR HUMANITY

We are told the story of Anna, a young girl who was raised in a context devoid of meaningful social contact. Kingsley Davis, a sociologist, studied the six-year-old girl and described her as being more an object than a person. What Anna had been deprived of was ***socialization***, or lifelong social experience, by which individuals develop human potential and learn the patterns of their culture. Socialization is the foundation of ***personality***, referring to a person's fairly consistent pattern of thinking, feeling, and acting. In Anna's case, personality just did not develop.

Human Development: Nature and Nurture

➢The Biological Sciences: The Role of Nature

Naturalists during the mid-nineteenth century, applying Charles Darwin's theory of evolution, claimed that all human behaviour was instinctive. Although this is no longer a dominant view, the thinking is still with us as people, for example, talk about "born criminals."

➢The Social Sciences: The Role of Nurture

Social scientists reject much of the biological argument and see human nature itself as shaped by cultural context.

Psychologist John Watson challenged the naturalistic perspective and developed an approach called behaviourism, claiming that all human behaviour was learned within particular social environments.

Contemporary social scientists do not argue that biology plays no role in shaping human behaviour. At the very least, human physical traits are linked to heredity. Also, certain characteristics such as intelligence, potential to excel in music and art, and personality characteristics seem to be influenced by heredity. The current position on this issue is that nurture is our nature.

Social Isolation

For obvious ethical reasons, research on the effects of social isolation has been limited to the study of animals. A few rare cases of human isolation, like Anna's, have been investigated.

➢Studies of Nonhuman Primates

Classic research by Harry and Margaret Harlow using rhesus monkeys has illustrated the importance of social interaction for other primates besides humans. Using various experimental situations with artificial "mothers" for infant monkeys, they determined that while physical development occurred within normal limits, emotional and social growth failed to occur. One important discovery was that monkeys deprived of mother-infant contact, if surrounded by other infant monkeys, did not suffer adversely. This suggested the importance of social interaction in general rather than specifically a maternal bond. A second conclusion was that monkeys who experienced short-term isolation (three months or less) recovered to normal emotional levels after rejoining other monkeys. Long-term separation appears to have irreversible negative consequences.

➢Studies of Isolated Children

The cases of Anna, Isabelle, and Genie, all of whom suffered through years of isolation and neglect as young children, are reviewed. Each case suggests that while humans are resilient creatures, extreme social isolation results in irreversible damage to normal personality development.

UNDERSTANDING SOCIALIZATION

Sigmund Freud: The Elements of Personality

While trained as a physician, Freud's most important contribution was the development of psychoanalysis and the study of personality development.

➢Basic Human Needs

Freud saw biological factors having a significant influence on personality, though he rejected the argument that human behaviour reflected simple biological instinct. He conceived instincts as general urges and drives. He claimed humans had two basic needs or drives: ***eros***, a need for bonding and ***thanatos***, which related to a drive for death.

➢Freud's Model of Personality

Freud's perspective combined both these basic needs and the influence of society into a unique model of personality. He argued the personality is comprised of three parts. One is the ***id***, rooted in biology and representing the human being's basic needs, which are unconscious and demand immediate satisfaction. Another, representing the conscious attempt to balance innate pleasure-seeking drives of the human organism and the demands of society, he labelled the ***ego***. Finally, the human personality develops a ***superego,*** which is the operation of culture within the individual that ultimately defines, for the individual, moral limits.

➢Personality Development

There is basic conflict between the id and the superego, which the ego must continually try to manage. If the conflict is not adequately resolved, personality disorders result. Society's controlling influence on drives is referred to as ***repression***. Often a compromise between society and the individual is struck, where fundamentally selfish drives are redirected into socially acceptable objectives. This process is called ***sublimation***.

Id-centred children feel good only in a physical sense, but after three or four years, with the gradual development of the superego, they can begin to evaluate their behaviour by cultural standards.

While controversial, Freud's work highlights the internalization of social norms and the importance of childhood experiences in the socialization process and the development of personality.

Jean Piaget's Theory of Cognitive Development

A prominent psychologist of the twentieth century, Piaget's work centred on human ***cognition***, or how people think and understand. He was concerned with not just what a person knew, but how the person knows something. He identified four major stages of cognitive development.

➢The Sensorimotor Stage

The ***sensorimotor stage*** is described as the level of human development in which the world is experienced only through sensory contact. This stage lasts for about the first two years of life. The understanding of symbols does not exist during this period. The child experiences the world only in terms of direct physical contact.

➢The Pre-operational Stage

The ***pre-operational stage*** was described by Piaget as the level of human development in which language and other symbols are first used. This stage extends from the age of two to the age of six. Children continue to be very egocentric during this time, having little ability to generalize concepts.

➢The Concrete Operational Stage

The third stage in Piaget's model is called the ***concrete operational stage*** and is described as the level of human development characterized by the use of logic to understand objects or events. This period typically covers the ages of seven to eleven. Cause-and-effect relationships begin to be understood during this period. The ability to take the perspective of other people also emerges.

➢The Formal Operational Stage

The fourth stage is the ***formal operational stage*** and is described as the level of human development characterized by highly abstract and critical thought. This stage begins about age twelve. The ability to think in hypothetical terms is also developed.

Some critics suggest that the model may not fit traditional societies and that, even in our own society, as many as a third of adults do not reach the final stage.

Lawrence Kohlberg's Theory of Moral Development

Kohlberg used Piaget's theory as a springboard for a study on moral reasoning. He suggests a ***preconventional stage*** based on pain and pleasure, a ***conventional stage*** (in the teenage years), where right and wrong is understood within cultural norms, and a ***postconventional stage,*** where abstract critique of the social order is possible.

Kohlberg's theory may not apply equally well in all societies and it would appear that many North Americans do not reach the final stage of moral development. His research subjects were also all boys.

Carol Gilligan's Theory of Gender and Moral Development

Gilligan, as a response to the gender-limited work of Kohlberg, concludes that males and females make moral judgments in different ways. Males use a ***justice perspective:*** "It's wrong if the rules define it that way". Females use a ***care and responsibility perspective:*** "It's wrong if it damages relationships." Her recent research on self-esteem demonstrates that female self-esteem begins to slip during adolescence as they encounter more authority figures who are men. Her research is covered in the **Thinking About Diversity Box** (p. 114).

George Herbert Mead's Theory of the Social Self

Mead's analysis is often referred to as ***social behaviourism,*** where he focuses on mental processes.

➢The Self

Mead understood the basis of humanity to be the ***self,*** a dimension of personality composed of an individual's self- conception. For Mead, the self was a totally social phenomenon, inseparable from society. The connection between the two was explained in a series of steps, the emergence of the self through social experience, based on the exchange of symbolic intentions, and occurring within a context in which people take the role of the other, or take their point of view into account during social interaction.

➢The Looking-Glass Self

The process of taking the role of the other can be understood using Charles Horton Cooley's concept of the ***looking-glass self.*** This term focuses on the idea that a person's self-conception is based on the response of others.

➢The I and The Me

The capacity to see one's self has two components, namely: (1) the self as subject by which we initiate social action, and (2) the self as object, concerning how we perceive ourselves from the perspective of others. The subjective part of the self Mead labelled the "I." The objective aspect Mead called the "Me." All social interaction is seen as the continuous interplay of these two aspects of the self.

➢Development of the Self

Mead emphasized that the key to developing the self was social experience. Mead saw infants as responding to others only in terms of imitation. As the use of symbols emerges the child enters a ***play*** stage, in which role-taking occurs. Initially, the roles are modelled after significant others, especially parents. Through further social experience children enter the ***game*** stage where the simultaneous playing of many roles is possible. The final stage involves the development of a ***generalized other,*** or widespread cultural norms and values used as a reference in evaluating ourselves.

Figure 5-1 (p. 115) illustrates the development of the self as a process of gaining social experience. Although Mead's work is criticized as being radically social he helps us to understand the importance of symbolic interaction to the development of self.

Erik H. Erikson's Eight Stages of Development

Erikson offers a broader view of socialization, suggesting that personality continues to change throughout life. His eight stages begin in infancy and end in old age.

Some are critical of the apparent rigidity of the model, but it does force us to examine the influence of agencies of socialization other than the family.

AGENTS OF SOCIALIZATION

The Family

The family is identified as the most important agent of socialization. The process of socialization within this institution is both intentional and unconscious. While parenting styles vary, the most important aspect in parent-child relations seems to be ***attention*** paid by parents to their children. The family is the initial source for transmission of culture to the child.

From an early age children learn from their families that social class exists and that it is associated with different behaviour patterns and different values. Research also shows that affluent parents are more likely to provide their children with "cultural capital" that advances learning and creates a sense of confidence. Racial and ethnic background of the family also contributes to the development of social identity for children. The **Thinking About Diversity Box** (p. 118) reveals the complexity of ethnic or racial socialization.

The School

School exposes children to people from a diversity of social backgrounds; however, they are likely to cluster in playgroups made up of one race, class, and gender.

Gender

Schools and families together socialize children into gender roles. Boys engage in more aggressive behaviour than girls and are prepared for occupational roles in engineering and science. Schools also teach many things informally through a "hidden curriculum," which rewards children from rich families as opposed to those from poor families.

The Peer Group

Peer group socialization typically occurs outside the context of adult supervision. A ***peer group*** is defined as a social group whose members have interests, social position, and age in common. Some research provides evidence suggesting that the conflict between parents and their adolescent children is more apparent than real. A major feature operative during adolescence is referred to as ***anticipatory socialization***, or the process of social learning directed toward gaining a desired position.

The Mass Media

The ***mass media*** are impersonal communications directed to a vast audience. This includes television, newspapers, and radio, although television has become the dominant medium, such that children spend more hours watching television than they spend in school or in interacting with their parents. The message includes class, gender, and racial biases but, on the other hand, the producers tend to be more liberal than the average Canadian or American. **Figure 5-2** (p. 121) demonstrates the pervasiveness of television ownership and the **Media Perspectives Box** (p. 122) discusses the portrayal of racial minorities and women in television productions. While historically, minority groups and women were under-represented and portrayed stereotypically, there has been massive change in the last few years so that minorities and women play a more dominant role and are portrayed, more often, in a fair and sympathetic fashion.

Although television and other mass media can be magnificent sources for entertainment and learning, there has developed a concern over media violence and media bias and its impact upon behaviour, especially of children. There is, as yet, no consensus about the existence of a cause-and-effect relationship.

SOCIALIZATION AND THE LIFE COURSE

While focus is given to childhood in terms of the significance of socialization, this process is lifelong. Social experience is structured during different stages of the life course.

Childhood

Nike is criticized for the employment of children in the production of sneakers since ***childhood*** in Canadian culture lasts roughly the first twelve years of life, a period characterized by freedom from responsibilities. While most suggest childhood is an expanding period in technologically advanced societies, some research, especially on affluent families, suggests it actually may be getting shorter. The "hurried child" pattern reflects this idea.

Adolescence

This period emerged as a distinct life cycle stage in industrial societies. This period corresponds roughly to the teen years. The social turmoil often associated with this stage appears to be the result of inconsistencies in the socialization process, as opposed to physical changes. Examples concerning the status of teens in relation to voting and drinking are discussed, along with the fact that social class also plays a role because working-class youth are often working at age eighteen, while middle-class individuals may be in graduate school at thirty.

Adulthood

Adulthood is a period when most of our life's accomplishments occur, and, especially toward the end of this stage, people reflect upon what they have accomplished.

Early adulthood lasts approximately from the early 20s to age 40. While personality is largely set by this time, certain dislocations, like unemployment, divorce, or a serious illness can result in significant changes to the self. This period is dominated by meeting day-to-day responsibilities and achieving goals set earlier in life. The juggling of conflicting priorities also characterizes this period especially for women who work but who are expected to maintain the functions of mother and housewife. Recently the term "adultescent" has been used to describe those who are living with their parents at 30 years of age or older.

Middle adulthood lasts roughly between the ages of 40 and 60. A distinctive quality of this period is reflection on personal achievements in light of earlier expectations. While working men and women are often forced to recognize their failure to realize earlier expectations, women must also confront their physical decline in a society that is less generous, in this respect, to them as compared to men.

Old Age

This period begins during the mid-60s. The status of the aged varies greatly cross-culturally. In rapidly changing modern societies, the aged tend to be defined as marginal or even obsolete. This period is quite different from previous ones as it is characterized by the leaving of roles instead of entering new ones. As the proportion of elderly people increases, as it will rather dramatically over the next thirty years, the anti-elderly bias will surely decline.

Death and Dying

As the proportion of people in old age increases, we will likely be more comfortable with the idea of death. More people now make legal and financial preparations for a surviving spouse. The work of Elisabeth Kübler-Ross describes the transition from denial to acceptance of death.

THE LIFE COURSE: PATTERNS AND VARIATIONS

The life course is largely a social construction and each stage contains characteristic problems that are, however, affected by the dynamics of class, race, ethnicity, and gender.

Life experience also varies because of when people were born. Age cohorts or generations are likely to have experienced cultural and economic trends that other cohorts have not. Those born in the 1940s and 1950s faced economic expansion, while today's youth face economic uncertainty.

RESOCIALIZATION: TOTAL INSTITUTIONS

A ***total institution*** is defined as a setting in which individuals are isolated from the rest of society and manipulated by an administrative staff. Erving Goffman has identified three distinct qualities of such institutions: (1) they control all aspects of the daily lives of the residents, (2) they subject residents to standardized activities, and (3) they apply formal rules and rigid scheduling to all activities. This structure is designed to achieve the policy of ***resocialization***, or deliberate control of an environment to radically alter an inmate's personality. This is understood as a two-part process—the destruction of the individua"s self-conception, and the systematic building of another one. A process known as ***institutionalization*** often occurs whereby residents become dependent on the structure of the institution and are unable to function outside the institution. The **Thinking It Through Box** (p. 127) describes how Ontario's first boot camp can be conceptualized as a total institution.

KEY CONCEPTS

Define each of the following concepts on a separate sheet of paper. Check the accuracy of your answers by referring to the glossary section in the text, as well as by referring to italicized definitions located throughout the chapter.

adolescence
adulthood
anticipatory socialization
childhood
cohort
concrete operational stage
death and dying
ego
formal operational stage
generalized other
hidden curriculum
id
looking-glass self
mass media
old age
peer group
personality
pre-operational stage
resocialization
self
sensorimotor stage
significant others
socialization
superego
total institution

STUDY QUESTIONS

True-False

1. T F John Watson was a nineteenth-century psychologist who argued that human behaviour was largely determined by heredity.

2. T F Social scientists agree that personality characteristics have some genetic component.

3. T F The Harlows' social isolation research on rhesus monkeys illustrates that while short-term isolation can be overcome, long-term isolation appears to cause irreversible emotional and behavioural damage to the monkeys.

4. T F Freud envisioned biological factors as having little or no influence on personality development.

5. T F Freud claimed that the superego represents the human being's basic drives.

6. T F At the pre-operational stage, according to Piaget, a child cannot judge size, weight, or volume.

7. T F Carol Gilligan argues that girls make moral judgments from a justice perspective.

8. T F Mead's concept of the generalized other refers to widespread cultural norms and values used as a reference in evaluating ourselves.

9. T F An ever larger proportion of Canadians claims multiple ethnic or racial origins, thereby diluting the impact of ethnic socialization.

10. T F The concept "hidden curriculum" relates to the important informal cultural values being transmitted to children in school.

11. T F Kübler-Ross describes the first phase of dying as acceptance.

12. T F A rigidly controlled total institution usually instils in its inmates the desire and capacity to adjust to the outside world.

Multiple Choice

1. The story of Anna illustrates the significance of __________ in personality development.

   (a) heredity
   (b) social experience
   (c) physical conditions
   (d) ecological forces
   (e) historical processes

2. Freud identified two basic needs or drives. One was the death instinct, which he referred to as ____________.

   (a) eros
   (b) thanatos
   (c) superego
   (d) id
   (e) ego

3. Freud called culture existing within the individual ________________.

(a) thanatos
(b) eros
(c) the ego
(d) the id
(e) the superego

4. According to Piaget, which of the following best describes the formal operational stage of cognitive development?

(a) the level of human development in which the world is experienced only through sensory contact
(b) the level of human development characterized by the use of logic to understand objects and events
(c) the level of human development in which language and other symbols are first used
(d) the level of human development characterized by highly abstract thought
(e) none of the above

5. In Kohlberg's final stage of moral development, the postconventional level, individuals ________________________.

(a) conceptualize rightness as what feels good to them
(b) define right and wrong in terms of what is consistent with cultural norms
(c) are capable of arguing that what is conventional may not be right
(d) (all of the above)
(e) (none of the above)

6. Gilligan finds that girls' __________ slips away as they pass through adolescence.

(a) self-esteem
(b) sense of responsibility
(c) self-awareness
d) justice perspective
e) superego development

7. The concept of the looking-glass self refers to ___________________________.

(a) Freud's argument that through psychoanalysis we can uncover our unconscious
(b) Piaget's view that through biological maturation and social experience individuals become able to logically hypothesize about thoughts without relying on concrete reality
(c) Watson's behaviourist notion that one can see through to a person's mind only by observing their behaviour
(d) Cooley's idea that a person's self-conception is based on responses of others

8. In which of Erikson's eight stages of development do we find the challenge of intimacy versus isolation?

(a) toddler
(b) pre-adolescent
(c) young adulthood
(d) middle adulthood
(e) none of the above

9. Research shows that affluent parents provide ________________________ for their children in the socialization process.

a) an emphasis on obedience and authority
b) an emphasis on good judgment and creativity
c) an exposure to physical punishment
d) an exposure to limited leisure opportunities
e) none of the above

10. Recent studies in Canada on television violence have concluded that ________________.

(a) television violence increases aggressive behaviour in children
(b) the link between television violence and children's behaviour is inconclusive and contradictory.
(c) there is a link between violence on television and violence in society
(d) (all of the above)
(e) (a and c above)

11. In industrial societies, the stage of life often associated with emotional and social turmoil is called ____________________.

(a) childhood
(b) adolescence
(c) middle adulthood.
(d) old age
(e) (none of the above)

Fill in The Blank

1. In the absence of social experience, _____________ does not emerge at all.

2. The approach called ____________, developed by John Watson in the early twentieth century provided a perspective that stressed learning rather than instincts as the key to personality development.

3. According to Freud, the _____________ represents the human being's basic drives that are unconscious and demand immediate satisfaction.

4. Piaget's work centred on human _____________.

5. Carol Gilligan's research finds that girls' ___________ starts to slip away as they pass through adolescence.

6. Mead called the objective element of self the ____________.

7. _______________ give young people the opportunity to discuss interests that may not be shared by adults.

8. The highest number of television sets per person exists in __________.

9. A prison or mental hospital is an example of a ____________.

10. The deliberate manipulation of the environment in a prison, for example, has the ultimate goal of _______________.

Definition and Short Answer

1. Briefly review the history of the nature-nurture debate concerning human development.
2. Review the cases of social isolation described in the text. What are the effects of social isolation on non-human primates? What are the effects of social isolation on children?
3. According to Freud, what are the basic components of personality?
4. According to Piaget, what are the stages of cognitive development? What are the characteristics of each stage?
5. What do Kohlberg and Gilligan have to say about moral development?
6. What is Mead's theory of personality development? What are the stages identified in his model. What is the "self" and how does it develop?
7. How does Erikson broaden our understanding of socialization?
8. What are the major agents of socialization? Briefly describe how each influences human development.
9. What influence does social class have on family socialization practices?
10. How is our conception of death likely to change over the next quarter century?
11. How do the media portray minorities?
12. What is a total institution? Provide an example.

Answers to Study Questions

True-False

1. F (p. 109)
2. T (p. 109)
3. T (p. 110)
4. F (p. 111)
5. F (p. 111)
6. T (p. 112)
7. F (p. 113)
8. T (p. 115)
9. T (p. 118)
10. T (p. 119)
11. F (p. 125)
12. F (p. 126)

Multiple Choice

1. b (p. 108)
2. b (p. 111)
3. e (p. 111)
4. d (p. 112)
5. c (p. 112)
6. a (p. 114)
7. d (p. 114)
8. c (p. 116)
9. b (p. 117)
10. d (pp. 121-123)
11. b (p. 124)

Fill in the Blank

1. personality (p. 108)
2. behaviourism (p. 109)
3. id (p. 111)
4. cognition (p. 112)
5. self-esteem (p. 114)
6. me (p. 114)
7. peer groups (p. 120)
8. Sweden (p. 121)
9. total institution (p. 126)
10. resocialization (p. 126)

ANALYSIS AND COMMENT

Go back through the chapter and write down in the spaces below key points from each of the following boxes.

THINKING ABOUT DIVERSITY: RACE, CLASS, AND GENDER

"The Importance of Gender in Research"
Key Points

THINKING ABOUT DIVERSITY: RACE, CLASS, AND GENDER.

"Ethnic and Racial Identities: Evidence of Renewal and Dilution"
Key Points:

MEDIA PERSPECTIVES

"How Do the Media Portray Minorities?"
Key Points:

THINKING IT THROUGH

"Ontario's First Boot Camp as a Total Institution: 1997-2003"
Key Points:

SUGGESTED READINGS

Classic Sources

George Herbert Mead. 1962; orig. 1934. *Mind, Self, and Society from the Standpoint of a Social Behaviorist.* Charles W. Morris, ed. Chicago: University of Chicago Press.
Compiled after Mead's death by his students, this paperback presents Mead's analysis of the development of self.

Margaret Mead. 1961; orig. 1928. *Coming of Age in Samoa.* New York: Dell.
While still in her early twenties, Margaret Mead completed what is probably the best-known book in anthropology, in which she argues that the problems of adolescence are socially created rather than rooted in biology.

Contemporary Sources

Grace Craig. 1995. *Human Development.* 7th. Ed. Englewood Cliffs, NJ: Prentice Hall.
This book is a good general reference for understanding socialization across the life course.

George H. Hill, Lorraine Raglin, and Charles Floyd Johnson. 1990. *Black Women and Television.* New York: Garland.
Mary Ellen Brown, ed. 1990. *Television and Women's Culture: The Politics of the Popular.* 1990. Newbury Park, CA: Sage Publications.
The first of these two books about television highlights African-American women and cites interesting "firsts." The second, a collection of thirteen essays, delves into the subject of television and women, as actors and as audience.

John R. Seeley (*et al.*). 1963. *Crestwood Heights: A Study of the Culture of Suburban Life.* New York: Wiley.
A classic book on socialization in an elite community in Canada.

Margrit Eichler. 1988. *Families in Canada Today: Recent Changes and Their Policy Consequences.* 2nd. Ed. Toronto: Gage.
The impact of Canadian public policy on family life is the focus of Eichler's book.

Craig McKie and Keith Thompson. 1990. *Canadian Social Trends.* Toronto: Thompson Educational Publishing.
A brief summary of a variety of analyses of timely data collected via the Canadian census.

Jean-Yves Soucy with Annette, Cecile, and Yvonne Dionne. 1996. *Family Secrets.* Toronto: Stoddart.
This is the most recent book on the Dionne family.

Global Sources

Alba N. Ambert and Marie D. Alvarez, eds. 1992. *Puerto Rican Children on the Mainland: Interdisciplinary Perspectives.* New York: Garland.
This collection of essays sketches a statistical portrait of Puerto Ricans on the U.S. mainland and investigates distinctive dimensions of socialization among young people.

M.E.J. Wadsworth. 1991. *The Imprint of Time: Childhood, History, and Adult Life.* New York: Clarendon Press.
Long-term studies of cohorts are difficult and, therefore, rare in social science. This book reports on an ongoing study of more than 5000 men and women living throughout Britain, all born in 1946 and interviewed periodically since then.

Meg Luxton. 1980. *More than a Labour of Love.* Toronto: Women's Press.
A detailed examination of the lives of three generations of women in Flin Flon, Manitoba.

CHAPTER 6

Social Interaction in Everyday Life

CHAPTER OUTLINE

I. **Social Structure: A Guide to Everyday Living**
II. **Status**
    A. Status Set
    B. Ascribed Status and Achieved Status
    C. Master Status
III. **Role**
    A. Role Set
    B. Role Conflict and Role Strain
    C. Role Exit
IV. **The Social Construction of Reality**
    A. The Thomas Theorem
    B. Ethnomethodology
    C. Reality Building: Class and Culture
V. **Dramaturgical Analysis: "The Presentation of Self"**
    A. Performances
        1. An Application: The Doctor's Office
    B. Nonverbal Communication
        1. Body Language and Deception
    C. Gender and Performances
    D. Idealization
    E. Embarrassment and Tact
VI. **Interaction in Everyday Life: Three Applications**
    A. Emotions: The Social Construction of Feeling
        1. The Biological Side of Emotions
        2. The Cultural Side of Emotions
        3. Emotions on the Job
    B. Language: The Social Construction of Gender
        1. Language and Power
        2. Language and Value
        3. Language and Attention
    C. Reality Play: The Social Construction of Humour
        1. The Foundation of Humour
        2. The Dynamics of Humour: "Getting It"
        3. The Topics of Humour
        4. The Functions of Humour
        5. Humour and Conflict
VI. **Making the Grade**
VII. **Key Points**
VIII. **Key Concepts**
IX. **Applications and Exercises**
X. **MySocLab**

LEARNING OBJECTIVES

- To identify the characteristics of social structure
- To distinguish the different types of statuses and roles and the interconnection among them.
- To describe the importance of role in social interaction
- To explain the social construction of reality
- To understand the theoretical approach within the symbolic-interaction paradigm known as ethnomethodology
- To know the importance of performance, nonverbal communication, idealization, and embarrassment to the "presentation of self
- To describe dramaturgical analysis
- To be able to use gender and humour as illustrations of how people construct meaning in everyday life

CHAPTER REVIEW

The chapter begins with a description of how men and women deal differently with being lost. Women will ask for directions; often men will not. Such a vignette can be subjected to sociological analysis through the examination of ***social interaction***, the process by which people act and react in relation to others.

SOCIAL STRUCTURE: A GUIDE TO EVERYDAY LIVING

The social structural aspects of a society provide a guide for behaviour. Once the signposts are learned, the overall nature of the interaction process is clarified.

STATUS

One of the basic elements of social structure is ***status***, a recognized social position that an individual occupies. Each position is part of social identify that helps define our relationship to others.

Status Set

No person holds only one status position. He or she holds many. All the statuses that a person holds at a given time are called a status set. One can be a female, a student, a daughter, and a wife among others.

Ascribed and Achieved Status

Sociologists distinguish two ways in which statuses are obtained. An ***ascribed status*** is a social position that is received at birth or involuntarily assumed later in the life course. In contrast, an ***achieved status*** refers to a social position that is assumed voluntarily and that reflects personal ability and effort. Most often there is a combination of ascribed and achieved factors in each of our statuses.

Master Status

A ***master status*** is defined as a status that has an exceptional importance for social identity, often shaping a person's entire life. In our society, one's occupation often comprises this position. **The Thinking It Through box** (p. 134) points out that physical disability becomes the master status for many people. Ascribed statuses such as gender or mental illness are other examples of positions that can act as a person's master status.

ROLE

The concept ***role*** refers to patterns of expected behaviour attached to a particular status. Role performance can differ somewhat from the expectations society attaches to a role.

Role Set

Generally, a person has many more roles than statuses, as each status typically has multiple roles attached. Robert Merton defines a ***role set*** as a number of roles attached to a single status. **Figure 6-1** (p. 135) provides an illustration of a status set and role set. Roles people use to define their lives differ from society to society. **Global Map 6-1** (p. 136) shows how housework performed by women varies globally.

Role Conflict and Role Strain

The concept ***role conflict*** refers to incompatibility among the roles corresponding to two or more statuses. Even the roles attached to a single status can create problems for an individual. ***Role strain*** is the incompatibility among roles corresponding to a single status.

Role Exit

Role exit is the process by which people disengage from social roles that have been central to their lives. "Exes" often retain self-images from an earlier role that may interfere with the development of a new sense of self.

THE SOCIAL CONSTRUCTION OF REALITY

While statuses and roles structure our lives, we as individuals have considerable ability to shape patterns of interaction with others. The phrase ***social construction of reality*** refers to the process by which individuals creatively shape reality through social interaction. Social interaction is understood as a process of negotiation which generates a changing reality. **Figure 6-2**, (p. 137), for example, describes the proportion of first unions that are common law over a twenty-year period in Canada.

The Thomas Theorem

One observation made by sociologists is that situations that are defined as real become real in their consequences. This has become known as the ***Thomas theorem*** as constructed by W.I. Thomas.

Ethnomethodology

One approach to understanding the ways humans shape reality is called ***ethnomethodology,*** which is based on the symbolic-interaction paradigm. Harold Garfinkel coined the term, which is defined as the study of the way that people make sense of their everyday lives. Garfinkel did research in which he had students deliberately "break the rules" of ordinary social interaction. This approach highlights awareness of many unspoken agreements that underlie various interaction situations.

Reality Building: Class and Culture

People build reality from the surrounding culture. Social background in a given society affects how individuals see reality and certainly reality is affected by the circumstances of different global cultures**.** The **Media Perspectives Box** (p. 140) shows how perceptions of disability can change over time and the **Thinking Critically Box** (p. 149) indicates how information technology has an impact on our sense of reality.

DRAMATURGICAL ANALYSIS: "THE PRESENTATION OF SELF"

Another approach to understanding the social interaction of everyday life is ***dramaturgical analysis,*** as developed by Erving Goffman. This approach is defined as the analysis of social interaction in terms of theatrical performances. Goffman theorized that statuses and roles are used to create impressions. Central to this analysis is the process called the ***presentation of self***, meaning the ways in which individuals, in various settings, attempt to create specific impressions in the minds of others. This process is also referred to as ***impression management***. The **Media Perspectives Box** (p. 140) offers the opportunity of evaluating "presentation of self" for those in a negative "master status" of disability.

Performances

Goffman referred to the conscious and unconscious efforts of people in conveying information about themselves as ***performances***. These would include dress, tone of voice, objects being carried, etc.

➢An Application: The Doctor's Office

This is an interesting analysis of physicians and their offices. Conversations with patients are discussed to illustrate the notion that the doctor is in charge.

Nonverbal Communication

Novelist William Sansom's description of a fictional character named Mr. Preedy walking across a beach in Spain is used to illustrate the process of ***nonverbal communication***. This concept refers to communication using body movements, gestures, and facial expressions rather than spoken words. Types of smiles, eye contact, and hand movements can convey particular meanings.

➢Body Language and Deception

Performances can sometimes be deceiving when actors say something in order to hide an untruth. But such deceptions are difficult to maintain because the performance may break down as gestures or body movements suggest inconsistencies.

Gender and Performances

Gender is a central element in personal performances especially with regard to demeanour, personal space, facial expression, and touching.

Demeanour refers to the way we carry ourselves. It tends to vary depending on an individual's power. Given that men are more likely than women to be in positions of dominance, it is suggested that women must craft their performances more formally and display appropriate deference.

Power is also a key to the use of space. Masculinity has been traditionally associated with greater amounts of ***personal space***, or the surrounding area over which a person makes some claim to privacy. Also, men tend to intrude on a woman's space more often than women intrude on a man's space.

Women tend to maintain interactions through sustaining eye contact longer than men do, while men tend to stare more. For both Aboriginal men and women, however, staring is discourteous and only fleeting eye contact is maintained. Meanings associated with smiling also seem to vary with gender as do touching patterns, with men tending to touch women more than women touch men. Various rituals are created in which men tend to express their dominance over women. None of these meanings attached to performance help people to communicate online, as is explored in the **Applying Sociology Box** (p. 142).

Idealization

Goffman suggests that we attempt to idealize our intentions when it comes to our performances. The context of a hospital involving physicians making their rounds with patients is used to illustrate how people, in this case doctors, try to convince people they are abiding by ideal cultural standards, when, in fact, less noble reasons are often involved.

Embarrassment and Tact

As hard as we may try to craft perfect performances, slip-ups do occur and may cause embarrassment, or the recognition that we have failed through our performance to convince our audience. Audiences will often ignore flaws in performances, using tact to enable the performance to continue. This is because embarrassment causes discomfort for all present.

While life is not a scripted play, to some extent, Shakespeare's "All the world's a stage" idea does portray our relationships within social structure.

INTERACTION IN EVERYDAY LIFE: THREE APPLICATIONS

Emotions: The Social Construction of Feeling

Emotions or feelings are an important personal element, but emotions also are guided by society.

➢The Biological Side of Emotions

Ekman finds that six basic emotions vary little across cultures and can be seen as biologically programmed. They are happiness, sadness, anger, fear, disgust, and surprise.

➢The Cultural Side of Emotions

Culture provides the trigger for emotions: where it is displayed, how it is valued, and who should express it (gender for example).

➢Emotions on the Job

Most people express their emotions more freely at home because employers establish emotional scripts for employees.

Language: The Social Construction of Gender

Language conveys both obvious and not so obvious meanings. Gender is a trigger for differential definition in at least three ways.

➢Language and Power

One example of this is that males tend to attach female pronouns to valued objects, consistent with the concept of possession. Another illustration is women changing their name when they marry. When they fail to do so, the husband is seen by some as lacking in control.

➢Language and Value

Language conveys different levels of status in many subtle ways. Typically, the masculine terms carry higher status.

➢Language and Attention

The English language seems to almost ignore what is feminine. This is reflected in our pronoun usage and, indeed, in our national anthem. However, efforts exist in the language lately (often grammatically incorrect) to provide gender-neutral pronouns.

Reality Play: The Social Construction of Humour

Another example of the sociological importance of everyday interaction is in the analysis of humour. The issue of why something is funny is seldom analyzed critically by people.

➢The Foundation of Humour

Humour emerges out of ambiguity and double meanings involving two differing definitions of the situation, a contrasting of the ***conventional*** and the ***unconventional***. The key to a good joke seems to lie in the opposition of realities. **The Media Perspectives Box** (p. 147) demonstrates the impact of mixed meanings in newspaper headlines. The humour performance is also important. If precision and timing are missing, the joke can fall flat.

➢The Dynamics of Humour: "Getting It"

To get the joke, the listener must understand the two realities: the conventional and the unconventional. People derive satisfaction and even "insider status" by being able to "piece together" the realities to "get the joke," and even if they don't get it, they make out as if they do.

➢The Topics of Humour

While humour is universal, what is viewed as funny is not. Yet, humour is everywhere closely tied to what is controversial. There is, however, a fine line between what is funny and what is "sick."

➢The Functions of Humour

The universality of humour reflects its function as a safety valve. Sentiments can be expressed that might be dangerous to relationships if taken seriously.

➢Humour and Conflict

While humour can liberate it can also oppress as jokes about gays and "ethnics" attest. Often, however, minorities will joke about themselves as well as the powerful. Humour offers all some freedom from reality.

KEY CONCEPTS

Define each of the following concepts on a separate sheet of paper. Check the accuracy of your answers by referring to the text, as well as by referring to italicized definitions located throughout the chapter.

achieved status
ascribed status
dramaturgical analysis
ethnomethodology
master status
nonverbal communication
personal space
presentation of self
role
role conflict
role exit
role set
role strain
social construction of reality
social interaction
status
status set
Thomas theorem

STUDY QUESTIONS

True-False

1. T F A status is a social position that a person holds.

2. T F A status set refers to all the roles a person plays during his or her lifetime.

3. T F Illness can operate as a master status.

4. T F Statuses vary by culture but roles do not.

5. T F The process by which people disengage from important social roles is called role exit.

6. T F Role strain refers to conflict among the roles connected to two or more statuses.

7. T F Women tend to be more sensitive than men to nonverbal communication.

8. T F Women commonly intrude on the personal space of men.

9. T F Ekman reports that people the world over recognize and express six basic emotions.

10. T F The essence of humour lies in the contrast between two incongruous realities, the conventional and the unconventional.

Multiple Choice

1. A social position that someone receives involuntarily is called a(n) _________________.

   (a) ascribed status
   (b) achieved status
   (c) master status
   (d) status set
   (e) role set

2. Which of the following is not a structural component of social interaction?

   (a) master status
   (b) role
   (c) value
   (d) role set
   (e) ascribed status

3. The behaviour expected of someone who holds a particular status is called a ___________.

   (a) master status
   (b) role
   (c) performance
   (d) dramaturgy
   (e) nonverbal communication.

4. The tension among the roles connected to a single status refers to ________________.

   (a) role conflict
   (b) role strain
   (c) status overload
   (d) status inconsistency
   (e) role set

5. When a mother is experiencing difficulty in parenting her children because of the demands of her occupation, she is experiencing ____________________.

   (a) status diffusion
   (b) role strain
   (c) role conflict
   (d) role exit
   (e) (none of the above)

6. The Thomas theorem states that ________________________________.

   (a) roles are only as important as the statuses to which they are attached
   (b) statuses are only as important as the roles to which they are attached
   (c) the basis of humanity is built upon the dual existence of creativity and conformity
   (d) common sense is only as good as the social structure within which it is embedded
   (e) situations defined as real are real in their consequences

7. The methodology used by ethnomethodologists to study everyday interaction involves __________________.

   (a) conducting surveys
   (b) unobtrusive observation
   (c) secondary analysis
   (d) breaking the rules
   (e) experimentation

8. The physicians private office and examination rooms were referred to by Goffman as the __________________.

   (a) front region
   (b) formal performance area
   (c) back region
   (d) informal performance area

9. When members of an audience help a performer to recover from a flawed performance, they are practising __________________.

   (a) idealization
   (b) embarrassment
   (c) emotional privation
   (d) control
   (e) tact

10. Which of the following is not an example provided in the text to illustrate how language functions to define the sexes?

   (a) attention
   (b) value
   (c) effectivity
   (d) power
   (e) none of the above

11. What is quickly eroding our traditional economy and is likely to reshape university classes and textual materials?

(a) "sick" jokes
(b) idealization
(d) gender dislocation
(d) information technology
(e) lack of government spending

Fill in the Blank

1. The process by which people act and react in relation to others is termed ________________________.

2. A ___________ is a social position that an individual occupies within society.

3. An ______________ status is one that someone assumes voluntarily and that reflects ability and effort.

4. ___________ _____________is the process by which people disengage from important social roles.

5. The _________ theorem states that situations that are defined as real are real in their consequences.
6. ___________________ is the study of the way people make sense of their everyday lives.

7. __________________ analysis is defined as the analysis of social interaction in terms of theatrical performance.

8. ____________ _________ refers to the area around a person over which some claim to privacy is made.

9. Goffman describes embarrassment simply as _________________.

10. As people socially construct their emotions as part of everyday reality, they are engaged in a process called ________________ ___________.

Definition and Short Answer

1. Suggest how you, in interaction with people who have a physical disability as a master status, might make them feel comfortable.

2. Refer to **Figure 6-1** (p. 135) and using it as a model, diagram your own status and role sets. Identify points of role conflict and role strain.

3. How does culture act as a trigger for emotion?

4. What are the three ways in which language functions to define the sexes differently? Provide an illustration for each.

5. What is ethnomethodology? Provide an illustration of how a researcher using this approach would study social interaction.

6. Define the concept idealization.

7. Discuss the issue of gender and personal performances as reviewed in the text. Provide illustrations from your own experience to demonstrate the points being made about the respective patterns of male and female social interaction.

8. What are the basic characteristics of humour? Write a joke and analyze how it manifests the characteristics discussed in the textbook.

9. How is technology changing the reality of Canadian society?

10. Take the role of disadvantaged people in your society and construct some jokes that you think they would see as humourous with respect to those who are powerful.

Answers to Study Questions

True-False

1. T (p. 132)
2. F (p. 132)
3. T (p. 133)
4. F (p. 134)
5. T (p. 135)
6. F (p. 135)
7. T (p. 141)
8. F (p. 141)
9. T (p. 144)
10. T (p. 146)

Multiple Choice

1. a (p. 133)
2. c (pp. 132-135)
3. b (p. 134)
4. b (p. 135)
5. c (p. 135)
6. e (p. 137)
7. d (p. 138)
8. c (p. 139)
9. e (p. 143)
10. c (p. 145)
11. d (p. 149)

Fill in the Blank

1. social interaction (p. 132)
2. status (p. 132)
3. achieved (p. 133)
4. role exit (p. 135)
5. Thomas (p. 137)
6. ethnomethodology (p. 137)
7. dramaturgical (p. 138)
8. personal space (p. 141)
9. losing face (p. 143)
10. emotion management (p. 144)

ANALYSIS AND COMMENT

Go back through the chapter and write down in the spaces below key points from each of the following boxes.

THINKING IT THROUGH

"Physical Disability as Master Status"
Key Points:

MEDIA PERSPECTIVES

"Disease and Disability in Hollywood Film: Twenty Years of Change"
Key Points:

APPLYING SOCIOLOGY

"Social Interaction: Working Online"
Key Points:

MEDIA PERSPECTIVES

"Double Take: Real Headlines That Make People Laugh"
Key Points:

THINKING CRITICALLY

"Is Technology Changing Our Reality?"
Key Points:

SUGGESTED READINGS

Classic Sources

Erving Goffman. 1959. *The Presentation of Self in Everyday Life.* Garden City, NY: Doubleday Anchor Books.
Erving Goffman's first book is his best-known work.

Peter L. Berger and Thomas Luckmann. 1967. *The Social Construction of Reality: A Treatise in the Sociology of Knowledge.* Garden City, NY: Doubleday Anchor Books.
This book elaborates on the argument that individuals generate meaning through their social interaction.

Contemporary Sources

Adam Phillips. 1994. *On Flirtation.* Cambridge: Harvard University Press.
Flirtation allows us to experiment, and shows that life lacks an overall rigid plan.

William Rathje and Cullan Murphy. 1991. *Rubbish: The Archeology of Garbage.* New York: HarperCollins.
Researchers at the University of Arizona learned a great deal about people by studying their garbage.

Robert Prus and C.R.D. Sharper. 1977. *Road Hustler: Career Contingencies of Professional Card and Dice Hustlers. Lexington, MA: Lexington Books.*
The authors observed and participated in hustling in order to write this rich and detailed description of the life of professional hustlers.

Peter W. Archibald. 1978. *Social Psychology as Political Economy.* Toronto: McGraw-Hill Ryerson.
This book examines the political economy in social psychology interactions.

Elliott Leyton. 1986. *Hunting Humans: The Rise of the Modern Multiple Murderer.* Toronto: McClelland & Stewart.
This book is a fascinating inside account of the multiple murderer.

Global Sources

Catherine A. Lutz. 1988. *Unnatural Emotions: Everyday Sentiments on a Micronesian Atoll and Their Challenge to Western Theory.* Chicago: University of Chicago Press.
This report of research on a Pacific island points up how emotions, and the way people think about them, are culturally variable.

Michele Fine and Adrian Ash. 1990. *Women with Disabilities.* Philadelphia: Temple University Press.
How do people define others with physical disabilities? How do these individuals construct their own identity? This book provides some insights.

Jack Haas and William Shaffir. 1977. "The Professionalization of Medical Students: Developing Competence and a Cloak of Competence." *Symbolic Interaction*, 1:71-88.
Haas and Shaffir studied medical students at McMaster University in Hamilton. The article above describes some processes through which they become "professional."

Christie Davies. 1990. *Ethnic Humor Around the World: A Comparative Analysis.* Bloomington: Indiana University Press.
Relatively little attention has been paid to the sociological analysis of humour. This book applies a global perspective to the issue.

References

Daniel Albas and Cheryl Albas. 1993. "Disclaimer Mannerisms of Students: How to Avoid Being Labelled as Cheaters." ***Canadian Review of Sociology and Anthropology, Vol. 30, No. 4: 451-67.***

CHAPTER 7 Groups and Organizations

CHAPTER OUTLINE

I. Social Groups
- A. Primary and Secondary Groups
- B. Group Leadership
  - 1. Two Leadership Roles
  - 2. Three Leadership Styles
- C. Group Conformity
  - 1. Asch's Research
  - 2. Milgram's Research
  - 3. Janis's "Groupthink"
- D. Reference Groups
  - 1. Stouffer's Research
- E. In-groups and Out-groups
- F. Group Size
  - 1. The Dyad
  - 2. The Triad
- G. Social Diversity: Race, Class, and Gender
- H. Networks

II. Formal Organizations
- A. Types of Formal Organizations
  - 1. Utilitarian Organizations
  - 2. Normative Organizations
  - 3. Coercive Organizations
- B. Origins of Formal Organizations
- C. Characteristics of Bureaucracy
- D. Organizational Environment
- E. The Informal Side of Bureaucracy
- F. Problems of Bureaucracy
  - 1. Bureaucratic Alienation
  - 2. Bureaucratic Inefficiency and Ritualism
  - 3. Bureaucratic Inertia
- G. Oligarchy

III. The Evolution of Formal Organizations
- A. Scientific Management
- B. The First Challenge: Race and Gender
  - 1. Patterns of Privilege and Exclusion
  - 2. The "Female Advantage"
- C. The Second Challenge: The Japanese Work Organization
- D. The Third Challenge: The Changing Nature of Work
- E. The "McDonaldization" of Society
  - 1. McDonaldization: Three Principles
  - 2. Can Rationality be Irrational?

IV. The Future of Organizations: Opposing Trends
V. Making the Grade
VI. Key Points
VII. Key Concepts
VIII. Applications and Exercises
IX. MySocLab

LEARNING OBJECTIVES

- To explain the differences among categories, crowds, primary groups, and secondary groups
- To identify the various types of leaders associated with social groups
- To compare and contrast the research of Asch, Milgram, and Janis on group conformity
- To explain the importance of reference groups to group dynamics by understanding Stouffer's research on soldiers
- To distinguish between in-groups and out-groups
- To explain the relevance of group size to the dynamics of social groups
- To discover what characteristics predict which people will join particular groups or network with each other
- To identify the types of formal organizations
- To identify the primary characteristics of bureaucracy
- To compare and contrast the small group and the formal organization on the basis of their respective activities, hierarchies, norms, criteria for membership, relationships, communications, and focuses
- To understand the influence of the external environment on the functioning of an organization
- To identify the outcomes of the informal side of bureaucracy
- To explain the limitations of bureaucracy
- To understand oligarchy, the rule of many by the few
- To understand the evolution of formal organizations from "scientific management" to "flexible organization"

- To comprehend the various challenges to unbridled scientific management, namely race and gender, competition primarily from the Japanese, and the changing nature of work
- To understand what is meant by the McDonaldization of society

CHAPTER REVIEW

The introduction to this chapter illustrates how the principles of "fast food" preparation, started by McDonalds, are linked to the changing nature of social groups and formal organizational structures of society. This chapter provides insight into the extent to which social groups, from families to large-scale bureaucratic structures, have meaning in our lives.

SOCIAL GROUPS

A ***social group*** is defined as two or more people who identify and interact with one another. While we each have our own individuality, the "us" feeling that can only be achieved in social groups is central to our existence as human beings.

Not all collections of individuals are social groups. People who share a status in common are defined as a ***category***, but the vast majority never interact with one another.

A crowd is a temporary cluster of individuals who may or may not interact. Ordinarily they are too transitory to qualify as a social group, although occasionally they may become group-like.

Primary and Secondary Groups

Charles Horton Cooley studied the extent to which people have personal concern for each other in social interaction settings. He distinguished between primary and secondary groups. ***Primary groups*** are defined as a typically small social group in which relationships are both personal and lasting. They are characterized as ends in and of themselves, they are critical in the socialization process, and members are considered unique and not interchangeable.

Secondary groups are defined as large and impersonal social groups usually based on a specific interest or activity. They are typically short term with narrowly defined relationships and are seen as a means to an end. The distinction in real life is not always as clear as these definitions might suggest. The **Summing Up Table** (p. 156) provides a summary of the key differences between primary and secondary groups.

Group Leadership

Leadership plays a critical role in group dynamics. Secondary groups are more likely to identify formal leaders.

➢Two Leadership Roles

Research reveals that there are usually two types of leaders in social groups. ***Instrumental leadership*** refers to group leadership that emphasizes the completion of tasks. ***Expressive leadership*** emphasizes collective well-being. This differentiation is also linked to gender, with men typically taking the instrumental role and women taking the expressive role in leadership positions especially in the family, although increased equality has blurred this distinction.

➢Three Leadership Styles

Three decision-making styles are identified. One is ***authoritarian*** leadership, which focuses on instrumental concerns. This type of leader makes decisions on his or her own, demanding strict compliance from subordinates. Another type is the ***democratic*** leader who takes a more expressive approach, seeking to include all members in the decision-making process. A third type is labelled ***laissez-faire***. Leaders using this approach tend to downplay their power, allowing the group to function on its own. Look at the **Applying Sociology Box** (p. 157) to estimate the type of leadership style most likely to develop in the DJ subculture.

Group Conformity

Group conformity is a dimension of group dynamics where members seek the satisfaction of being like other members. The Reena Virk murder is used to illustrate that members of groups will exhibit extreme violence in order to fit in with group expectations. Three research projects illustrate the importance of group conformity to the sociological understanding of group processes.

➢Asch's Research

Solomon Asch conducted an experiment in which "naïve" subjects were asked to answer questions concerning the length of lines. Accomplices of the experimenter comprised the rest of the group, who purposely gave incorrect answers. Often the naive subject would give a "wrong" answer in order to conform. **Figure 7-1** (p. 158) illustrates an example of the cards used in this experiment. The experiment found that one-third of the subjects would compromise their judgment to agree with the group.

➢Milgram's Research

Stanley Milgram conducted an experiment that naive subjects believed was about learning and memory. The naive subject played the role of a "teacher" and the accomplice played the role of a "learner." If learners failed to correctly remember word pairs given by the teacher, the teacher was instructed by Milgram (a legitimate authority figure) to electrically shock the learner. His research suggests that people comply with almost blind obedience to authority figures. Further, if encouraged by others in a group situation, subjects were likely to administer even higher voltage shocks, indicating that even "ordinary" individuals can elicit conformity behaviour.

➢Janis's "Groupthink"

Irving Janis researched the actions of high government officials by examining historical documents. He theorized that even experts in groups can be led to engage in behaviour that violates common sense. Janis discusses three factors htat affect decision-making processes and create ***groupthink***, an adoption of a narrow consensus view caused by group conformity. The lack of acceptance that Quebec might vote to secede in the 1995 referendum is a recent Canadian example of "groupthink."

Reference Groups

The term ***reference group*** signifies a social group that serves as a point of reference for people making evaluations and decisions. These groups can be primary or secondary. They are a major factor involved in anticipatory socialization processes.

➢Stouffer's Research

Samuel Stouffer conducted research on the morale and attitudes of soldiers in World War II in order to investigate the dynamics of reference groups. Stouffer found what appeared to be a paradox: Soldiers in branches with higher promotion rates were more pessimistic about their own chances of being promoted than soldiers in branches with lower rates of promotion. This is explained, however, by the identification of the groups against which the soldiers measured their progress. In relative terms, those soldiers in branches with higher rates felt deprived.

In-groups and Out-groups

Two other kinds of groups provide us with standards against which we evaluate ourselves. An ***in-group*** is a social group commanding a member's respect and loyalty. This group exists in relation to ***out-groups***, or social groups toward which one feels competition or opposition. This dichotomy allows us to sharpen boundaries between groups and to highlight their distinctive identities. The operation of the group dynamics created by these distinctions affects broader social patterns in society, such as social inequality between whites and visible minorities.

Group Size

Group size significantly influences how members socially interact. As a group's membership is added to arithmetically, the number of possible relationships expands rapidly. **Figure 7-2** (p. 160) provides an illustration.

➢The Dyad

The dyad has two members and is characterized by intensity and instability. Marriages in Canada are a good example.

➢The Triad

The triad is composed of three members and often has more stability although the "third wheel" phenomenon is always a possibility.

As groups grow larger they become more stable because the loss of a member does not threaten the group. Larger groups, however, have less emotional intensity and greater formality.

Social Diversity: Race, Class, and Gender

This section focuses on the research by Peter Blau, who identifies three ways in which the structure of social groups regulates intergroup association. The three factors include group size, heterogeneity of group members, and physical boundaries.

Networks

The term ***network*** refers to a web of weak social ties that links people who identify and interact little with one another. Little sense of membership is felt by individuals in the network and only occasionally do they come into contact. Demographic characteristics, such as age, education, gender, and residence patterns influence the likelihood of a person's involvement in networks. New information technology has generated a global network of immense size. **Global Map 7-1** (p. 162) shows the extent of the internet and the **Thinking It Through Box** (p. 164) examines the origins and possible future of cyberspace, which offers immense networking capabilities unencumbered by formal usage rules. There is some evidence to support the notion that "who you know" in your network is just as important as "what you know."

FORMAL ORGANIZATIONS

Today our lives seem focused around ***formal organizations***, large, secondary groups that are organized to achieve their goals efficiently. In a society like Canada, these are vast organizations whose cultures remain unchanged as members come and go.

Types of Formal Organizations

Amitai Etzioni uses the variable of how members relate to the organization as a criterion for distinguishing three types of formal organizations.

➢Utilitarian Organizations

Utilitarian organizations provide material benefits for members in exchange for labour. Most people must join at least one organization in order to "make a living""

➢Normative Organizations

People join ***normative organizations*** to pursue some goal they consider morally worthwhile. Voluntary associations like the PTA and the Lions Club would be examples. Canadian students are increasingly involved in volunteer activities.

➢Coercive Organizations

Coercive organizations serve as a form of punishment (prisons) or treatment (psychiatric hospitals). People are separated from the rest of society within distinct physical boundaries and are labelled as inmates or patients.

Origins of Formal Organizations

Formal organizations date back thousands of years. The type of formal organization called ***bureaucracy,*** however, emerged as a result of changes occurring in societies in Europe and North America during the industrial revolution.

Characteristics of Bureaucracy

A bureaucracy is an organizational model rationally designed to perform complex tasks efficiently. Our telephone system is an example of the scope and capacity of bureaucratic organizations.

Max Weber identified six basic characteristics or elements of the ideal bureaucracy. These include specialization, hierarchy of offices, rules and regulations, technical competence, impersonality, and formal, written communications.

In contrast to small groups, like families, that have a personal character, the organizational model of bureaucracy limits unpredictability and promotes efficiency. The **Summing Up Table** (p. 167) differentiates between the qualities of bureaucracies and small groups. The internet is in some ways like a formal organization, but it escapes many elements of bureaucracy. See the **Media Perspectives Box** (p. 168).

Organizational Environment

Organizational environment refers to a range of factors outside an organization that affect its operation. These include technology, politics, the economy, current events (September 11, 2001), population patterns, and other organizations.

The Informal Side of Bureaucracy

While in principle bureaucracy has a highly formal structure, in reality not all behaviour in bureaucracies fits precisely the organizational rules. While it is the position or office that is supposed to carry the power, the personalities of the occupants are also important factors. Sometimes leaders also seek to benefit personally, as in the Enron situation. In addition, employees often establish informal networks, aided by the use of e-mail.

Problems of Bureaucracy

Although bureaucratic structures are widespread in today's society, there are concerns about dehumanization, alienation, and threats to democracy and personal freedom.

➢Bureaucratic Alienation

The efficiency goals of the organization reduce human beings to small pieces of a large machine, leaving both worker and client feeling alienated.

➢Bureaucratic Inefficiency and Ritualism

The image of red tape is closely tied to bureaucracies. ***Bureaucratic ritualism*** signifies a preoccupation with rules and regulations as ends in themselves rather than as means to organizational goals. This process, often referred to as "red tape," tends to reduce performance and stifle the creativity of members.

➢Bureaucratic Inertia

Bureaucracies seem to have lives of their own. ***Bureaucratic inertia*** refers to the tendency of bureaucratic organizations to persist over time whether there is any reason for their existence beyond the jobs of its members.

Oligarchy

Robert Michels observed the fact that ***oligarchy***, or the rule of the many by the few, was a typical outgrowth of bureaucracy. He suggested that individuals in high levels within a bureaucratic hierarchy tend to accumulate power and use it to promote their own objectives thereby endangering democratic principles. **Canada Map 7-1** (p. 171) illustrates the size of government bureaucracy in Canada.

THE EVOLUTION OF FORMAL ORGANIZATIONS

The rigid top-down organizational system identified by Weber led to the adoption of an organizational model called ***scientific management***. Various challenges to this model led to a new model called the *flexible organization.*

Scientific Management

Early in the twentieth century, Frederick Taylor suggested that scientific management, the application of scientific principles to the operation of organizations, was the answer to inefficiency. Analysis of task, application of methods to more efficiently manage the task, and incentives to workers for higher productivity were the way to lower prices and higher wages. The capacity to make these decisions rested with the managers alone. As decades passed, formal organizations faced several challenges including race and gender, rising competition, and the changing nature of work.

The First Challenge: Race and Gender

Organizations were excluding women and minorities in their hiring practices, resulting in less competence and less efficiency.

➢Patterns of Privilege and Exclusion

Excluding women and minorities shuts out over half the population and even if they are represented in small numbers, they feel excluded from advancement, thereby reducing their contribution to the organization. With open opportunities the organization's leaders value the contributions of all.

➢The "Female Advantage"

Much research has shown that women try to understand issues more than men and are better at communication and sharing information. They are more flexible leaders who welcome contributions from workers and focus on interconnectedness in the organization. Overall, they make organizations more flexible and open.

The Second Challenge: The Japanese Work Organization

By the 1980s, most products made in Japan were better than those made in the United States, notably the automobile.

William Ouchi found that Japanese organizations emphasized collectivity more than the individualism found in North America. The Japanese hired in groups giving all workers equal responsibilities. They also hired for life, training workers in all aspects of the organization. They also involved their workers in the corporate decisions through quality circles and helped organize their social lives. These factors contributed to loyalty and quality products. The **Thinking Globally Box** (p. 174) looks at Canadian efforts to adopt the Japanese organizational model.

The Third Challenge: The Changing Nature of Work

The repetitive tasks of the industrial world that made things have moved to the post-industrial world where we process information. Many large-scale organizations now need workers who are given the opportunity to be creative, often in competitive work teams. Organizations are flatter rather than pyramidal (See **Figure 7-3,** p. 175) and there is less rigidity and more flexibility. But, the post-industrial society also creates low-skill service jobs, as well as high-skill creative jobs. So many organizations are still characterized by a rigid chain of command.

Large organizations have grown in power and intrusiveness. Look at the **Thinking Critically Box** (pp. 176-77) for the potential impact on personal privacy.

The "McDonaldization" of Society

McDonald's has become pervasive with over 31 000 restaurants worldwide (1300 in Canada) and the Canadian branch in Pushkin Square in Moscow is the busiest McDonald's in the world. The principles of the model infuse other organizations such as Tim Hortons and Canadian Tire.

➤McDonaldization: Three Principles

What is McDonald's? It is fast therefore ***efficient***. It is consistent, therefore it has *uniformity*. It is the same everywhere in the world, therefore it has ***predictability*** and it is rigidly controlled through ***automation***. It can be a comforting break from the "real world." Automatic teller machines, automatic hatcheries, and laser scanners in grocery stores are the latest examples of these principles applied elsewhere.

➤Can Rationality Be Irrational?

Does such rationality lead to dehumanization and loss of creativity and ultimately to a system that controls people rather than the reverse?

THE FUTURE OF ORGANIZATIONS: OPPOSING TRENDS

The top-down bureaucratic organization identified by Weber has given way to the flatter, more flexible model that prizes communication and creativity. These organizations value creative freedom and they are more productive. There is as well, however, the large-scale service organization that creates routine "McJobs" that look much like the jobs Taylor described a century ago.

Organizations facing global competition "downsize" to contain costs such that some people are much better off in the new organizational environment, while others struggle to hold their jobs and survive.

KEY CONCEPTS

Define each of the following concepts on a separate sheet of paper. Check the accuracy of your answers by referring to the key concepts section at the end of the chapter in the text, as well as by referring to italicized definitions located throughout the chapter.

bureaucracy	bureaucratic ritualism
bureaucratic inertia	category
coercive organization	oligarchy
crowd	organizational environment
dyad	out-group

expressive leadership
formal organizations
groupthink
humanizing organizations
in-group
instrumental leadership
network
normative organization
Parkinson's law
Peter principle
primary group
reference group
scientific management
secondary group
social group
triad
utilitarian organization

STUDY QUESTIONS

True-False

1. T F While people who know each other well, such as family members or neighbours, are often identifiable as groups, a crowd can never be considered a group.

2. T F Instrumental leadership tends to focus upon the completion of tasks.

3. T F Janis called the tendency of group members to conform by adopting a narrow view of some issue, "dumbing down."

4. T F Stouffer's research on soldier's attitudes toward their own promotions during World War II demonstrates the significance of reference groups in making judgments about ourselves.

5. T F According to research by Georg Simmel, larger groups tend to be more stable than small groups, such as dyads.

6. T F The more internally heterogeneous a group is, the more likely its members are to interact with members of other groups.

7. T F Most people join normative organizations for material rewards.

8. T F Studies of corporations document that the qualities and quirks of individuals have a tremendous impact on organizational outcomes.

9. T F Approximately 85% of the world's population has access to the internet.

10. T F The tedious preoccupation with organizational routines and procedures is called "red tape."

11. T F Weber's ideas on bureaucracy took hold in an organizational model called *flexible organization.*

12. T F Helgesen finds that women are more flexible leaders who typically allow subordinates greater autonomy.

13. T F The introduction of Total Quality Management at firms in Canada has led to improvements in worker involvement and company profile.

14. T F McDonaldization tends to limit human creativity, choice, and freedom.

Multiple Choice

1. A social group characterized by long-term personal relationships usually involving many activities is a ________.

   (a) primary group
   (b) secondary group
   (c) category
   (d) aggregate
   (e) normative organization

2. Which of the following is not true of primary groups?

   (a) They provide help for their members.
   (b) They are focused around specific activities.
   (c) They are valued in and of themselves.
   (d) They are viewed as ends in themselves.

3. Which of the following theorists differentiated between primary and secondary groups?

   (a) Max Weber
   (b) Amitai Etzioni
   (c) Emile Durkheim
   (d) Charles Horton Cooley
   (e) George Herbert Mead

4. The type of leadership that allows the group to function more or less on its own is called __________________.

   (a) authoritarian
   (b) democratic
   (c) utilitarian
   (d) laissez-faire
   (e) normative

5. What researcher found that approximately one-third of subjects will conform and answer incorrectly a perceptually obvious question?

   (a) Solomon Asch
   (b) Charles Horton Cooley
   (c) Stanley Milgram
   (d) Irving Janis
   (e) Rosabeth Moss Kanter

6. Whose research shows that people are likely to follow the lead of not only legitimate authority figures but also groups of ordinary people?

   (a) Solomon Asch
   (b) Stanley Milgram
   (c) Samuel Stouffer
   (d) Irving Janis
   (e) George Simmel

7. A "fuzzy" group that brings people into occasional contact but without a sense of belonging is called a(n) ________________.

   (a) triad
   (b) homogeneous group
   (c) network
   (d) cybergroup
   (e) coercive group

8. The structure of our society now turns on the operation of vast corporations and other bureaucracies that sociologists describe as ____________.

   (a) rigid organizations
   (b) conventional organizations
   (c) customary organizations
   (d) informal organizations
   (e) formal organizations

9. Which of the following is ***not*** typical of a bureaucratic organization?

   (a) Membership is based upon technical competence.
   (b) Relationships are typically primary in nature
   (c) Communications are formal.
   (d) The focus is task oriented.
   (e) The hierarchy is clearly defined.

10. Which of the following are factors outside an organization that affect its operation?

    (a) changing technology
    (b) dramatic current events
    (c) economic trends
    (d) all of the above
    (e) a and b above

11. The tendency of bureaucratic organizations to perpetuate themselves is called ____________.

(a) oligarchy
(b) bureaucratic inertia
(c) bureaucratic alienation
(d) bureaucratic inefficiency
(e) bureaucratic ritualism

12. Formal organizations in Japan ____________________.

(a) pay all age cohorts approximately the same
(b) tend to offer life security
(c) do not interfere in the worker's recreational environment
(d)(a and b above)
(e) (b and c above)

13. The tremendous number of files and databases maintained in an information-based society creates a threat to ___________________.

(a) the credit card industry
(b) privacy
(c) large accumulations of wealth
(d) nepotism

14. Which of the following is ***not*** one of the principles of McDonaldization?

(a) efficiency
(b) uniformity
(c) creativity
(d) control

Fill in the Blank

1. A _________ is defined as two or more people who identify and interact with one another.

2. Political organizations are examples of ____________ groups.

3. _______________ leadership makes a point of including everyone in the decision-making process.

4. The tendency of group members to conform, resulting in a narrow view of some issue is called _______________

5. A(n) ____________ is a social group towards which a member feels respect and loyalty.

6. A _______________ is a more stable social group than a dyad.

7. Networks of _________________ include more relatives.

8. _________________ thrives in the hierarchical structure of bureaucracy and reduces the accountability of leaders to other personnel or categories.

9. Tannen finds that female managers have a greater ________________ ________________ than male managers.

10. Because of global competition, organizations are often eager to cut costs by ____________.

Definition and Short Answer

1. Differentiate between the qualities of bureaucracies and small groups. In what ways are they similar?

2. Critically analyze the research on group conformity.

3. What are the factors in group decision-making processes that lead to "groupthink"?

4. What are the major limitations of bureaucracy? Provide an example for each.

5. Discuss the informal side of bureaucracy.

6. Provide two examples of a normative organization.

7. What are the factors that have led to the change from "scientific management" to "flexible organization"?

8. Does the Japanese organizational model work in North America?

9. What impact has McDonaldization had on Canadian society?

10. What will be the impact of computerization and large organization on personal privacy?

11. Discuss the opposing trends in organizational development.

Answers to Study Questions

True-False

1. F (p. 155)
2. T (p. 156)
3. F (p. 159)
4. T (pp. 159–160)
5. T (p. 161)
6. T (p. 161)
7. F (p. 165)
8. T (p. 167)
9. F (p. 168)
10. T (p. 169)
11. F (p. 170)
12. T (p. 172)
13. T (p. 174)
14. T (p. 178)

Multiple Choice

1. a (p. 155)
2. b (p. 155)
3. d (p. 155)
4. d (p. 157)
5. a (p. 158)
6. b (p. 159)
7. c (p. 161)
8. e (pp. 164-165)
9. b (pp. 165-166)
10. d (pp. 166-167)
11. b (pp. 169-170)
12. d (p. 172)
13. b (pp. 176-177)
14. c (pp. 177-178)

Fill in the Blank

1. social group (p. 154)
2. secondary (p. 156)
3. democratic (p. 157)
4. groupthink (p. 159)
5. in-group (p. 160)
6. triad (p. 161
7. women (p. 163)
8. oligarchy (p. 171)
9. information focus (p. 172)
10. downsizing (p. 178)

ANALYSIS AND COMMENT

Go back through the chapter and write down in the spaces below key points from each of the following boxes.

APPLYING SOCIOLOGY

"The Club DJ: Local Musician, Global Ties"
Key Points

THINKING IT THROUGH

"Virtual Community: Building Networks through Cyberspace"
Key Points:

MEDIA PERSPECTIVES

"The Internet: The Unregulated Medium"
Key Points:

THINKING GLOBALLY

"The Japanese Model: Will it Work in North America?"
Key Points:

THINKING CRITICALLY

"Computer Technology, Large Organizations, and the Assault on Privacy"
Key Points:

SUGGESTED READINGS

Contemporary Sources

Richard H. Hall. 1991. *Organizations: Structures, Processes, and Outcomes*. Englewood Cliffs, NJ: Prentice Hall.
Cecilia L. Ridgeway. 1983. *The Dynamics of Small Groups*. New York: St. Martin's Press.
These two books delve into many of the issues addressed in this chapter.

Arthur G. Miller. 1986. *The Obedience Experiments: A Case Study of Controversy in Social Science*. New York: Praeger.
Controversy has dogged the obedience experiments of Stanley Milgram for more than thirty years. This book reviews Milgram's work and related studies, and tackles the broad ethical questions such research raises.

Irving L. Janis. 1989. *Crucial Decisions: Leadership in Policymaking and Crisis Management*. New York: The Free Press.
This book, by the originator of the term "groupthink," examines organizational leadership.

Sally Helgesen. 1990. *The Female Advantage: Women's Ways of Leadership*. New York: Doubleday.
This intriguing book argues that women in managerial positions typically adopt a more humanized leadership style that works to the advantage of corporations.

Carl E. Larson and Frank M. J. LaFasto. 1989. *Teamwork: What Must Go Right/What Can Go Wrong*. Newbury Park, CA: Sage.

This brief book spells out strategies for effectively organizing people into task groups.

Michael Herzfeld. 1991. *The Social Production of Indifference: Exploring the Roots of Western Bureaucracy*. New York: Berg.
James Q. Wilson. 1989. *Bureaucracy: What Government Agencies Do and Why They Do It*. New York: Basic Books.
The first of these books challenges the conventional belief that traditional social patterns run counter to bureaucracy, revealing how both are shaped by the same cultural forces. The second, by a renowned organizational researcher, brings together essays showing that government bureaucracies are far more varied than Weber's model suggests.

Rosabeth Moss Kanter. 1989. *When Giants Learn to Dance: Mastering the Challenges of Strategy, Management, and Careers in the 1990s*. New York: Simon and Schuster.
Alvin Toffler. 1985. *The Adaptive Corporation*. New York: McGraw-Hill.
These two books exemplify the growing trend of applying sociological analysis to problems of corporate management. The first, by one of the best-

known sociologists in the field of formal organizations, examines the future of corporate organization. The second, by a noted futurist, argues that simply "doing more of the same" in a changing society will surely lead to declining business.

Nicole Woolsey Biggart. 1989. *Charismatic Capitalism: Direct Selling Organizations in America.* Chicago: The University of Chicago Press.
Challenging the notion that formal organizations are based on cool-headed, rational behaviour, some organizations deliberately foster emotional intensity among their members. This study highlights companies such as Mary Kay cosmetics and Amway products that have used emotional, motivational techniques successfully.

Canadian Sources

Barry Wellman. 1979. "The Community Question: The Intimate Networks of East Yorkers." *American Journal of Sociology* Vol. 84, No. 5: 1201-31.
This article deals with the "intimate networks" in a Toronto borough, revealing that these close ties extend throughout the metropolitan area and beyond.

Isabel Bassett. 1985. *The Bassett Report: Career Success and Canadian Women.* Toronto: Collins.
This analysis of factors affecting the careers of Canadian women is based on in-depth interviews and a Goldfarb poll commissioned by Bassett (a television journalist).

Diane Francis. 1986. *Controlling Interest: Who Owns Canada?* Toronto: McMillan. According to Diane Francis, corporate concentration is particularly alarming in Canada. Here she tells the story of the small number of families and corporations that effectively run our country.

John Anderson and M. Gunderson. 1982. *Union Management Relations in Canada.* Don Mills, ON: Addison-Wesley.
This collection of articles dealing with Canadian industrial relations includes Canada-U.S.-Europe comparisons.

Dianne Collier. 1994. *Hurry Up and Wait: An Inside Look at Life as a Canadian Military Wife.* Carp, ON: Creative Bound.
Canada's military complex very effectively controls the lives of its military men, but it also makes tremendous demands upon military wives and children. This very readable book tells their story.

Global Sources

Boye De Mente. 1987. *Japanese Etiquette and Ethics in Business.* 5th ed. Lincolnwod, IL: NTC Business Books.
This is one of the better books contrasting formal organizations in the United States with those in Japan.

CHAPTER 8

Sexuality and Society

CHAPTER OUTLINE

I. **Understanding Sexuality**
II. **Sex: A Biological Issue**
  A. Sex and the Body
    1. Intersexual People
    2. Transsexuals
  B. Sex: A Cultural Issue
    1. Cultural Variation
    2. The Incest Taboo
III. **Sexual Attitudes**
  A. The Sexual Revolution
  B. The Sexual Counterrevolution
  C. Premarital Sex
  D. Sex between Adults
    1. Extramarital Sex
IV. **Sexual Orientation**
  A. What Gives us a Sexual Orientation?
    1. Sexual Orientation: A Product of Society
    2. Sexual Orientation: A Product of Biology
  B. How Many Gay People Are There?
  C. The Gay Rights Movement
V. **Sexual Issues and Controversies**
  A. Teen Pregnancy
  B. Pornography
  C. Prostitution
    1. Types of Prostitution
    2. A Victimless Crime?
  D. Sexual Assault
VI. **Theoretical Analysis of Sexuality**
  A. Structural-Functional Analysis
    1. The Need To Regulate Sexuality
    2. Latent Functions: The Case of Prostitution
  B. Symbolic-Interaction Analysis
    1. The Social Construction of Sexuality
    2. 2. Global Comparisons
  C. Social Conflict Analysis
    1. Sexuality: Reflecting Social Inequality
    2. Sexuality: Creating Social Inequality
    3. Queer Theory
VI. **Making the Grade**
VII. **Key Points**
VIII. **Key Concepts**
IX. **Applications and Exercises**
X. **MySocLab**

LEARNING OBJECTIVES

- To gain a sociological understanding of human sexuality focusing on both biological and cultural factors
- To become more aware of the sexual attitudes found in North America
- To be able to describe both the sexual revolution and sexual counterrevolution that occurred during the last half-century in North America
- To be able to discuss human sexuality as it is experienced across different stages of the human life course
- To be able to discuss issues relating to the biological and social causes of sexual orientation
- To be able to describe the demographics of sexual orientation in our society, including the research methods used to obtain such information about our population
- To gain a sociological perspective on several sexual controversies, including teen pregnancy, pornography, prostitution, and sexual assault
- To be able to discuss issues relating to human sexuality from the viewpoints offered by structural-functional, symbolic-interactionist, and social-conflict analyses.

CHAPTER REVIEW

UNDERSTANDING SEXUALITY

Sexuality is a common theme in our society, sometimes dominating everyday conversations and certainly producing huge profits for the sex industry. To some extent, however, sex has been a cultural taboo historically, thereby producing anxiety and a distinct lack of scientific understanding. That changed in the middle of the twentieth century, so much so that the transsexual relationship discussed in the opening scenario is readily accepted in the Canadian military.

SEX—A BIOLOGICAL ISSUE

Sex refers to the biological distinction between females and males. It is the means by which humans reproduce, resulting in the birth of 105 males for every 100 females.

Sex and the Body

At birth, males and females are distinguished by ***primary sex characteristics***, the genitals used for reproduction. At puberty additional sex differentiation produces ***secondary sex characteristics***, bodily differences, other than genitals, that distinguish males and females. Sex is different from gender, which is the cultural behavioural expectations for males and females.

➢Intersexual People

Occasionally hormone imbalances before birth produce *intersexual people*, human beings with some combination of male and female genitalia.

➢Transsexuals

These are people who feel they are one sex when biologically they are the other. Some have surgery to alter their genitals since they feel "trapped" in the wrong body. The **Media Perspectives Box** (p. 186) deals with a similar issue. A twin boy had his penis severed during circumcision and the decision was made to alter him surgically and raise him as a girl. He was given a female ***gender identity*** through socialization, but he was never satisfied and ultimately received a gender reassignment and lived at one time as a married man.

Sex: A Cultural Issue

While sexuality has a biological foundation, its expression is widely variant.

➢Cultural Variation

Norms of types of intercourse, and with whom one can have sex, vary by culture and over time in a single culture.

➢The Incest Taboo

One cultural universal with respect to sex is the ***incest taboo***, a norm forbidding sexual relations or marriage between certain relatives. The relatives are not the same in all societies but the taboo operates everywhere to protect the social organization of the family.

SEXUAL ATTITUDES

North American attitudes about sexuality have been inconsistent, a mixture of European rigidity that suggested sex existed inside marriage for reproductive purposes, and a commitment to individuality that suggested people should be able to do what they wish, as long as others are not harmed. The balance in this mixture shifted over time. Canadians have become more accepting of nonmarital sex and homosexuality but increasingly non-accepting of extramarital sexuality. (See **Table 8-1** p. 188 with respect to attitudes toward nonmarital sex, extramarital sex, and homosexuality.)

The Sexual Revolution

Migration to towns and cities helped to create the "Roaring Twenties" with its relaxed sexual standards. Alfred Kinsey's studies of sexuality in the United States opened up the topic to scientific analysis and the findings suggested people were less conventional than previously thought. In the 1960s youth culture dominated as the boomers came of age. **Figure 8-1** (p. 189) shows how much change took place among female boomers compared to previous generations with respect to premarital partners. As well, the "double standard" (where men are permitted and women are not) to engage in premarital sex has declined considerably. The pill gave women the opportunity to engage in sex without elaborate preparation. The patterns in global use of contraceptives are identified in **Global Map 8-1** (p. 191).

The Sexual Counterrevolution

Not everyone thought the sexual revolution was productive for society. A counterrevolution set in, calling for a return to family values. The movement to sexual responsibility meant that some were abstaining from sex before marriage or limiting their sexual partners. The fear of sexually transmitted diseases (STDs), was probably another precipitating factor.

Premarital Sex

The sexual revolution and counterrevolution have resulted in more favourable attitudes about premarital sexuality in Canadians than in Americans, as indicated in **Table 8-2 (**p. 192). Women have certainly increased their participation in premarital sexuality (almost as high as the male rates), but they are much more likely than men to adhere to a "love" standard rather than a "fun" standard.

Sex Between Adults

Canadians are active sexually but age is a determining factor. Sexual activity peaks in the 30s and declines thereafter. A recent international study of those over 40 years of age found high levels of sexual satisfaction, especially in those countries with higher gender equality.

Extramarital Sex

Eight-five to ninety percent of Americans and Canadians say extramarital sexuality is wrong, but behavioural studies indicate 25% of men and 10% of women have engaged in extramarital sexuality. A recent Ipsos-Reid poll in Canada found that another small percentage would cheat if they thought they would not get caught.

SEXUAL ORIENTATION

Sexual orientation refers to an individual's preference in terms of sexual partners: same sex, other sex, either sex, neither sex. Although the norm is ***heterosexuality*** (other), ***homosexuality*** (same sex) is not uncommon, and ***bisexuality*** (either sex) and ***asexuality*** (neither sex) are also known. In some societies, homosexual relations have not only been tolerated, but preferred. **Figure 8-2** (p. 193) describes each of these sexual orientations in relation to the others.

What Gives Us A Sexual Orientation?

➢Sexual Orientation: A Product of Society

There are some historical and cultural examples that suggest that homosexuality is a social construction.

➢Sexual Orientation: A Product of Biology

Some genetic research and brain structure research suggests a biological origin to sexual orientation.

If the biological explanation is correct, gay and lesbian people should expect legal protection from discrimination like other minorities.

How Many Gay People Are There?

Given that sexuality doesn't always fit into neat categories and that not all individuals are willing to reveal their sexual orientation, it is difficult to estimate the extent of homosexuality. At one time, a one in ten estimate was made but recent surveys indicate that the numbers of people who consider themselves exclusively homosexual is much less than that. **Figure 8-3** (p. 194) shows 1994 data from the U.S.

The Gay Rights Movement

Homophobia, the dread of close personal interaction with people thought to be gay, lesbian, or bisexual, is certainly on the decline in Canada and the United States, to a large extent because of the success of the gay rights movement. In 1969 Canada removed from the Criminal Code homosexual activity that took place in private between consenting adults. Benefits were extended to partners in same-sex relationships, and in 2001 Toronto's Metropolitan Community Church successfully married homosexuals by publishing the banns for three Sundays prior to marriage. Court decisions in 2003 struck down marriage laws in Ontario, British Columbia, and Quebec and in 2005, Paul Martin's Liberal government made same-sex marriage legal throughout Canada. The **Thinking About Diversity Box** (p. 196) describes the changes in Canada with respect to same-sex marriages.

SEXUAL ISSUES AND CONTROVERSIES

Teen Pregnancy

Sexuality without social maturity often leads to pregnancy. These mothers are at high risk of not finishing school, which often leads to them and their children living in poverty. The rate of teen pregnancy, however, has declined considerably in the last several years. Over half of teen pregnancies end in *abortion,* the deliberate termination of a pregnancy**.** The **Thinking It Through Box** (p. 204) looks at the issue of abortion.

Pornography

In Canada the issue of *pornography*, sexually explicit material that causes sexual arousal, is linked to the illegality of ***obscenity***, which involves undue exploitation of sex and violation of community standards. Traditionally, pornography was judged on moral grounds but increasingly it is seen as a ***power issue*** because women are depicted as sexual objects.

Canada attempts to balance free expression with objectionable sexual materials.

Prostitution

Prostitution is the selling of sexual services. It is illegal in most American states but not in Canada, where it is soliciting or communicating for the purpose of prostitution in a public place that is illegal. **Map 8-2** (p. 198) shows the global distribution of prostitution.

➢Types of Prostitution

Call girls control their own dates but brothel workers or street walkers are under the control of madams or pimps.

➢A Victimless Crime?

Many consider prostitution a victimless crime, but many women become trapped and victimized. The homicide rate is high and the Pickton Trial in Vancouver brings attention to the disappearance of the sixty-three women in the mid-1990s, the majority of whom were prostitutes.

Sexual Assault

In Canada, rape is called sexual assault and the reported cases are only a fraction of the total. Most rapes are not committed by strangers but by people who know the victim. The **Applying Sociology Box** (p. 200) describes the mythology and the reality of rape in North America.

THEORETICAL ANALYSIS OF SEXUALITY

The **Applying Theory Table** (p. 201) highlights the key insights of each approach.

Structural Functional Analysis

This analysis highlights the contribution any social pattern makes to the overall operation of the society.

➢The Need to Regulate Sexuality

The need to regulate reproduction for the maintenance of the family unit is clear. Free sexual expression and "illegimate" reproduction would not provide appropriate protection for children.

➢Latent Functions: The Case of Prostitution

While prostitution spreads disease and exploits women, it does serve to meet the sexual needs of some who might not otherwise be successful.

Symbolic-Interaction Analysis

Realities regarding sexuality vary by context and time.

➢The Social Construction of Sexuality

While structural functional approaches to understanding sexuality focus on continuity rather than change, symbolic-interactionist approaches demonstrate how social construction leads to changes in definition.

Prior to the separation of sex and reproduction, a premarital virginity norm was in place. Today, 87% of nonmarried Canadians say they engage in sex.

➢Global Comparisons

A normative behaviour in Canada, male circumcision, is rare in many other parts of the world.

Social-Conflict Analysis

Sexuality can both reflect and contribute to patterns of inequality.

➢Sexuality: Reflecting Social Inequality

Prostitution is a transaction involving two people, but the prostitute is arrested more often than the male client.

➢Sexuality: Creating Social Inequality

To some extent pornography leads to women being perceived as sexual objects and playthings of men.

➢Queer Theory

This theory challenges an allegedly heterosexual bias in sociology and asserts that our society is characterized by ***heterosexism***, a view stigmatizing anyone who is not heterosexual as "queer."

Structural-functionalism tends to ignore change, symbolic-interaction over-emphasizes differences and change, and social-conflict analysis underestimates the reduction in inequality that has occurred and forgets that sexuality is not a power issue for everybody.

KEY CONCEPTS

Define each of the following concepts on a separate sheet of paper. Check the accuracy of your answers by referring to the key concepts in the text, as well as by referring to italicized definitions located throughout the chapter.

abortion
asexuality
bisexuality
gender identity
heterosexuality
heterosexism
homophobia
homosexuality
incest taboo
intersexual people
pornography
primary sex characteristics
prostitution
queer theory
secondary sex characteristics
sex
sexual orientation
transsexuals

STUDY QUESTIONS

True-False

1. T F Social scientists long considered sex off limits for research. It was not until the middle of the twentieth century that researchers turned attention to this pervasive dimension of social life.

2. T F Secondary sex characteristics are those that develop during puberty.

3. T F Intersexual people are those who feel they are one sex even though biologically they are the other.

4. T F The traits that females and males, guided by their culture, incorporate into their personalities, are called gender identity.

5. T F Almost any sexual practice shows considerable variation from one society to another.

6. T F Every known culture has some form of *incest taboo*—It is a cultural universal.

7. T F The gender "double standard" for premarital sexuality has narrowed for those who came of age during the Sexual Revolution.

8. T F Among Canadian university students, males are more likely than females to endorse the recreational aspect of premarital sex.

9. T F The percentage of Canadians saying that extramarital sex is "always wrong" decreased from 60% to 50% between 1975 and 1995.

10. T F Sexual orientation refers to the biological distinction of being female or male.

11. T F Pornography refers to sexually explicit material that causes sexual arousal.

12. T F A common myth is that most victims of rapes are raped by strangers.

13. T F Heterosexism is a view that labels anyone who is not heterosexual as "queer."

14. T F According to survey research, over 40% of adults in the U.S. and Canada think that a woman should be able to obtain a legal abortion for any reason if she wants to.

Multiple Choice

1. ________________refers to the biological distinction between females and males.

(a) Gender
(b) Sex
(c) Sexual orientation
(d) Human sexuality
(e) Sex characteristics

2. ______________ are people who feel they are one sex even though biologically they are of the other sex.

(a) Hermaphrodites
(b) Transvestites
(c) Homophobics
(d) Transsexuals

3. During the last century, people witnessed profound changes in sexual attitudes and practices. The first indications of this change occurred in the _____________.

(a) 1920s
(b) 1940s
(c) 1960s
(d) 1970s
(e) 1980s

4. Although 90% of Americans consider extramarital sex as "almost always wrong," __________ % of married men have had at least one extramarital sexual experience.

(a) 10
(b) 15
(c) 20
(d) 25
(e) 50

5. ________________ refers to a person's preference in terms of sexual partner: same sex, other sex, either sex, neither sex.

(a) Sexual orientation
(b) Sex
(c) Gender
(d) Sexual response

6. Attitudes towards homosexuality are changing. Which of the following statements are correct with respect to that change?

(a) By 2003, only 48% of Canadians felt homosexuality was wrong.
(b) In 1969, Canada removed from the Criminal Code homosexual activity that took place in private between consenting adults.
(c) By 1998, Canada had extended benefits to same-sex couples in committed relationships.
(d) All of the above
(e) a and b above

7. Strictly speaking, pornography is legal in Canada. It is _________ that is illegal.

(a) smut
(b) snuff
(c) obscenity
(d) erotica
(e) X-rated videos

8. Which of the following is ***inaccurate*** about prostitution?

   (a) Most prostitutes are women.
   (b) Most prostitutes offer heterosexual services.
   (c) Call girls are the lowest prestige type of prostitution.
   (d) Prostitution is greatest in poor countries where patriarchy is strong.

9. Which of the following is/are evidence of a societal need to regulate sex?

   (a) Most societies condemn married people for having sex with someone other than their spouse.
   (b) Every society has some form of incest taboo.
   (c) Historically, the social control of sexuality was strong, primarily because sex commonly led to childbirth.
   (d) All of the above
   (e) (a) and (b) above

10. Which of the following is inaccurate concerning the perspective offered by the structural-functionalist paradigm?

    (a) It helps us to appreciate how sexuality plays an important part in how society is organized.
    (b) It focuses attention on how societies, through the incest taboo and other cultural norms, have always paid attention to who has sex with whom, especially who reproduces with whom.
    (c) This approach pays considerable attention to the great diversity of sexual ideas and practices found around the world.
    (d) All of the above are accurate.

11. Which of the following is a criticism of the symbolic-interactionist paradigm?

    (a) It fails to take into account how social patterns regarding sexuality are socially constructed.
    (b) It fails to help us appreciate the variety of sexual practices found over the course of history and around the world.
    (c) It fails to identify the broader social structures that establish certain patterns of sexual behaviours cross-culturally.
    (d) None of the above are criticism of symbolic-interactionism

12. About _____________% of Canadians and Americans would prohibit abortion under any circumstances.

    (a) 5
    (b) 7
    (c) 12
    (d) 20
    (e) 37

Fill in the Blank

1. ____________ refers to the biological distinction between females and males.

2. ____________ sex characteristics refer to bodily differences, apart from the genitals, that distinguish biologically mature females and males.

3. Human beings with some combination of female and male genitalia are referred to as _______.

4. One cultural universal—an element found in every society the world over—is the ________________, a norm forbidding sexual relations or marriage between certain relatives.

5. The most recent studies in the U.S. targeting men and women born in the 1970s show that ________ percent of men and _______percent of women had premarital sexual intercourse by their senior year in high school.

6. Some research suggests that sexual orientation is rooted in biology. Simon LeVay links sexual orientation to the structure of the __________ _________.

7. Canada made same-sex marriage legal in the year ____________.

8. _______ describes the dread of close personal interaction with people thought to be gay, lesbian, or bisexual.

9. Although there is much debate about crossing the line from acceptable erotica to unacceptable obscenity, there is not much doubt about one area, and that is _____________________.

10. At the bottom of the sex-worker hierarchy are ___________ __________.

11. Communicating for the purposes of prostitution is against the law in Canada, but many people consider it a ____________ crime.

12. _______% of female Canadian students have experienced sexual assault.

Definition and Short Answer

1. What are the important anatomical differences between males and females? In what ways are these differences important in terms of the relative statuses and roles of women and men in social institutions such as the family and the economy?

2. What evidence do we have that sexual practices vary culturally?

3. What are the functions served by the incest taboo for both individuals and society as a whole?

4. When was the sexual revolution? What social and cultural factors influenced this revolution? What was the sexual counterrevolution? What social and cultural factors helped bring it about?

5. How would you summarize our society's attitudes concerning premarital sex?

6. What is the evidence that sexual orientation is a product of society? What is the evidence that it is a product of biology?

7. How has the gay rights movement influenced Canadian attitudes towards gay people?

8. To what extent would you agree that pornography today is less a moral issue than it is an issue concerning power? Why?

9. Is prostitution really a victimless crime? Why?

10. Why is it important for society to regulate sexuality?

11. What evidence do symbolic-interactionists use to suggest sexuality is socially constructed?

12. Social-conflict theorists argue that sexuality is at the root of inequality between women and men. How is this so?

13. Discuss the differences between the "pro-choice" and "pro-life" proponents of abortion.

Answers to Study Questions

True-False

1. T (p. 184)
2. T (p. 185)
3. F (p. 185)
4. T (p. 186)
5. T (p. 186)
6. T (p. 187)
7. T (pp. 189-190)
8. T (p. 191)
9. F (p. 192)
10. F (p. 193)
11. T (p. 197)
12. T (p. 200)
13. T (p. 203)
14. T (p. 204)

Multiple Choice

1. b (p. 185)
2. d (p. 185)
3. a (p. 189)
4. d (p. 192)
5. a (p. 193)
6. d (p. 195)
7. c (p. 197)
8. c (pp. 197-198)
9. d (p. 201)
10. c (pp. 201-202)
11. c (p. 202)
12. a (p. 204)

Fill in the Blank

1. Sex (p. 185)
2. Secondary (p. 185)
3. Intersexual people (p. 185)
4. incest taboo (p. 187)
5. 76, 66 (p. 191)
6. human brain (p. 193)
7. 2005 (p. 195)
8. Homophobia (p. 195)
9. child pornography (p. 197)
10. street walkers (p. 198)
11. Victimless (p. 199)
12. 17 (p. 200)

ANALYSIS AND COMMENT

Go back through the chapter and write down in the spaces below key points from each of the following boxes.

MEDIA PERSPECTIVES

"The Boy Who Was Raised as a Girl"
Key Points

THINKING ABOUT DIVERSITY: RACE, CLASS, AND GENDER

"Same-Sex Marriage in Canada"
Key Points:

APPLYING SOCIOLOGY

"Date Rape: Exposing Dangerous Myths"
Key Points:

THINKING IT THROUGH

"The Abortion Controversy"
Key Points:

SUGGESTED READINGS

Classic Sources

Edgar Gregersen. 1983 ***Sexual Practices. The Story of Human Sexuality.*** **New York: Franklin Watts.**
This book contains a vast amount of material on cross-cultural sexual practices, along with fascinating illustrations.

Vern L. Bullough. 1994. ***Science in the Bedroom: A History of Sex Research.*** **New York: Basic Books.**
Details about sex research from the Ancient Greeks to Hirschfield, Ellis, and Freud.

Richard von Kraft-Ebing. 1886. ***Psychopathia Sexualis.*** New York: Putnam (Reprint).

Contemporary Sources

Robert Michael, John Gagnon, Edward O. Laumann, and Gina Kolata. 1994. ***Sex in America: A Definitive Survey.*** **Boston: Little Brown.**
Contains the results of the National Health and Social Life Survey, conducted by the National Opinion Research Center.

Bernie Zilbergeld. 1999. ***The New Male Sexuality.*** **New York: Bantam Books.**
Insightful observations from the author's experiences as a sex therapist.

Glen Wilson. 1987. ***Varient Sexuality: Research and Theory.*** **Baltimore: Johns Hopkins University Press.**
Theoretical explanations for sexual variations.

Canadian Sources

Canadian Journal of Human Sexuality.
A quarterly journal that publishes recent research on human sexuality.

Alan King, Richard P. Beazley, Wendy K. Warren, Catherine A. Harkins, Alan S. Robertson, and Joyce L. Radford. 1988. ***The Canada Youth and AIDS Study.*** **Kingston Ont. Social program Evaluation Group, Queens University.**
This study examined whether a number of risk factors were associated with engaging in sexual intercourse.

Eleanor Maticka-Tyndale and Edward S. Herold. 1999. Condom Use on Spring Break Vacation: The Influence of Intentions, Prior Use, and Context. ***Journal of Applied Psychology*****, 29, 1010-1027.**
This article identifies recent research by these authors and others that deals with the relationship between sexual scripts and risk-taking sexual behaviours.

David Cruise and Alison Grifiths. 1997. ***On South Mountain: The Dark Secrets of the Golen Clan.*** **Toronto: Viking.**
A chilling tale of child sexual abuse within the Golen family of Nova Scotia.

Julian Roberts and Renate M Mohr. 1995. ***Confronting Sexual Assault: A Decade of Legal Change.*** **Toronto: University of Toronto Press.**
Discusses the issues leading up to changes in the offences relating to sexual assault and child sexual abuse.

Global Sources

Neil Miller. 1992. ***Out in the World: Gay and Lesbian Life from Buenos Aires to Bangkok.*** **New York: Random House.**
Fascinating accounts of gay and lesbian communities around the world.

Roberta Perkins and Gerry Bennett. 1985. ***Being a Prostitute.*** **London: Allen and Unwin.**
The story of a prostitue in Australia.

CHAPTER 9

Deviance

CHAPTER OUTLINE

I. **What Is Deviance?**
   A. Social Control
   B. The Biological Context
   C. Personality Factors
   D. The Social Foundations of Deviance
II. **The Functions of Deviance: Structural-Functional Analysis**
   A. Durkheim's Basic Insight
      1. An Illustration: The Puritans of Massachusetts Bay
   B. Merton's Strain Theory
   C. Deviant Subcultures
III. **Labelling Deviance: Symbolic-Interaction Analysis**
   A. Labelling Theory
      1. Primary and Secondary Deviance
      2. Stigma
      3. Retrospective and Projective Labelling
      4. Labelling Difference as Deviance
   B. The Medicalization of Deviance
      1. The Difference Labels Make
   C. Sutherland's Differential Association Theory
   D. Hirschi's Control Theory
IV. **Deviance and Inequality: Social-Conflict Analysis**
   A. Deviance and Power
   B. Deviance and Capitalism
   C. White-Collar Crime
   D. Corporate Crime
   E. Organized Crime
V. **Deviance, Race, Ethnicity, and Gender**
   A. Hate Crimes
   B. Deviance and Gender
VI. **Crime**
   A. Types of Crime
   B. Criminal Statistics
   C. The Street Criminal: A Profile
      1. Age
      2. Gender
      3. Social Class
      4. Race and Ethnicity
   D. Crime: Canadian, American, and Global Perspectives

VII. The Criminal Justice System
- A. Police
- B. Courts
- C. Punishment
  1. Retribution
  2. Deterrence
  3. Rehabilitation
  4. Societal Protection
- D. Community-Based Corrections
  1. Probation
  2. Parole
  3. Sentencing Circle

VIII. Making the Grade
IX. Key Points
X. Key Concepts
XI. Applications and Exercises
XII. MySocLab

LEARNING OBJECTIVES

- To use the sociological perspective to explain deviance as a product of society
- To understand the biological and psychological explanations for deviance
- To understand the structural-functional, symbolic-interactionist, and social-conflict explanations of deviant behaviour
- To understand the works of Durkheim, Merton and Cloward and Ohlin within the structural-functional framework
- To understand labelling theory, differential-association theory, and control theory within the symbolic-interactionist framework
- To understand how power affects deviant definitions from within the social-conflict perspective
- To explain how gender and race have an impact on deviant definitions
- To know how crime is defined and how age, gender, social class, race, and ethnicity are related to differential distributions of crime
- To know the limitations of criminal statistics
- To identify and explain the elements of our criminal justice system
- To understand community-based corrections

CHAPTER REVIEW

This chapter addresses questions concerning deviance. For example, why do societies create laws: Why are some people more likely than others to be accused of violations? Not all individuals fit the definition of street criminals, Martha Stewart being an example.

WHAT IS DEVIANCE?

Deviance is the recognized violation of cultural norms. It is a very broad concept and many characteristics are used by members of society in identifying deviance. One familiar type of deviance is ***crime***, or the violation of norms formally enacted into criminal law. A special category of crime is ***juvenile delinquency***, or the violation of legal standards by the young.

It is pointed out that deviance can be negative or positive, but in that it stems from ***difference,*** it causes us to react to another person as an "outsider."

Social Control

Social control is defined as attempts by society to regulate the behaviour of individuals. Much of it is an informal effort by significant others, but a very formal response comes from the ***criminal justice system***, or a societal reaction to alleged violations of the law through the use of police, courts, and prison officials.

The Biological Context

A century ago most human behaviour was explained by biological instincts. Understandably early attempts to understand deviance emphasized biological causes.

Early work by Cesare Lombroso and later, William Sheldon, suggested that criminals possessed distinctive physical traits or body types. Today there continues to be genetic research with attempts to isolate a predisposition to criminality. While it may be true that biology affects some behaviour, the majority of current research focuses upon social influences.

Personality Factors

Psychological explanations of deviance concentrate on personality abnormalities, and like biological theories are focused on "individualistic" characteristics.

Containment theory suggests that nondelinquents have personalities that intervene in any social impulse towards deviance. Longitudinal research by Reckless and Dinitz in the 1960s supported this notion.

Since most serious crime, however, is committed by people who are psychologically normal, the limitations of this theoretical approach are obvious. What is also ignored is the different likelihoods of being labelled as deviant, depending upon a person's location within the power structure of society.

The Social Foundations of Deviance

Deviance is not simply a matter of free choice or personal failings. Both conformity and deviance are shaped by society and this is evident in three ways: Deviance exists only in relation to cultural norms; people become deviant as others define them that way; and both norms and the way people define rule breaking involve social power.

THE FUNCTIONS OF DEVIANCE: STRUCTURAL-FUNCTIONAL ANALYSIS

Durkheim's Basic Insight

While on the surface deviance may appear to be only harmful for society, Emile Durkheim asserted that deviance is an integral part of all societies and serves four major functions. These include affirming cultural values and norms, clarifying moral boundaries, promoting social unity, and encouraging social change. The **Thinking About Diversity Box** (p. 213) offers an example of how rapid social change can have a negative impact.

➢An Illustration: The Puritans of Massachusetts Bay

Kai Erikson's historical research on this highly religious society supports Durkheim's theory concerning the functions of deviance. For these people, deviance helped clarify various moral boundaries. Over time, he noted, what was defined as deviant changed as social and environmental conditions changed. What remained constant, however, was the proportion of people viewed as deviant.

Merton's Strain Theory

Merton uses strain theory to point out imbalances between socially endorsed "means" available to different groups of people and the widely held goals and values in society. As a result of this structured inequality of opportunity, some people are prone to deviant responses. Four adaptive strategies are identified by Merton: innovation, ritualism, retreatism, and rebellion. **Figure 9-1** (p. 214) outlines the components of this theory. Conformity, or the acceptance of both cultural goals and means is seen as the result of successful socialization and the opportunity to pursue these goals through socially approved means. The text discusses Rocco Perri's life as an example of Merton's "innovation" mode of adaptation for those experiencing social marginality.

Merton finds that many people respond to the strain by abandoning success goals through ritualistic maintenance of rules. Others reject the goals of success and the means, and retreat into drugs or alcohol perhaps. The final group rejects both goals and means but replaces them with others through rebellion.

Deviant Subcultures

Researchers Richard Cloward and Lloyd Ohlin have attempted to extend the work of Merton utilizing the concept of relative opportunity structure. They argue that criminal deviance occurs when there is limited opportunity to achieve success accompanied by accessible illegitimate opportunities. They further suggest that criminal subcultures emerge to organize and expand systems of deviance. Again, Rocco Perri's life is an example. In poor and highly transient neighbourhoods "conflict subcultures" (i.e., violent gangs) are more often the form this process takes. Those who fail to achieve success even through criminal means are likely to fall into "retreatist subcultures" (e.g., alcoholism).

Albert Cohen found that deviant subcultures occur more often in the lower classes and are based on values that oppose the dominant culture.

Finally, Elijah Anderson finds that most young people conform to conventional values but some, because of neighbourhood crime, hostility from police, and indifference by their own parents, decide to live by a "street code."

LABELLING DEVIANCE: SYMBOLIC-INTERACTION ANALYSIS

The symbolic-interaction approach focuses upon deviance as a flexible process.

Labelling Theory

Labelling theory, the assertion that deviance and conformity result from the response of others, stresses the relativity of deviance. Of critical significance to proponents of this perspective is the process by which people label others as deviant.

➢Primary and Secondary Deviance

Edwin Lemert has distinguished between the concepts of ***primary deviance***, initial acts of deviance that may provoke little action, and ***secondary deviance***, repeated norm violations that lead the individual to accept the deviant definition.

➢Stigma

Erving Goffman suggested secondary deviance is the beginning of a "deviant career." This is typically a consequence of acquiring a ***stigma***, or a powerful negative social label that radically changes a person's social identity and self-concept. Some people may go through a "*degradation ceremony*," like a criminal prosecution, where a community formally condemns the person for deviance allegedly committed.

➢Retrospective and Projective Labelling

Retrospective labelling is the interpretation of someone's past consistent with present deviance. In this case, other people selectively rethink the "deviant's" past, arguing all the evidence was there that would predict the person's problem.

Projective labelling is the projection of a deviant identity into the future, so that escape from stigma is difficult.

➢Labelling Difference as Deviance

Thomas Szasz argues that the concept "mental illness" should not be applied to people. He says that only the "body" can become ill, and mental illness is therefore a myth. Szasz suggests that the label mental illness is attached to people who are different and who disturb the status quo of society. It acts as a justification for forcing people to comply with cultural norms.

The Medicalization of Deviance

Over the last fifty years, the field of medicine has had a tremendous influence on how deviance has been understood and explained. The ***medicalization of deviance*** relates to the transformation of moral and legal issues into medical matters. Instead of seeing conformity and deviance as matters of "bad" and "good," we conceive the dichotomy as one of "well" versus "sick." The general view of alcoholism in our society in recent years is a good illustration of this process.

➢The Difference Labels Make

If a medical definition is used, there are profound consequences. Rather than the police, clinical specialists will respond and the response will be in a treatment rather than punishment mode. Finally, while a moral response would make the perpetrator responsible, a medical response suggests that the person is incompetent, leaving others to make treatment decisions.

Sutherland's Differential Association Theory

Edwin Sutherland suggests that deviance is learned through association with others. Accordingly, a person's likelihood of violating norms is dependent upon the frequency of association with those who encourage norm violation.

Hirschi's Control Theory

Hirschi's point is that what really requires explanation is conformity. He suggests conformity results from four types of social controls: attachment, opportunity, involvement, and belief. Once again, a person's position in the social structural system is important in determining one's likelihood of being involved in subcultural deviance. Those with little to lose become rule-breakers.

The symbolic-interactionist approach ignores why society defines certain activities as deviant in the first place. It also glosses over the fact that certain behaviours are defined as deviant almost everywhere, suggesting that cultural relativity is not appropriate to all behavioural acts. As well, not all, even well-orchestrated, labels are accepted by the individuals named, and in some instances the label is not avoided but eagerly sought.

DEVIANCE AND INEQUALITY: SOCIAL-CONFLICT ANALYSIS

Deviance and Power

Social inequality serves as the basis of social-conflict theory as it relates to deviance. Certainly less powerful people in society are more likely to be defined as deviant. This pattern is explained in three ways: First, the norms of society generally reflect the interests of the powerful. Second, even if the behaviour of the powerful is questioned, they have the resources to resist deviant labels. And third, laws and norms are usually never questioned, being viewed as "natural," even if inherently unfair.

Deviance and Capitalism

Steven Spitzer has suggested that deviant labels are attached to people who interfere with capitalism. Four qualities of capitalism are critical to recognize in order to understand who is labelled as deviant. These are private ownership, production labour, respect for authority, and acceptance of the status quo. He differentiates between two types of problem populations. One is represented by non-productive, but non-threatening members of society. Another is characterized by people perceived as directly threatening to the capitalist system. Spitzer says that capitalism itself creates these groups, though the individuals themselves are blamed for their own problems.

White-Collar Crime

The concept ***white-collar crime***, or crimes committed by persons of high social position in the course of their occupations, was defined by Edwin Sutherland in the 1940s. This type of crime involves powerful people taking illegal advantage of their occupational position. While it is estimated that the harm done to society by white-collar crime is greater than street crime, most people are not particularly concerned about this form of deviance. This is in part illustrated by the fact that violators who are caught have traditionally been dealt with in civil court rather than criminal court.

Until recently, white-collar criminals, if successfully prosecuted, rarely went to jail. The **Media Perspectives Box** (pp. 220-221) does indicate, however, that "crime in high places" is now receiving more public attention.

Social-conflict theory focuses our attention on the significance of power and inequality in understanding how deviance is defined and controlled. However, some weaknesses of this approach have been identified. The assumption that the rich and powerful directly create and control cultural norms is questionable given the nature of our political process. Second, this approach suggests that only when inequality exists is there deviance, yet even economically egalitarian societies exhibit types of deviance, and as Durkheim has pointed out, deviance can be functional.

The **Applying Theory Table 9-1** (p. 222) summarizes the major contributions of each of the sociological explanations of deviance.

Corporate Crime

When whole companies break the law, *corporate crime*, illegal actions of a corporation or people acting on its behalf, takes place. It could be knowingly selling dangerous products or deliberately polluting the environment. The public is often unaware of the violations and the perpetrators usually go unpunished.

Organized Crime

Organized crime is a business supplying illegal goods or services such as illegal drugs, prostitution, and credit card fraud. The Italian Mafia was one of the first in North America but almost any ethnic category can be involved today.

DEVIANCE, RACE, ETHNICITY, AND GENDER

Power strongly predicts the shape of deviance in society.

Hate Crimes

A hate crime is a criminal act against a person or a person's property by an offender motivated by racial or other bias. **Figure 9-2** (p. 222) shows recent data on victims of hate crime in Canada. A full 25% is directed against Jewish people or institutions.

Deviance and Gender

The inclusion of gender in the study of deviant behaviour has been insignificant especially in the structural-functional and conflict perspectives. Only in the labelling approach has the gender issue been examined carefully and it has been found that the behaviour of males and females are evaluated by different standards. Further, because of their position within the power structure, men often escape responsibility when they victimize women. The rates of crime and violence are much higher for men. The **Thinking It Through Box** (pp. 224-225) looks at the link between masculinity and violence in hockey.

CRIME

Crime is the violation of criminal law statutes. In Canada they are enacted by the federal government.

Crime is composed of the act itself and criminal intent or "*mens rea*." Degree of intent is important with respect to determining the seriousness of a crime.

Types of Crimes

In Canada information on crime is obtained from the Uniform Crime Reporting System in a Statistics Canada publication, *Canadian Crime Statistics*. ***Violent crimes***, crimes against people that involve violence or the threat of violence, include murder, manslaughter, sexual assault, and robbery among others. ***Property crimes***, crimes that involve theft of property belonging to others, including theft over $5,000, theft under $5,000, fraud, and possession of stolen goods, among others, is the second major crime category. A third type are ***victimless crimes***, violation of laws in which there is no readily apparent victim, such as prostitution and gambling. This category is often a misnomer since the young runaway lured into prostitution could readily be seen as a victim of circumstance.

Criminal Statistics

Canada's crime statistics indicate a steady increase in violent and property crimes from 1962 to 1992, followed by a clear decline through 2004. **Figure 9-3** (p. 223) indicates these changes. Our homicide rates are less than one-quarter the American rates, but there is a substantial differential between the provinces as indicated in the **Canada Map 9-1** (p. 226).

It should be noted that official crime statistics are far from accurate and seriously underestimate the real levels. Homicides are almost always brought to the attention of police, but sexual assault and property crime are often not. Victimization reports indicate that real rates of crime are much higher than official statistics indicate. There is increasing evidence that men may be victims of assault as often as women.

The Street Criminal: A Profile

The likelihood of engaging in crime increases sharply during adolescence and declines thereafter. In Canada, 20- to 34-year-olds are 25% of the population, but 62% of prison inmates.

Statistics indicate crime to be predominantly a male activity. In Canada 85%-90% of arrests involve males and 97% of prison inmates are male. While recent evidence suggests the disparity is shrinking, women are still involved primarily in victimless crimes and shoplifting. There is also, of course, the reluctance to define women as criminal. The Karla Homolka case is noteworthy since she was permitted to make a *plea bargain*, a legal negotiation in which the prosecution reduces a defendant's charge in exchange for a guilty plea. She received a manslaughter conviction in exchange for giving evidence against her husband.

While most people believe that poor people simply commit more crime, the situation is actually more complex. Research suggests crime exists across all social strata; it is the types of crimes committed that vary. Those who are victimized by crime are also disproportionately at the lower economic levels of society.

The relationship between race and crime is a complex one, but certainly Blacks and Aboriginal people are grossly overrepresented with respect to arrests and incarceration. Prejudice would appear to play a role, as these categories of race are more likely to be reported by citizens and arrested by police. Race is also related to social class, which itself leads to over-criminalization. Finally, white-collar crimes, committed primarily by middle-class Whites are underreported and often not counted in official crime statistics. The recent report of the Commission on Systemic Racism in the Ontario Criminal Justice System reports that Blacks are treated more harshly at every stage in the justice system.

Crime: Canadian, American, and Global Perspectives

Relative to European societies, the United States has a very high crime rate, and Canada is also relatively high by world standards. The U.S. rates are affected by an emphasis on individual economic success, the weakening of family support systems, and high levels of unemployment, which create categories of chronically poor people along with a high proportion of privately owned guns. All these factors, except guns, are in place in Canada, suggesting that we can expect an increase in our crime rates unless social change reduces the impact of these factors. The recent diminution of Canada's social safety net may accelerate this change. Crime rates, however, are actually falling.

The Canadian government's recent gun-control legislation is a recognition of the danger associated with widespread availability of guns. **Figure 9-4** (p. 228) shows the death rates by handguns for six countries, and **Figure 9-5** (p. 229) shows Canadian firearm homicides by type of firearm. Firearm homicide rates have been declining since 1991. **Table 9-1** (p. 228) shows statistics for Canadian homicide by method, for 2000 to 2004.

The terrorist attacks in New York in 2001 and the increasing flow of illegal drugs have meant that Canada must respond to criminal activities somewhat in concert with other countries, especially the United States. Airport security and the flow of illegal drugs from Canada is of concern to Americans.

THE CRIMINAL JUSTICE SYSTEM

The criminal justice system is comprised of three component parts. These are the following:

Police

The police represent the point of contact between the public and the criminal justice system. They are responsible for maintaining public order by uniformly enforcing the law. However, particularly because of the relatively small number of police in our population, they must exercise much discretion about which situations receive their attention. In Ontario police are less likely to make an arrest when their actions are not observed or if they feel an individual is trustworthy. Perhaps that is why Blacks and Aboriginal people are disproportionately arrested and why greater numbers of police are found in areas of large income disparities and large numbers of minorities.

Courts

It is within this component of the system that guilt or innocence is determined. In practice, a large number of cases are dealt with through ***plea bargaining,*** where the prosecution reduces the charge in exchange for a guilty plea. This saves the court time and expense but it abuses protection for defendants and perhaps for the public as well .Note the public response to Karla Homolka's successful plea bargaining.

Punishment

Approaches to punishment have changed over time. Children and juveniles are treated differently in the Canadian justice system and capital punishment was abolished in 1976. **Global Map 9-1** (p. 231) shows a global trend away from the death penalty.

The four justifications for using punishment include ***retribution***, subjecting an offender to suffering comparable to that caused by the offence; ***deterrence***, the attempt to discourage criminality through punishment; ***rehabilitation***, reforming the offender to preclude subsequent offences; and ***social protection***, rendering an offender incapable of further offences either temporarily, during a period of incarceration, or permanently by execution. These justifications of punishment are summarized in the **Summing Up Table** (p. 232).

While these justifications are widely recognized, demonstrating their consequences is very problematic. Their relative effectiveness is questioned given the high ***criminal recidivism*** rates, or subsequent offences by people previously convicted of crimes. Likewise, specific deterrence expectations associated with capital punishment are shown to have no effect.

Community-Based Corrections

It is apparent that prisons do little to rehabilitate most offenders and they are very expensive. An alternative is community-based corrections, where the correction programs operate in the community, rather than in prison. They are less expensive, reduce crowding in prisons, and allow for supervision of the convicts. The goal is reform, not punishment.

➢Probation

The offender remains in the community under the supervision of a probation officer.

➢Parole

The prisoner is released from prison to serve the rest of his or her sentence in the community under the supervision of a parole officer.

➢Sentencing Circles

This is a community-based program for Aboriginal offenders. Sentencing circles, which include the victim, are intended to start the healing process for the accused, the victim, and the community.

All these programs are less expensive than prisons, but there is not much evidence that they significantly reduce recidivism. The **Thinking Critically Box** (pp. 233-234) looks at the issue of "what can a society do about crime."

KEY CONCEPTS

Define each of the following concepts on a separate sheet of paper. Check the accuracy of your answers by referring to the key concepts in the text, as well as by referring to italicized definitions located throughout the chapter.

community-based corrections
control theory
corporate crime
crime
criminal justice system
criminal recidivism
deterrence
deviance
differential association
hate crime
juvenile delinquency
labelling theory
medicalization of deviance
organized crime
plea bargain
primary deviance
projective labelling
property crimes
rehabilitation
retribution
retrospective labelling
secondary deviance
social control
social protection
stigma
victimless crimes
violent crimes
white-collar crime

STUDY QUESTIONS

True-False

1. T F Deviance is the recognized violation of cultural norms.

2. T F William Sheldon posited that body structure might predict criminality.

3. T F The vast majority of serious crimes are committed by people whose psychological profiles are not normal.

4. T F Durkheim suggests that society creates deviants to mark its changing moral boundaries.

5. T F According to Cloward and Ohlin, deviance or conformity grows out of the relative opportunity structure that frames young people's lives.

6. T F Primary deviance is when an individual engages in repeated norm violations and begins to take on a deviant identity.

7. T F Thomas Szasz argues that mental illness is a myth and is a label used by the powerful in society to force people to follow dominant cultural norms.

8. T F Sutherland contends that a person's tendency towards deviance or conformity depends upon his or her relationship with the mother.

9. T F Hirschi suggests that people who have little to lose from deviance are most likely to become rule breakers.

10. T F The social-conflict perspective suggests that even the powerful do not have the resources to resist deviant labels.

11. T F The Italian Mafia are responsible for almost all organized crime in North America.

12. T F The most likely targets of hate crime in Canada are Muslims.

13. T F The homicide rates in Canada are highest in Manitoba.

 Multiple Choice

1. This researcher discerned that criminals had distinctive physical features:

   (a) Sheldon Glueck
   (b) Walter Miller
   (c) Cesare Lombroso
   (d) Charles Goring
   (e) Emile Durkheim

2. Which of the following is not a social foundation of deviance according to our authors?

   (a) Deviance exists in relation to cultural norms.
   (b) People become deviant in that others define them that way.
   (c) Both norms and the way people define social situations involve social power.
   (d) All are identified as foundations of deviance.
   (e) None are identified as foundations of deviance.

3. Which of the following is ***not*** one of the functions that Durkheim suggested deviance serves?

   (a) Deviance affirms cultural values.
   (b) Responses to deviance clarify moral boundaries.
   (c) Responses to deviance attack social unity.
   (d) Deviance encourages social change.

4. Kai Erikson's historical research on the Puritans of Massachusetts Bay supports which of the following?

(a) Durkheim's structural-functional perspective concerning the functions of deviance
(b) The psychological theory of containment
(c) The genetic inbreeding theory of deviance
(d) The body structure theory of deviance
(e) The social conflict theory of deviance

5. Merton's strain theory has been criticized for __________________________.

(a) explaining only some forms of deviance
(b) ignoring the dislocation between goals and means in society
(c) limiting the definition of success to wealth
(d) (a and b above)
(e) (a and c above)

6. What is the term for the behaviour of an individual who engages in repeated norm violation and begins to take on a deviant identity?

(a) retreatist deviance
(b) ritualistic deviance
(c) rebellious deviance
(d) secondary deviance
(e) primary deviance

7. When people begin interpreting someone's past consistent with present deviance, they are engaging in____________________.

(a) primary deviance
(b) secondary deviance
(c) labelling
(d) retrospective labelling
(e) opportunity

8. Crimes committed by persons of high social position in the course of their occupations is called ______________________.

(a) white-collar crimes
(b) capitalist deviance
(c) power crime
(d) harmless burden
(e) victimless crime

9. Violent and property crime in Canada peaked in ________________.

(a) the early 1920s
(b) the late 1990s
(c) the early 1990s
(d) 1946
(e) the early 1960s

10. Crime rates in Canada are highest for ____________________.

    (a) individuals between the ages 25 and 44
    (b) males
    (c) Blacks and Aboriginal people
    (d) (a and b above)
    (e) (b and c above)

11. A legal negotiation in which the prosecution reduces a defendant's charge in exchange for a guilty plea is called __________________.

    (a) retribution
    (b) reduced levy
    (c) neutral deterrence
    (d) plea bargaining
    (e) reassessment

12. Which of the following is ***not*** one of the usual justifications for punishment?

    (a) retribution
    (b) sanctification
    (c) deterrence
    (d) rehabilitation
    (e) social protection

Fill in the Blank

1. The ____________ _____________ ____________ is a societal reaction to alleged violations of the law through the use of police, courts, and punishment.

2. Reckless and Dinitz developed ____________ theory, which posits that boys who developed a strong conscience and identified with cultural values would avoid deviant behaviour.

3. In Merton's _______ response, people resolve the strain of limited success by compulsive efforts to live "respectably."

4. Sometimes an entire community formally stigmatizes individuals through what Harold Garfinkel calls a _________ ______________.

5. In ___________ ________ Hirschi claims that the essence of social control lies in people's anticipation of the consequences of their behaviour.

6. Stephen Spitzer argues that deviant labels are applied to people who impede the operation of _______________.

7. The sale of illegal goods and services is called ___________ ______________.

8. The Canadian criminal justice system consists of three elements: ________________, ________________, and ______________.

9. In Canada young people under the age of eighteen years of age are seen to have a ________________ for crime

10. Canadian society has a high rate of ______________ ____________________, subsequent offences by people previously convicted of crime.

Definition and Short Answer

1. According to Hirschi's control theory, there are four types of social controls. What are these? Provide an example of each.

2. According to Merton's strain theory, what are the four deviant responses by individuals to dominant cultural patterns?

3. What are the functions of deviance according to Durkheim?

4. What characteristics are likely to have people labelled as being a member of a "problem population" according to Spitzer?

5. How do researchers using the differential association theory explain deviance?

6. What is meant by the term "medicalization of deviance"?

7. Is the masculinity of violence in Canadian hockey related to the expression of male violence in society?

8. What are the four justifications for the use of punishment against criminals?

9. What are the social foundations of deviance? Illustrate each.

10. Summarize the basic explanations of deviance using each of the following perspectives: social-conflict, symbolic-interactionism, and structural-functionalism.

Answers to Study Questions

True-False

1. T (p. 210)
2. T (p. 211)
3. F (p. 211)
4. T (p. 213)
5. T (p. 214)
6. F (p. 216)
7. T (p. 216)
8. F (p. 217)
9. T (p. 217)
10. F (p. 218)
11. F (p. 220)
12. F (p. 222)
13. F (p. 226)

Multiple Choice

1. c (p. 210)
2. d (pp. 211-212)
3. c (p. 212)
4. a (pp. 213-214)
5. e (p. 214)
6. d (p. 216)
7. d (p. 216)
8. a (p. 219)
9. c (pp. 223)
10. e (pp. 225-227)
11. d (p. 226)
12. b (p. 230)

Fill in the Blank

1. criminal justice system (p. 210)
2. containment (p. 211)
3. ritualism (p. 214)
4. degradation ceremony (p. 216)
5. control theory (p. 217)
6. capitalism (p. 218)
7. organized crime (p. 220)
8. the police, the courts, punishment (p. 229)
9. lower capacity (p. 230)
10. criminal recidivism (p. 232)

ANALYSIS AND COMMENT

Go back through the chapter and write down in the spaces below key points from each of the following boxes.

THINKING ABOUT DIVERSITY

"Suicide among Aboriginal People"
Key Points:

MEDIA PERSPECTIVES

"Crime in High Places "
Key Points:

THINKING IT THROUGH

"Dangerous Masculinity: Violence and Crime in Hockey"
Key Points:

THINKING CRITICALLY

"What Can Be Done About Crime?"
Key Points:

SUGGESTED READINGS

Contemporary Sources

Eileen B. Leonard. 1982. *Women, Crime, and Society: A Critique of Theoretical Criminology.* New York: Longman.

Thompson Educational Publishing.
These three books are valuable efforts to incorporate gender into the study of deviance. The first explains how women have virtually been ignored up to the present in studies of crime; the second applies labelling theory to gender issues; the third looks at women as victims.

Charles W. Thomas. 1987. *Corrections in America: Problems of the Past and the Present.* Newbury Park, CA: Sage.
D. Owen Carrigan. 1991. *Crime and Punishment in Canada: A History.* Toronto: McClelland a& Stewart.
These two books present the history and many contemporary controversies surrounding crime and punishment in Canada and the United States.

Robert M. Bohm. 1991. *The Death Penalty in America: Current Research.* Cincinnati, OH: Anderson Publishing.
This book offers eight essays dealing with the death penalty.

Bernard J. Gallagher III. 1991. *The Sociology of Mental Illness.* 3rd ed. Englewood Cliffs, NJ: Prentice Hall.
This sociological account of mental illness delves into who in the United States is affected by such conditions and the social role of the mental patient.

Anne Campbell. 1991. *The Girls in the Gang.* 2nd ed. Cambridge, MA: Basil Blackwell.
Most research about youth gangs is by and about men. Anne Campbell provides a rare and insightful account of young women in New York street gangs.

Edwin M. Schur. 1983. *Labelling Women Deviant: Gender, Stigma, and Social Control.* Philadelphia: Temple University Press.
Walter S. DeKeseredy and Ronald Hinch. 1991. *Woman Abuse: Sociological Perspectives.* Toronto: University of Toronto Press.
Robert B. Edgerton. 1976. *Deviance: A Cross-Cultural Perspective.* Menlo Park, CA: Cummings.
This book shows the relativity of deviance, illustrating the extent to which the definition of deviant behaviour varies with time and across cultures.

Daniel Wolf. 1991. *The Rebels: A Brotherhood of Outlaw Bikers.* Toronto: University of Toronto Press.
A professor of anthropology reports on field work that involved riding for three years with a biker gang.

Canadian Sources

David Suzuki and Peter Knudtson. 1989. *Genetics: The Clash between the New Genetics and Human Values.* Cambridge, MA: Harvard University Press.

Global Sources

Ikuyo Sato. *Kamikaze Biker: Parody and Anomy in Affluent Japan.* Chicago: University of Chicago Press, 1991.
In the tradition of Emile Durkheim, this account of juvenile delinquency in Japan highlights the breakdown of traditional social controls that often accompany material affluence.

CHAPTER 10

Social Stratification

CHAPTER OUTLINE

LEARNING OBJECTIVES

- To understand the four basic principles of social stratification
- To differentiate between two systems of stratification: caste and class, and to be able to provide historical and cross-cultural examples of each
- To know the relationship between culture, ideology, and stratification
- To differentiate between the structural-functional, social-conflict, and symbolic-interactionist perspectives of stratification
- To understand the views of Max Weber concerning the various dimensions of social class
- To know the synthesis approach to understanding social stratification put forward by Lenski
- To understand the link between theories of social class and value judgments
- To understand the limitations of the relationship between intelligence and social class

CHAPTER REVIEW

WHAT IS SOCIAL STRATIFICATION?

Social inequality, characterized by the unequal distribution of valued resources, is found in every society. Some of the inequality is the result of individual differences in ability and effort, but much of it also relates to societal structures. ***Social stratification*** refers to a system by which categories of people in society are ranked in a hierarchy. This chapter opens with an illustration of the sinking of the *Titanic* to show the consequences of social inequality in terms of who survived the disaster and who did not. One of the children who died, but was not initially identified, was discovered to be a relative of one of the authors, Linda Gerber. Sociological and personal reality often overlap. (See the **Thinking About Diversity Box** (p. 242) for confirmation.) Four principles are identified that help explain why social stratification exists. First, social stratification is a characteristic of society and not merely of individuals. Second, social stratification is universal but variable. Third, it persists over generations. And, fourth, it is supported by patterns of belief.

CASTE AND CLASS SYSTEMS

Sociologists distinguish between two general systems of social stratification based on the degree of social mobility representative of the system.

The Caste System

A ***caste system*** is a system of social stratification based on ascription. Pure caste systems are "closed" with no social mobility.

➢An Illustration: India

The Indian system consists of four major castes and hundreds of sub-caste groups. Four factors underlie this ascriptive process. First, birth determines one's occupation. Second, marriage unites people of the same social ranking. Third, people interact daily with "their own kind." Fourth, powerful cultural beliefs support the maintenance of the system.

➢Caste and Agrarian Life

Caste systems are much more typical of agrarian societies where lifelong agricultural routines depend upon a rigid sense of duty and discipline. The **Thinking Globally Box** (p. 243) outlines another caste system, in South Africa, that is challenged by democratic reform but still based on race.

The Class System

Representative of industrial societies, ***class systems*** are defined as systems of social stratification based on both birth and individual achievement. Social categories are not as rigidly defined as in the caste system. Individual ability, promoted by open social mobility, is critical to this system.

Meritocracy

Meritocracy refers to social stratification based on personal merit. A pure meritocracy would reward a person based on ability and merit and therefore make good use of human potential. Family wealth, however, maintains some elements of caste and provides some order and stability through the family institution.

Status Consistency

Status consistency refers to the degree of consistency of a person's social standing across various dimensions of social inequality. Class systems have lower levels of status consistency.

Ascription and Achievement: England

England represents a society where caste qualities of its agrarian past still are interwoven within the modern day industrial class system.

➢The Estate System

England's agrarian past, with deep historical roots, was based on a caste-like estate system. Three estates, the first (clergy), the second (nobility), and the third (commoners) comprised this system. The law of ***primogeniture,*** by which property could only be inherited by the eldest son, helped maintain this system. The Industrial Revolution allowed some commoners in the cities to amass wealth sufficient to rival the power of the nobility and led to the blurring of social rankings.

➢England Today

Aspects of their feudal past persist today. For example, a monarch still stands as Britain's head of state, and descendants of traditional nobility still maintain inherited wealth and property. Power in government, however, resides in the House of Commons, which is primarily composed of people who have achieved their positions. Today, about 25% of the British population falls into the middle class, and 50% into the working class. Almost 25% are "poor." Although their stratification system is based primarily on class, social mobility is less likely than in the United States or Canada. The greater rigidity of this class system is reflected in very distinct linguistic patterns.

Another Example: Japan

Like Great Britain, Japan mixes both caste and meritocracy in their social stratification system.

➢Feudal Japan

For many centuries of agrarian feudalism, Japan was one of the most rigidly stratified cultures in the world. An imperial family maintained a network of regional nobility called ***shoguns.*** A warrior caste, called ***samurai***, fell just below the nobility. The majority of people were commoners, like serfs in feudal Europe. There was an additional ranking, however, called ***burakumin***, or outcasts, who were below the commoners.

➢Modern Japan

Industrialization and intercultural contact have dramatically changed Japan over the last century. The nobility lost its legal standing after World War II. For many though, tradition is still revered and family background continues to remain important in determining social status. Traditional male dominance, for example, remains well embedded.

Classless Societies? The Former Soviet Union

Some nations, like Russia, have claimed to be classless.

The Russian Revolution

The Soviet Union, guided by the ideas of Karl Marx after 1917, claimed to be a classless society because of the elimination of private ownership of the productive components of society. Yet, it remained socially stratified as occupations generally fell into four major categories: high government officials, the intelligentsia, manual labourers, and rural peasantry. Even so, it had less economic inequality than capitalist societies.

The Modern Russian Federation

The reforms spurred by Mikhail Gorbachev's economic program of restructuring, known as ***perestroika***, were significant. The efforts to elevate living standards through economic reform ultimately led to the overthrow of the ruling class, the Communist party.

While there has been greater social mobility in the last century than in capitalist societies, the last decade has brought economic turbulence and a significant downward mobility. This kind of mobility is what sociologists call ***structural social mobility***, where the shift is due to changes in the society and economy rather than to individual effort. The privatization of business leaves a larger gap between rich and poor.

China: Emerging Social Classes

China, like Russia, experienced a revolution and all property was placed in the hands of the state. All work was declared equal but social classes persisted with Communist party officials at the top, followed by factory managers and professionals, industrial workers, and rural peasants. After the death of Mao, the state loosened its grip on the economy, but maintained central political control. New economic growth has created a wealthy elite but most of the economic development has not reached China's rural interior. **Figure 10-1** (p. 249) indicates that China has substantially greater inequality than Canada.

Ideology: The Power Behind Stratification

Despite the mal-distribution of resources in systems characterized by social inequality, social hierarchies are remarkably persistent, at least in part because of ***ideology***, cultural beliefs that serve to justify patterns of inequality.

➢Plato and Marx on Ideology

Plato and Marx both recognize that ideologies exist in all societies to justify whatever stratification scheme is in place. Marx was critical, however, of inequality that channelled wealth and power into the hands of a few.

➢Historical Patterns of Ideology

Ideology changes with a society's economy and technology. The caste system initially ensured that the necessary lifelong labour would take place. Industrial capitalism rewards people who perform better and some aspects of a meritocracy occur. Early sociologists, like Herbert Spencer, talked about the "survival of the fittest." While it is difficult to change social stratification, challenges do arise, such as women questioning the notion of a "woman's place."

THE FUNCTIONS OF SOCIAL STRATIFICATION

The Davis-Moore Thesis

The Davis-Moore thesis asserts that some degree of social stratification is even a social necessity. They theorize that certain tasks in society are of more value than others, and in order to ensure the most qualified people fill these positions, they must be rewarded better than others.

Melvin Tumin suggests that the functional importance of tasks is difficult to measure. Should Barry Bonds make $20 million a year to play baseball? The **Applying Sociology Box** (pp. 252-253) addresses this question. Second, caste-like systems prevent some from developing their abilities, and not all societies attach the same importance to money. The **Media Perspectives Box** (p. 254) suggests different notions exist in Europe than in North America.

STRATIFICATION AND CONFLICT

Karl Marx: Class and Conflict

Marx's view of social stratification is based on his observations of industrialization in Europe during the nineteenth century. He saw a class division between the ***capitalists*** (owners of the means of production) and the ***workers*** (proletariat). The huge differences in rewards for these categories would lead to misery and ultimately a revolution to overthrow the capitalists. As influential as Marx's thinking has been for sociological understanding of social stratification, it does overlook its motivating value. The insight provided by the Davis-Moore thesis perhaps explains, in part, the low productivity characteristic of former socialist economies. Supporters of Marx still contend, however, that people are not inherently selfish and could be motivated to perform social roles for more intrinsic rewards.

Why No Marxist Revolution?

The overthrow of the capitalist system has not occurred for at least four central reasons as identified by Dahrendorf. First, the capitalist class has become fragmented over the last century, with numerous stockholders assuming ownership. Second, the proletariat has been significantly changed by the "white-collar revolution." A century ago the vast majority of workers in North America had ***blue-collar occupations***, or work involving mostly manual labour. Today, most members of the labour force hold ***white-collar occupations***, or they work at tasks that involve mostly mental activity. Most of this change has occurred through structural social mobility. A third factor involves the fact that the workers' conditions have improved through labour organizations. Finally, legal protection has been widely expanded for workers.

➢A Counterpoint

The value of Marx's perspective is still significant. There continues to be exploitation of workers, and a small percentage of people control the vast majority of wealth in our society. As well, there exists in capitalist societies an urban underclass and Aboriginal peoples in Canada, who live in desperate poverty.

Max Weber: Class, Status, and Power

Max Weber viewed Marx's ideas of social class as being too simplistic. Weber theorized that there were three dimensions of social inequality: class, status, and power.

➢The Socioeconomic Status Hierarchy

Weber theorized that a single individual's rankings on the three dimensions might be quite different, thus, a multidimensional aspect of social inequality was important to him. The term used today to reflect this idea is ***socioeconomic status*** referring to a composite social ranking based on various dimensions of social inequality.

➢Inequality in History

Weber noted that each of the three dimensions of social inequality predominates at different points in history. In agrarian societies status or social prestige stand out, while industrialization and capitalism place more focus on class. Finally, with increasing bureaucratization, power becomes centred in the hands of bureaucrats, whether the society be capitalist or socialist.

Although Weber's multidimensional approach remains influential, the enormous wealth of privileged Canadians contrasts sharply with the grinding poverty of the poor.

STRATIFICATION AND INTERACTION

Marx and Weber focused on the macro-level, the way a whole society is stratified, but people interact with others of similar social standing on a daily basis. Some of those interactions have a message about desired social standing: The term *conspicuous consumption* describes the buying and using of products to make "statements about one's social position."

The **Applying Theory Table** (p. 257) summarizes the three theoretical approaches to social stratification.

STRATIFICATION AND TECHNOLOGY: A GLOBAL PERSPECTIVE

The Lenski model of sociocultural evolution (outlined in Chapter 4) can help us to understand the varying degrees of inequality found in the world.

In the technologically simple hunter/gatherer societies, no categories of people have more than others.

As technology advances to produce horticultural, pastoral, and agrarian societies, a surplus in resources is created and inequality grows.

Further technological change leads to the creation of industrial societies where education allows for literacy and political participation, which pushes inequality downwards.

The Kuznets Curve (Figure 10-2, p. 258)

This curve suggests that technological progress first sharply increases but then moderates the intensity of stratification.

Global Map 10-1 (p. 259) generally supports the notion expressed in Kuznets Curve, where less income inequality is found in the highly industrialized countries. It may well be, however, that the Information Revolution will increase the economic polarization in Canada.

SOCIAL STRATIFICATION: FACTS AND VALUES

A quote from a Kurt Vonnegut novel describes a fictional America in the later twenty-first century represented by absolutely no social inequality. It highlights the significant social meaning social inequality actually has for us in our everyday lives.

Theoretical explanations contain both fact and value positions, as comparison between the structural-functional and social-conflict paradigms illustrates. The same facts can be perceived and understood differently. The **Thinking It Through Box** (p. 260) discusses the link between intelligence and social class where, indeed, value positions influence how apparent facts can be perceived differently.

KEY CONCEPTS

Define each of the following concepts on a separate sheet of paper. Check the accuracy of your answers by referring to the key concepts in the text, as well as by referring to italicized definitions located throughout the chapter.

blue-collar occupations
caste system
class system
conspicuous consumption
Davis-Moore thesis
ideology
Kuznets curve
meritocracy
social mobility
social stratification
socioeconomic status
status consistency
structural social mobility
white-collar occupations

STUDY QUESTIONS

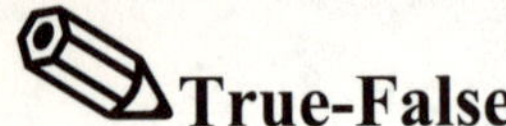

True-False

1. T F Age and class were found to be important predictive characteristics with respect to who died when the *Titanic* sank.

2. T F Ascription is fundamental to social stratification systems based on castes.

3. T F The "unknown child" of the *Titanic* disaster was the godson of one of the authors of your text, Linda Gerber.

4. T F Caste systems today are more typical of industrial societies.

5. T F In England today social mobility occurs as often as it does in Canada and the United States.

6. T F Economic inequality in China is greater than in Canada.

7. T F Herbert Spencer argued that society had a responsibility to treat all citizens equally economically.

8. T F The Davis-Moore thesis is a component of the social-conflict perspective of social stratification.

9. T F The revolutionary developments that Marx considered inevitable have now materialized.

10. T F Max Weber developed a unidimensional model of social stratification, which was dominant in the early part of this century.

11. T F The symbolic-interaction approach to stratification argues that the products we consume make a statement about social position.

12. T F The Kuznets curve projects greater social inequality as industrial societies advance through technological change.

13. T F Kurt Vonnegut, Jr. warns that social equality can be dangerous in practice.

14. T F The authors of *The Bell Curve: Intelligence and Class Structure in American Life* suggest that only 30% of human intelligence is transmitted genetically.

Multiple Choice

1. Which of the following principles is not a basic factor in explaining the existence of social stratification?

   (a) Social stratification is universal and variable.
   (b) Social stratification persists over generations.
   (c) Social stratification is supported by patterns of belief.
   (d) Social stratification is a characteristic of society, not simply of individuals.
   (e) All are basic factors in explaining social stratification.

3. In South Africa today, ______________________________.

   (a) Blacks have economic equality
   (b) residential segregation has disappeared
   (c) living conditions are much better in Soweto
   (d) one-third of Blacks have no work
   (e) (none of the above is true)

3. In England during the Middle Ages, the clergy were often referred to as the ___________.

   (a) first estate
   (b) second estate
   (c) third estate
   (d) fourth estate

4. In feudal Japan, the caste that was composed of soldiers was called __________________.

   (a) shoguns
   (b) samurai
   (c) *burakumin*
   (d) lords
   (e) *suffei*

5. A shift in the social position of large numbers of people due primarily to changes in the society itself rather than individual effort is called ________________________.

   (a) *apparatchik*
   (b) gateway behaviour
   (c) *perestroika*
   (d) structural social mobility
   (e) meritocratic stratification

6. The thesis that social stratification has beneficial consequences for the operation of a society was posited by ____________________.

   (a) Marx and Engels
   (b) Goethe
   (c) Davis and Moore
   (d) Mantle and Maris
   (e) Plato and Socrates

7. Tumin criticizes "functional importance" theories of stratification because __________.

   (a) it is difficult to measure functional importance
   (b) stratification does not necessarily guarantee the development of individual talent
   (c) social inequality promotes conflict
   (d) (all of the above)
   (e) (a and b above)

8. The Marxist revolution has not occurred because of ______________________.

   (a) the development of white-collar work
   (b) more extensive worker organizations
   (c) less extensive legal protections for workers
   (d) (a and b above)
   (e) (a and c above)

9. A composite ranking based on various dimensions of social inequality is called ______________________.

   (a) social prestige
   (b) socioeconomic status
   (c) social stratification
   (d) Weberian multidimension
   (e) (none of the above)

10. The buying or using products because of the statement they make about social position is called ______________________.

    (a) caste behaviour
    (b) Kuznets application
    (c) conspicuous consumption
    (d) upward social mobility
    (e) (none of the above)

Fill in the Blank

1. ________________________ is a change in a person's position in a social hierarchy.

2. A __________ is a system of social stratification based on ascription.

3. When people marry others of the same rank, the marriage is called __________________.

4. In feudal Great Britain, the law of _________________ mandated that only the eldest son inherited his parents' property.

5. Below the commoners in feudal Japan were the lowest social strata called ______________________.

6. ___________ is a set of cultural beliefs that justify patterns of inequality.

7. ____________________ claimed that the Davis-Moore argument in favour of social stratification ignores how class can prevent the development of individual talent.

8. According to Marx, __________________ society reproduces the class structure in each new generation.

9. The three dimensions of Weber's model of social stratification are termed ____________, ____________, and ___________.

10. Lenski argues that the level of _____________ representative of a society is a very significant factor in determining the nature of social stratification in that society.

Definition and Short Answer

1. What are the four basic principles that help explain the existence of social stratification?

2. Briefly describe the social stratification system of England today.

3. According to information provided in the text, why hasn't the Marxist revolution occurred?

4. What are the basic qualities of a caste system?

5. What is meant by the concept "structural social mobility?"

6. What are the components of Weber's multidimensional model of social stratification?

7. What are the basic tenets of the Davis-Moore thesis?

8. How do structural-functionalist, social-conflict, and interactionist theorists differ in terms of helping us understand social stratification?

9. Discuss Lenski's sociocultural evolution perspective and how it relates to a global and historical understanding of social stratification.

10. Are rich people really smarter?

Answers to Study Questions

True-False

1. T (p. 240)
2. T (p. 241)
3. T (p. 242)
4. F (p. 244)
5. F (p. 246)
6. T (p. 249)
7. F (p. 250)
8. F (p. 250)
9. F (p. 251)
10. F (p. 255)
11. T (p. 257)
12. F (p. 258)
13. T (p. 258)
14. F (p. 260)

Multiple Choice

1. e (p. 241)
2. d (p. 243)
3. a (p. 250)
4. b (p. 246)
5. d (p. 248)
6. c (p. 250)
7. d (pp. 250-251)
8. d (pp. 251-252)
9. b (p. 255)
10. c (p. 256)

Fill in the Blank

1. social mobility (p. 241)
2. caste (p. 241)
4. endogamous (p. 244)
5. primogeniture (p. 245)
5. burakumin (p. 247)
6. ideology (p. 249)
7. Melvin Tumin (p. 251)
8. capitalist (p. 251)
9. class, status, power (p. 255)
10. technology (p. 257)

ANALYSIS AND COMMENT

Go back through the chapter and write down in the spaces below key points from each of the following boxes.

THINKING ABOUT DIVERSITY: RACE, CLASS AND GENDER

"The *Titanic*: Personal and Canadian Connections"
Key Points:

THINKING GLOBALLY

"Race As Caste: A Report from South Africa"
Key Points:

APPLYING SOCIOLOGY

"Salaries: Are the Rich Worth What They Earn?"
Key Points:

MEDIA PERSPECTIVES

"Love of Leisure, and Europe's Reasons"
Key Points:

THINKING IT THROUGH

"The Bell Curve Debate: Are Rich People Really Smarter?"
Key Points:

SUGGESTED READINGS

Classic Sources

Lilian Breslow Rubin. 1976. *Worlds of Pain: Life in the Working-Class Family. New York: Basic Books.*
Based on interviews with fifty working-class families, Rubin skillfully explores the effects of social stratification on everyday life.

C. Wright Mills. 1956. *The Power Elite.* New York: Oxford University Press.
In this treatise written in the Marxist tradition, Mills argues that American society is dominated by a small, well-integrated group that controls the economy, the government, and the military.

Contemporary Sources

Charles E. Hurst. 1992. *Social Inequality: Forms, Causes, and Consequences.* Needham Heights, MA: Allyn and Bacon
Michael D. Grimes. 1991. *Class in Twentieth-Century American Sociology: An Analysis of Theories and Measurement Strategies.* New York: Praeger.
The first of these two books explores a number of issues raised in this chapter. The second, an historical account, traces how sociology has grappled with the study of social stratification.

David B. Grusky, ed. 1992. *Social Stratification: Class, Race, and Gender in Sociological Perspective.* Boulder, CO: Westview.
This collection of essays brings together a number of influential points of view concerning social diversity and hierarchy.

Margaret S. Clark, ed. 1991. *Prosocial Behaviour.* Newbury Park, CA: Sage.
Discussions about social hierarchy often revolve around the thorny question of whether, by nature, individuals are selfish or altruistic. This collection of a dozen essays presents comparative evidence of the existence of altruism in every culture.

Russell Jacoby and Naomi Glauberman, eds. 1995. *The Bell Curve Debate: History Documents, Opinions.* New York: Times Books.
Presenting the ideas of dozens of scholars and journalists, this is an excellent collection of commentary and analysis of the Bell Curve thesis—the alleged link between intelligence and social class.

Canadian Sources

James Curtis, Edward Grabb, Neil Guppy, and Sid Gilbert, eds. 1993. *Social Inequality in Canada.* Toronto: Prentice Hall Canada.
This collection of reprinted articles approaches social inequality from a number of perspectives.

Monica Boyd, John Goyder, Frank E. Jones, Hugh A. McRoberts, Peter Pineo, and John Porter. 1981. "Status Attainment in Canada: Findings of the Canadian Mobility Study." *Canadian Review of Sociology and Anthropology*, Vol. 18:657-673.
John Porter and a number of colleagues set out to

replicate and expand upon work by Blau and Duncan on American status attainment. This paper shows that Canada's social mobility rate is almost identical to that of the United States.

Lorne Tepperman. 1976. "A Simulation of Social Mobility in Industrial Societies." ***Canadian Review of Sociology and Anthropology,*** **Vol. 13:26-42.**
The rate of mobility in a society is largely a function of the shape or structure of its stratification system. Tepperman develops a model that deals with shifts in the shape of both stratification systems and social mobility with industrialization.

Global Sources

Sven E. Olsson. 1990. ***Social Policy and Welfare State in Sweden.*** **Lund, Sweden: Arkiv.**
This analysis of social stratification in Sweden points out the role of culture and national politics in the creation of this nation's extensive welfare system.

Sidney Verba with Steven Kelman, Gary R. Orren, Ichiro Miyake, Joji Watanuki, Ikuo Kabashima, and G. Donald Ferree, Jr. 1987. ***Elites and the Idea of Equality: A Comparison of Japan, Sweden, and the United States.*** **Cambridge, MA: Harvard University Press.**
This book compares social equality in three distinctive societies.

James Curtis and Lorne Tepperman, eds. 1994. ***Haves and Have Nots: An International Reader on Social Inequality.*** **Englewood Cliffs, NJ: Prentice Hall.**
This collection of essays by Canadian authors presents a global survey of social stratification.

CHAPTER 11 Social Class in Canada

CHAPTER OUTLINE

I. **Dimensions of Social Inequality**
   - A. Income
   - B. Wealth
   - C. Power
   - D. Occupational Prestige
   - E. Schooling

II. **Canadian Stratification: Merit and Caste**
   - A. Ancestry
   - B. Race and Ethnicity
   - C. Gender

III. **Social Classes in Canada**
   - A. The Upper Class
     - 1. Upper-Upper Class
     - 2. Lower-Upper Class
   - B. The Middle Class
     - 1. Upper-Middle Class
     - 2. Average-Middle Class
   - C. The Working Class
   - D. The Lower Class

IV **The Difference Class Makes**
   - A. Health
   - B. Values and Attitudes
   - C. Family and Gender

V. **Social Mobility**
   - A. Social Mobility in Canada

VI **Poverty in Canada**
   - A. The Extent of Canadian Poverty
   - B. Who are the Poor?
     - 1. Age
     - 2. Education
     - 3. Race and Ethnicity
     - 4. Gender and Family Patterns
   - C. Explaining Poverty
     - 1. One View: Blame the Poor
     - 2. Counterpoint: Blame Society
   - D. The Working Poor
   - E. Homelessness

VII. **Making the Grade**

VIII. **Key Points**

IX. **Key Concepts**

X. **Applications and Exercises**

XI. **MySocLab**

LEARNING OBJECTIVES

- To understand the extent of social inequality in Canada
- To explain the role of income, wealth, power, occupational prestige, gender, and education in the Canadian class system
- To identify and trace the significance of various ascribed statuses for the construction and maintenance of social stratification in Canada
- To describe the general characteristics of the upper, middle, working, and lower classes. in Canadian society
- To understand that Aboriginal peoples run the gamut of the Canadian class system
- To understand the impact of social class on health, values and attitudes, family, and gender in Canadian society
- To understand the nature of intragenerational and intergenerational social mobility
- To distinguish between relative and absolute poverty
- To explain the causes of poverty
- To describe the demographics of poverty in Canada
- To understand the debate over who has responsibility for poverty
- To explain the reasons for the existence of homelessness
- To understand the impact of welfare on those who receive it and the society that supplies it

CHAPTER REVIEW

The chapter begins with a description of a young, single-parent mother moving homes for the third time in seven months. Her welfare has been cut by the Ontario government and she has lost her funding for a college program she hoped would raise her out of poverty.

Hers is a common story that demonstrates the power of stratification to positively or negatively imprint people's lives regardless of their personal talents or ambitions. The popular perception of a bulging middle class does not square with reality.

DIMENSIONS OF SOCIAL INEQUALITY

Canadians tend to underestimate the amount of social inequality in our society; there is a general belief that equality of opportunity allows individual initiative to decide who gets ahead. Certainly, compared to most other societies, Canadians perceive themselves to be well off. In reality, however, we tend to interact with those who are close to us in the class system, insulating us from the true dimensions of social inequality. Although money is an important component of inequality, ***socioeconomic status*** encompasses, as well, power, occupational prestige, and schooling.

Income

An important dimension of social inequality is ***income***. The average family income in 2004 was $76,000, part of a sustained recovery from 1993 (**Figure 11-1,** p. 267). **Table 11-1** (p. 268) shows the disparity in earnings between the top and bottom 20% of Canadian earners, with the top 20% of families receiving 43.6% of the income, while the bottom 20% of families receive 5.2% of the income. While the disparity is larger in the U.S., the Canadian numbers are moving closer to the American distribution. **Canada Map 11-1** (p. 269) indicates, as well, that income is not distributed equally across Canada. **Figure11-2** (p. 268) shows that the income disparity in Canada is at about the middle of high income countries.

Wealth

Wealth, which includes the total amount of money and valuable goods that a person or family controls, is even more unequally distributed than income.

Power

Wealth is an important source of power in our society. Do the wealthy, in part through social links, dominate political and economic decisions?

Occupational Prestige

Occupation, as well as being a major determinant of income, wealth, and power, is an important source of social prestige. Physicians have scored near the top for several decades and newspaper carriers near the bottom. In general, white-collar occupations are higher on prestige scales than blue-collar workers, but these differences are getting smaller. A recent study by John Goyder (see **Figure 11-3,** p. 270) indicates that fewer occupations are ranked at the top and bottom now compared to a quarter-century ago. The differences between male- and female-dominated jobs have lessened considerably.

Schooling

Education is an important determinant of labour force participation, occupation, and income and is highly valued in Canada and other industrial societies. Although education is generally conceived to be a right, there has not always been equal participation by women. Lately, however, women have completed more schooling than men. There is a strong correlation between educational completion and level of income.

CANADIAN STRATIFICATION: MERIT AND CASTE

Who we are at birth greatly influences what we later become.

Ancestry

Our point of entry into the system of social inequality is determined, in large part, by our ***ancestry***. Being born to privilege or poverty sets the stage for our future schooling, occupation, and income.

Race and Ethnicity

Race and ethnicity are important determinants of social position. **Figure 11-4** (p. 271) shows that Canadians of Japanese origin have the highest average incomes followed by English, French, Chinese, Black, and Aboriginal peoples. **Figure 11-5** (p. 272) looks only at those making $60 000 or more and the order is nearly the same, except that Aboriginal peoples are ranked higher than Blacks. The **Thinking About Diversity Box** (p. 273) indicates that while Aboriginal peoples as a group are at the bottom of the social class continuum, some are faring well in business ventures.

Gender

Women earn less income, accumulate less wealth, and enjoy less occupational prestige than men.

SOCIAL CLASSES IN CANADA

Despite the difficulty in clearly defining class levels in Canadian society because of low levels of status consistency and the fluidity provided by social mobility, it is possible to think of four general social classes in Canada. Increasingly, computer literacy is linked to employability. The **Thinking It Through Box** (p. 274) looks at computers and social class.

The Upper Class

Perhaps 3-5% of Canadians fall into this class. Much of their wealth is inherited. Their children go to private schools and they exercise great power in occupational positions. Although this group has historically been primarily of British origin, it is now more widely distributed.

➢Upper-Upper Class

One percent belongs to an upper-upper class distinguished primarily by "old money."

➢Lower-Upper Class

The remaining 2-4% fall into the lower-upper class and depend more on earnings than inherited wealth. They are, for the most part, the "nouveau riche."

The Middle Class

Roughly 40-50% of the Canadian population falls into this category. Because of its size, it has tremendous influence on patterns of Canadian culture. There is considerable racial and ethnic diversity in this class and it is not characterized by exclusiveness and familiarity. The top half of this category is termed the "upper-middle" class with family incomes of $50,000 to $100,000 earned from upper managerial or professional fields. The rest of the middle class (average middles) typically works in less prestigious white-collar occupations or highly skilled blue-collar jobs. According to the **Applying Sociology Box** (p. 277) the middle class dominate the Calgary Stampede.

The Working Class

This class comprises about one-third of the population and has lower incomes than the middle class and virtually no accumulated wealth. Their jobs provide less personal satisfaction.

The Lower Class

The remaining 20% of our population is identified as the lower class. In 2001 roughly 16% of the Canadian population were labelled as poor. Many are supported entirely by welfare payments, while others are among the "working poor" whose incomes are insufficient to cover necessities like food, shelter, and clothing. They typically live in less desirable neighbourhoods—often racially or ethnically distinct—and their children are often resigned to living the same hopeless lives of their parents.

THE DIFFERENCE CLASS MAKES

Health

Above-average family income leads to healthier children and adults, better access to medical care and longer lives.

Values and Attitudes

What class you are in can be linked to behaviour patterns and attitudes. Generally, the more affluent have greater tolerance for difference than the less affluent.

Family and Gender

Middle-class parents encourage creativity in their children while working-class parents encourage conformity. This is connected to where they imagine their children will work. Spousal relationships also differ, with more rigid role segregation in the working class as compared to more egalitarian relationships in the middle class, which also contains more emotional intimacy.

SOCIAL MOBILITY

Canada is characterized by a significant measure of social mobility. Social mobility can result from personal achievement or structural change in the society itself. It can be upward or downward and intragenerational or intergenerational. ***Intragenerational social mobility*** refers to a change in social position occurring during a person's lifetime. ***Intergenerational social mobility*** refers to upward or downward social mobility of children in relation to their parents.

Social Mobility in Canada

Canadians have generally expected that each new generation will do better than the last. Recent data suggest that while there is much upward and downward activity, on balance not much shift takes place between generations. Men experience more occupational inheritance than women and education is the key to occupational mobility in Canada. Divorce is a good predictor of downward social mobility for women but not men.

POVERTY IN CANADA

Social stratification creates "haves" and "have-nots." The "have-nots" can experience ***relative poverty***, a deprivation in relation to those who have more, or ***absolute poverty***, a deprivation of resources that is life threatening. Roughly one in seven of the world's population lives in conditions of absolute poverty, while few Canadians do.

The Extent of Canadian Poverty

In 1995, 15.7% of the Canadian population fell below the poverty line. That figure had fallen to 11.2% by 2004. Even so, recent United Nations' reports have criticized Canada for having so much poverty in a wealthy society. More than 800 000 different people make use of food banks each month.

Who are the Poor?

➢Age

A generation ago, the elderly were at the greatest risk for poverty, but today it is children. In 2004, 12.8% of children under 18 years of age were below the low-income cut-off point. This is much lower than figures from the mid-1990s. While poverty is declining in Canada, there are huge differences between family types as indicated in **Figure 11-6** (p. 282). Children in female lone-parent families are at greatest risk.

➢Education

People who have higher levels of education are considerably less likely to be unemployed and experience poverty conditions.

➢Race and Ethnicity

While British and French-background Canadians are not at the top of the income categories as measured by average male income (Welsh, Scottish, Jewish, and Japanese are higher), Blacks, West Indians, Latin Americans, some Asian groups, and Aboriginal peoples are clearly near the bottom. **Figure 11-7** (p. 283) also shows that recent immigrants are overrepresented in low-income categories.

➢Gender and Family Patterns

Women who head households bear the brunt of poverty. They are less likely to be employed and when they are, they earn less than men. **Figure 11-8** (p. 283) shows that female-headed, lone parent families have a low-average income. In fact**, Figure 11-9** (p. 284) demonstrates that 45.4% of these families fall below the poverty line. This situation has been described as the ***feminization_of poverty.***

Explaining Poverty

Sociologists generally agree that poverty is a product of social structure, but two distinct views about who is responsible are debated in the society.

➢One View: Blame the Poor

On one side are those who suggest that the poor are responsible for their own poverty. Oscar Lewis speaks of a ***culture of poverty*** where diminished expectations are the rule. Edward Banfield identifies a "living for the moment" orientation that guarantees a perpetuation of poverty.

➢**Counterpoint: Blame Society**

On the other side are those who suggest that society is primarily responsible for poverty. William Ryan holds that unequal distribution of resources is the problem and that any lack of ambition on the part of the poor is a consequence rather than a cause of their lack of opportunity.

There are advocates for both sides of this argument. Clearly individual initiative plays a role in shaping a person's social position, but many people work hard at minimum wages and find themselves below the poverty line. As well, a comprehensive child-care system would provide single-parent women with a better opportunity to seek training and/or find a job. Many of the poor depend on welfare. The **Thinking Critically Box** (p. 287) discusses Canada's welfare dilemma.

The Working Poor

Not all poor people are jobless. Many work at jobs, sometimes several jobs, that do not provide enough resources to move above the poverty line.

Homelessness

Although estimates of the level of homelessness are difficult to make, the familiar stereotypes of men sleeping in doorways and women carrying all their possessions in a shopping bag are no longer appropriate when there are examples of whole families who can no longer afford housing because of job loss. All homeless people have one thing in common, poverty. While many of them are poverty-stricken because of personal problems, there are an increasing number who find themselves homeless because of societal dislocation and government cutbacks. The **Media Perspectives Box** (p. 286) looks at the effort to count the homeless in Canada.

KEY CONCEPTS

Define each of the following concepts on a separate sheet of paper. Check the accuracy of your answers by referring to the text, as well as by referring to italicized definitions located throughout the chapter.

absolute poverty
culture of poverty
feminization of poverty
hidden injury of class
income
intergenerational mobility
intragenerational mobility
relative poverty
wealth

STUDY QUESTIONS

True-False

1. T F The income gap between the rich and the poor was greater in 2001 than any other time since 1961.

2. T F The income disparity between low-income and high-income groups is lower in Sweden than in Canada.

3. T F In 2000, incomes in Canada were highest in Ontario, the Yukon, and Northwest Territories.

4. T F In 2000, Canadians placed fewer occupations in the lowest and highest categories than they did in 1975.

5. T F The percentage of Aboriginal peoples who earned a high income more than doubled in the 1990s.

6. T F Almost all children from the upper-middle class receive a university education.

7. T F Because of poor eating habits, richer people do not live as long as poorer people.

8. T F Working-class parents encourage their children to express their individuality.

9. T F Occupational inheritance is more common for men than women.

10. T F In 2004, 11.2% of Canadians had incomes below the poverty line.

11. T F The family structure with the lowest income level is male-headed, lone-parent families.

12. T F Today the homeless are typically drug dependent men and women who sleep in doorways.

Multiple Choice

1. Statistics show that the incomes of Canadian families vary considerably. Which of the following statistics is accurate?

   (a) The average family income in 2004 was $40 000.
   (b) The top 20% of earners receive 60% of the total income distributed.
   (c) Wealth in Canada is more evenly distributed than income.
   (d) In 2001, the richest 20% of earners received 43.6% of the total income distributed.

2. Which of the following provinces had the highest median income in the year 2000?

   (a) Ontario
   (b) Alberta
   (c) British Columbia
   (d) Newfoundland
   (e) Manitoba

3. Which of these occupations is consistently at the top of occupational prestige rankings in the industrial, high-income countries?

   (a) university professors
   (b) nurses
   (c) physicians
   (d) lawyers
   (e) accountants

4. Canadians of ___________ origin have the highest average income in Canada.

   (a) English
   (b) French
   (c) Chinese
   (d) Aboriginal
   (e) Japanese

5. Which of the following is ***not*** true about social class in Canada?

   (a) The upper-upper class includes less than 1% of the Canadian population.
   (b) The lower-upper class is often referred to as the "nouveau riche."
   (c) Virtually all upper-middle class children receive a university education.
   (d) In the lower class, welfare dependency is often passed from one generation to the next.
   (e) Working-class children are taught by their parents to be independent and creative.

6. A change in the social position of children relative to that of their parents is called ____________.

   (a) individual social mobility
   (b) structural social mobility
   (c) intragenerational mobility
   (d) intergenerational mobility

7. In 2004, _____ % of the Canadian population were classified as poor.

   (a) 5.4 (b) 11.2 (c) 18 (d) 21.0 (e) 28.6

8. Which of the following groups experienced the highest percentage of people below the low-income cut-off?

   (a) Aboriginal
   (b) Black
   (c) Chinese
   (d) English
   (e) Japanese

9. The feminization of poverty in Canada is clearly related to ______________________.

   (a) female lone-parent families
   (b) sexual harassment in the workplace
   (c) the lower level of educational attainment of females
   (d) reduced female participation in the labour force

10. The fastest growing category of the homeless is now __________________.

    (a) male alcoholics
    (b) lone-parent females
    (c) children
    (d) the mentally ill
    (e) drug addicts

11. The tax write-offs to the affluent in Canadian society have been referred to by Canadian liberals as __________________.

    (a) corporate welfare
    (b) wealthfare
    (c) wealthy bums
    (d) snowbirditus
    (e) (none of the above)

Fill in the Blank

1. Socioeconomic status includes the dimensions of money, power, occupational prestige, and ______________.

2. While ______________ is defined as occupational wages or salaries from investments, ____________ refers to the total amount of money and goods that a person or family controls.

3. Women tend to be concentrated in _____ _____ jobs.

4. Women's salaries are most comparable in the ___________________ category as compared to men's.

5. The upper-upper class make up less than ____% of the total population.

6. The _____ _____ participate more extensively in the Calgary Stampede than other classes.

7. _____ social mobility refers to a change in social position occurring during a person's lifetime.

8. __________ poverty refers to a deprivation of resources that is life threatening.

9. In 2001, 45.4% of children living in _______________ ______________ __________ were living in poverty

10. Oscar Lewis claims that poor people become entrapped in a ___________ ______ ___________.

11. Since most census forms are mailed to home addresses, ______________ people fall through the cracks.

Definition and Short Answer

1. What are the reasons Canadians tend to underestimate the extent of social inequality in our society?

2. How is income distributed (by quintiles) in Canada? How has this distribution changed in the last forty years?

3. How does gender affect occupational status?

4. To what extent do ascribed statuses affect a person's place in our stratification system?

5. How do the four classes differ in lifestyle?

6. What is the reality of social mobility in Canadian society?

7. Who are the poor in Canadian society?

8. What is the "culture of poverty"?

9. How can society be identified as responsible for poverty?

10. What is meant by the "feminization of poverty"? To what extent is it a sizeable problem in Canada?

11. Who are the homeless in Canada?

Answers to Study Questions

True-False

1. T (p. 270)
2. T (p. 270)
3. T (p. 271)
4. T (p. 272)
5. T (p. 274)
6. T (p. 278)
7. F (p. 280)
8. F (p. 281)
9. T (p. 282)
10. T (p. 283)
11. F (pp. 284-285)
12. F (p. 287)

Multiple Choice

1. d (pp. 269-270)
2. a (p. 271)
3. c (p. 272)
4. e (p. 273)
5. e (pp. 277-281)
6. d (p. 282)
7. b (p. 283)
8. b (p. 284)
9. a (pp. 284-285)
10. c (p. 287)
11. b (p. 289)

Fill in the Blank

1. schooling (pp. 269)
2. income; wealth (pp. 269-271)
3. pink ghetto (p. 272)
4. self-employed professional (p. 272)
5. 1% (p. 277)
6. middle-class (p. 279)
7. intragenerational (p. 281)
8. absolute (p. 282)
9. female-headed, lone parent families (p. 285)
10. culture of poverty (p. 285)
11. homeless (p. 288)

ANALYSIS AND COMMENT

Go back through the chapter and write down in the spaces below key points from each of the following boxes.

THINKING ABOUT DIVERSITY

"Social Class and Aboriginal Peoples"
Key Points:

THINKING IT THROUGH

"Computers and Social Class"
Key Points:

APPLYING SOCIOLOGY

"Middle-Class Stampede"
Key Points:

MEDIA PERSPECTIVES

"Counting the Homeless in Toronto"
Key Points:

THINKING CRITICALLY

"The Welfare Dilemma"
Key Points:

SUGGESTED READINGS

Classic Source

John Porter. 1965. *The Vertical Mosaic: An Analysis of Class and Power in Canada.* Toronto: University of Toronto Press.
This sociological classic is still cited regularly in studies on social stratification.

Contemporary Sources

Susan A. Ostrander. 1984. *Women of the Upper Class.* Philadelphia: Temple University Press.
Lois Benjamin. 1991. *The Black Elite: Facing the Color Line in the Twilight of the Twentieth Century.* Chicago: Nelson-Hall.
The first of these books explains how the lives of privileged women differ from those of privileged men; the second argues that elite class standing does not override the significance of race in the United States.

Barbara Ehrenreich. 1990. *Fear of Falling: The Inner Life of the Middle Class.* New York: Harper Collins.
This readable and insightful book probes middle America during a time of economic decline.

Canadian Sources

James Curtis, Edward Grabb, Neil Guppy, and Sid Gilbert. 1988. *Social Inequality in Canada.* Scarborough, ON: Prentice Hall.
This collection of readings deals with various dimensions of social inequality, its causes, and consequences.

William K. Carroll. 1986. *Corporate Power and Canadian Capitalism.* Vancouver: University of British Columbia Press.
This book deals with Canadian capitalism and the people who control the economy.

Alfred A. Hunter. 1986. *Class Tells on Social Inequality in Canada.* 2nd. Ed. Toronto: Butterworths.
This study looks at various aspects of social class, including its interaction with gender and ethnicity.

Dwight Hamilton. 1996. "50 Richest Canadians: It's So Much Better to Be Rich." *The Financial Post Magazine,* January 1996: 14-28.

National Council of Welfare. 1990. *Women and Poverty Revisited.* Ottawa: Ministry of Supply and Services.
John R. Columbo. 1996. *The 1996 Canadian Global Almanac.* Toronto: Macmillan.
Susan Crompton. 1994. "Left Behind: Lone Mothers in the Labour Market." *Perspectives on Labour and Income.* Ottawa: Statistics Canada, Catalogue No. 75-001E.

Global Source

Robert Erikson and John H. Goldthorpe. 1992. *The Constant Flux: A Study of Class Mobility in Industrial Societies.* Oxford, U.K.: Clarendon Press.

CHAPTER 12

Global Stratification

CHAPTER OUTLINE

I. **Global Stratification: An Overview**
   - A. A Word about Terminology
   - B. High-Income Countries
   - C. Middle-Income Countries
   - D. Low-Income Countries

II. **Global Wealth and Poverty**
   - A. The Severity of Poverty
     - 1. Relative versus Absolute Poverty
   - B. The Extent of Poverty
   - C. Poverty and Children
   - D. Poverty and Women
   - E. Slavery
   - F. Explanations of Global Poverty

III. **Global Stratification: Theoretical Analysis**
   - A. Modernization Theory
     - 1. Historical Perspective
     - 2. Rostow's Stages of Modernization
     - 3. The Role of Rich Nations
   - B. Dependency Theory
     - 1. Historical Perspective
     - 2. The Importance of Colonialism
     - 3. Wallerstein's Capitalist World Economy
     - 4. The Role of Rich Nations
     - 5. Canada and Low Income Countries

IV. **Global Stratification: Looking Ahead**

V. **Making the Grade**

VI. **Key Points**

VII. **Key Concepts**

VIII. **Applications and Exercises**

IX. **MySocLab**

LEARNING OBJECTIVES

- To understand the nature of global income distribution between high-, medium-, and low-income societies
- To understand the nature of the differences with respect to industrial development between the three levels of societies
- To recognize the difference between relative and absolute poverty
- To comprehend the extensiveness of poverty in low-income countries
- To recognize the extent to which children and women are overrepresented among the poor of the world
- To identify and understand the explanations of global poverty
- To recognize that slavery still exists
- To identify and understand the two major theories used in explaining global inequality
- To identify the stages of modernization
- To understand the factors involved in dependency development
- To recognize Canada's relationship with low-income countries
- To identify the keys to combating global inequality over the next century

CHAPTER REVIEW

The nature of ***global stratification***, patterns of inequality in the world as a whole, is highlighted in the opening account of workers in a garment factory in Bangladesh. Not only do they needlessly perish in a fire, but they also earn a pittance compared to workers in Canada.

GLOBAL STRATIFICATION: AN OVERVIEW

Figure 12-1 (p. 293) identifies the distribution of world income where the richest 20% receives 80% of global income and the poorest 20% receives 1%. Placed in perspective, Canada's poorest people's living standard is higher than the majority of the earth's people.

A Word about Terminology

The traditional classification of countries with respect to economic development into first, second, and third worlds has been replaced because of the sweeping political changes in recent years, and because the lumping together into the third-world category of nations with widely divergent economic development was not satisfactory. The new classification of the 192 nations focuses on per-capita income development and divides nations into high-income, middle-income, and low-income categories.

High-Income Countries

These are the first countries to have industrialized. They are comprised primarily of Western Europe, North America, and New Zealand and Australia, along with Japan, Hong Kong, Singapore, and South Korea. Their total population is 18% of the world's population but they control over 80% of the world's income. Their people live primarily in urban areas and their productive technology is capital intensive. They are also at the forefront of computer technology. But even in high-income societies, many have low incomes. The **Thinking About Diversity Box** (p. 297) profiles striking poverty on the Texas border with Mexico.

Middle-Income Countries

While the high-income countries are characterized by per-capita income between $10 000 and $37 000, these countries are in the $2500 to $10 000 range. They have begun to industrialize, but at least a third of their residents are involved in agricultural production. Among this group are nations of the former Soviet Union and Eastern Europe, which have begun to introduce market systems. Also included are some Latin American, African, South American, and Asian countries, including China and India. These countries comprise 70% of the globe's population, but the usual amenities of the high-income countries are available to very few of these nations' citizens.

Low-Income Countries

The majority of people in these countries are abjectly poor and starvation is a recurrent feature of life. Twelve percent of the world's population lives in these countries, primarily in rural areas where the productivity levels are low. They are found primarily in Central and Eastern Africa, as well as Asia. **Global Map 12-1** (p. 295) shows the global distribution of the high-, medium-, and low-income societies.

GLOBAL WEALTH AND POVERTY

While deprivation exists in societies like Canada, the poorest countries are characterized by severe and extensive poverty. In the midst of the squalor of low-income societies, however, live enormously rich individuals.

The Severity of Poverty

The data presented in **Table 12-1** (p. 298) suggest why poverty is more ***severe*** in the low-income countries. This table compares the GDP and per-person income among countries from around the world for the year 2003. Further, a ***quality of life index*** measure is suggested for each nation. (Canadians enjoy a very high quality of life.) Significant differences are indicated. **Figure 12-2** (p. 298) shows the relative share of global income and population by world region.

Economic productivity is lowest where population growth is highest.

➢Relative versus Absolute Poverty

Every society experiences some level of poverty. In wealthy nations poverty is often viewed as a ***relative*** matter, but in the low-income countries, ***absolute*** poverty is much more critical. The people there typically lack the resources necessary to survive. **Global Map 12-2** (p. 300) shows the significant differences in median age of death depending upon the income level of countries. While the United Nations has a goal to reduce global poverty, the **Media Perspectives Box** (p. 301) indicates the extreme difficulties in even measuring it.

The Extent of Poverty

Poverty in the poor countries is also more ***extensive***. Most people there live in conditions far worse than the poor of Canada. These statistics boil down to one devastating fact: people are dying from a basic lack of nutrition. The magnitude of this tragedy is almost impossible to imagine with 40 000 people dying each day from starvation.

Poverty and Children

As in Canada, poverty worldwide hits children hardest. Many of the world's poor children live in the streets of cities forced to beg, steal, sell sex, or serve as couriers for drug gangs in order to survive.

Poverty and Women

While women in high-income countries like Canada face discrimination in the workforce and family, women in low-income countries fare far worse. They receive little schooling, they are responsible for most child-rearing and house maintenance, and they have little access to reproductive health care. About 70% of the world's poor are women.

Slavery

Although slavery was prohibited in Upper Canada in 1793, in the United States in 1865, and in 1948 by the United Nations Universal Declaration of Human Rights, almost 3% of humanity currently lives under conditions of slavery. Examples of current-day slavery include people living as chattel, abandoned children forced to work, debt bondage, servile forms of marriage, and human trafficking. The **Thinking Globally Box** (p. 303) describes the life of one slave in Mauritania.

Explanations of Global Poverty

Several factors are related to the severity and extent of poverty in low-income countries. These include the following:

1. technology
2. population growth
3. cultural patterns
4. social stratification
5. gender inequality
6. global power relationships

The **Applying Sociology Box** (p. 304) shows that poverty in poor societies is not responded to in the same way as in rich societies.

In terms of global power relationships, three key concepts are important. First, is the historical factor of ***colonialism***, or the process by which some nations enrich themselves through political and economic control of other nations. As a result of this, it is argued, many nations were exploited and remain underdeveloped. A second concept is ***neocolonialism***, referring to a new form of economic exploitation that does not involve formal political control. The argument here is focused on ***multinational corporations*** or large corporations whose operations span many different nations, and whose decisions are imposed on many countries.

GLOBAL STRATIFICATION: THEORETICAL ANALYSIS

The two dominant explanations for the unequal distribution of the world's wealth and power are ***modernization theory*** and ***dependency theory***.

Modernization Theory

Modernization theory maintains that global inequality reflects differing levels of technological development and cultural differences among societies.

➢Historical Perspective

A point made by these theorists is that until a few centuries ago, all people in the world were poor. The development of cities during the Middle Ages and the trade and exploration that emerged, coupled with the influence of the Industrial Revolution lifted the living standards of many societies. Therefore, ***affluence***, not deprivation, is what requires explanation.

This theory suggests that new technology is likely to be embraced only in certain societies. ***Tradition*** is the greatest barrier to economic development. This is consistent with Weber's theory of the influence of ideas on societal development. Calvinism in Europe toward the end of the Middle Ages moved society towards a focus on individualism and material affluence and an de-emphasis on kinship and community.

➢Rostow's Stages of Modernization

Modernization theorists argue that all societies are converging on one general form, the industrial model. According to W.W. Rostow, four general stages are followed by all societies:

1. The traditional stage, which is strongly tied to family and religion;

2. The take-off stage, during which time a limited market economy emerges. Progressive influences like foreign aid and advanced technologies are critical for poor nations to move through this stage;

3. The drive to technological maturity stage, represented today by Mexico, Puerto Rico, and the Republic of Korea, where societies experience rapid economic development, along with urbanization and specialization. Education becomes critical during this stage. The role of women begins to change and their status increases;

4. The high mass consumption stage, stimulated by mass production.

➢The Role of Rich Nations

Rather than seeing the high-income countries as part of the cause of global poverty, modernization theorists see it as part of the solution, in the following specific ways:

1. Assisting in population control through exportation of birth control technologies and the promotion of their use

2. Increasing food production by introducing "high-tech" farming methods (collectively referred to as the "Green Revolution")

3. Introducing industrial technology to increase productivity

4. Instituting programs of foreign aid, particularly in the form of investment capital.

There is international pressure on Canada to increase its foreign aid.

Proponents of modernization theory point out that several societies have demonstrated significant economic developments with the help of rich countries. Others argue, however, that modernization theory is just an attempt to defend and spread capitalism, and in many ways has fallen short in its own standards of success. Further, this approach tends to ignore historical changes that have impeded development. Other limitations involve a failure to make connections between rich and poor societies to see how a low-income country's development affects rich countries. Finally, the fact that this approach holds the high-income countries as the standard by which to judge all development is ethnocentric. Blaming the poor societies for their own poverty takes attention away from the negative effects of the behaviour of rich nations.

Dependency Theory

Dependency theory maintains that global poverty historically stems from the exploitation of poor societies by rich societies.

➢Historical Perspective

Dependency theorists argue that poor societies were better off in the past than they are today. They believe the economic positions of the rich and poor societies are interdependent and that the prosperity of high-income countries has come largely at the expense of low-income countries.

➢The Importance of Colonialism

European exploration of North America, Africa, and Asia led to colonization, which brought great wealth to countries like Britain and later, the United States. Indeed as **Figure 12-3** (p. 308) indicates, Africa's recent history is one of colonial domination. Although colonialism has largely disappeared, it has been replaced by neocolonialism. Political liberation has not been followed by economic autonomy.

➢Wallerstein's Capitalist World Economy

This model attempts to explain modern world inequality. A major point in this perspective is that the world economy, a global system, is beyond the control of traditional nations, and is dominated by capitalism. The rich nations are at the core of this world economy. This system perpetuates poverty in the rest of the world by creating and maintaining the dependency of these nations. This dependency is caused primarily by three factors:

1. narrow, export-oriented economies focused on raw materials,
2. a lack of industrial capacity, which means manufactured goods must be purchased, and
3. excessive foreign debt

➢The Role of Rich Nations

Dependency theorists argue that rich societies seize the wealth created in poor societies for their own purposes. Further, they argue the assumption of the relationship between population and poverty is spurious.

There is nothing inevitable about global hunger. There is sufficient food in most nations to feed their own people; but what poor nations do is grow crops to meet the demands of the rich nations, while ignoring their own needs. Critics argue, however, that there are weaknesses to this perspective. First, dependency theorists seem to assume all wealth obtained by rich nations is from poor nations. Second, those low-income nations with the closest ties to the rich nations are not the poorest. Third, while blaming world capitalism, dependency theorists ignore factors within the cultures of poor countries that lead to poverty, such as resistance to change and irresponsible political leadership. Fourth, some poor nations have advanced economically (note China and India). Finally, dependency theory does not produce clear policy-making alternatives, other than arguing for some kind of international socialism that certainly has not worked well at the national level.

➢Canada and Low-Income Countries

There is a tension in Canada's approach to development in low-income countries between the modernization and dependency models of understanding. While there has been a shift towards emphasizing self-sufficiency and improving the lives of the poor, there remains a desire to create an environment conducive to private-sector development and debt reduction. Despite its humanitarian goals, much of the aid is tied to potential for trade. Canadian universities are also extensively involved in overseas research and development, and are training more foreign students than a few years ago. The **Thinking It Through Box** (p. 312) is an example of Canadian research and activism in the Yucatán.

Recently, Canadians individually and through their government have responded generously to the tsunami disaster in the Indian Ocean and the devastation created by Hurricane Katrina in New Orleans. Some of our aid is also delivered militarily, as in Afghanistan.

GLOBAL STRATIFICATION: LOOKING AHEAD

Globalization of world economies has left many poor nations in grinding poverty and there has been loss of manufacturing jobs in high-income societies. Modernization and dependency theories can offer some level of understanding (see the **Applying Theory Table**, p. 310, for the basic principles).

Economic output has increased dramatically worldwide, but more of it in rich societies that become increasingly relatively better off than poor societies. There is less poverty overall, but the improvements are not equally spread out. Latin America is very mixed case, with significant economic output, but with approximately the same level of poverty in 2000 as was the case in 1970. Africa, especially south of the Sahara, has more poverty today (66% of the total) than in 1970 (11% of the total).

Governments have played a role in economic development, but not within a socialist framework.

Economic development in low-income societies puts great pressure on the environment as more resources are consumed.

Figure 12-4 (p. 313) demonstrates the continuing gap between rich and poor societies that may ultimately increase the risk of war and terrorism.

KEY CONCEPTS

Define each of the following concepts on a separate sheet of paper. Check the accuracy of your answers by referring to the text, as well as by referring to italicized definitions located throughout the chapter.

absolute poverty
colonialism
dependency theory
global stratification
modernization theory
multinational corporation
neocolonialism
relative poverty

STUDY QUESTIONS

True-False

1. T F The poorest 20% of the global population receives only 1% of all income.

2. T F High-income countries possessed the first economies to be transformed by the Industrial Revolution.

3. T F Middle-income countries are those with per-capita income ranging between $10 000 and $20 000.

4. T F In poor countries, half of all deaths occur among people less than 40 years of age.

5. T F Globally, women are disproportionately the poorest of the poor.

6. T F There are perhaps 90 000 slaves presently in Mauritania.

7. T F According to Mother Teresa, India has "happy poverty."

8. T F Modernization theory has guided the foreign policy of Canada for decades.

9. T F Dependency theory envisions global inequality in terms of the distribution of wealth.

10. T. F. Crop specialization in the Yucatán has left farmers vulnerable to losses owing to poor weather, pest attack, and plant diseases.

11. T F In Africa, especially countries south of the Sahara, living conditions have improved remarkably in the last thirty years.

12. T F The keys to combating global inequality during the next century lie in seeing it as partly a problem of technology and also a political issue.

Multiple Choice

1. Among middle-income countries the highest per-capita incomes are found in ___________.

   (a) Albania
   (b) Ecuador
   (c) Canada
   (d) Malaysia
   (e) Hong Kong

2. In low-income societies, _______ % of the people live in cities.

   (a) 33 (b) 42 (c) 50 (d) 70 (e) 93

3. In 2003, the quality of life index was highest in ________________.

   (a) Canada
   (b) the United States
   (c) France
   (d) Norway
   (e) Haiti

4. Overall gender inequality is _____________ in ________-income countries.

   (a) least, low
   (b) starkest, middle
   (c) least, middle
   (d) starkest, low
   (e) starkest, high

5. Which of the following is not discussed as an explanation of poverty in low-income countries?

   (a) gender inequality
   (b) population growth
   (c) technology
   (d) social stratification
   (e) all are discussed

6. Which of the following statements are ***correct*** with respect to slavery in Mauritania?

   (a) Slavery began there about 200 years ago.
   (b) After independence in 1946, Mauritania banned slavery.
   (c) In 1905, the French colonial rulers of Mauritania banned slavery.
   (d) All of the above
   (e) a and b above

7. Modernization theory identifies __________ as the greatest barrier to economic development.

   (a) population
   (b) religion
   (c) education
   (d) lack of work ethic
   (e) tradition

8. According to Rostow's modernization model, which stage is Thailand currently in?

   (a) traditional
   (b) take-off
   (c) drive to technological maturity
   (d) high mass consumption
   (e) residual-dependency

9. Which of the following is ***not*** a criticism of modernization theory?

   (a) There has been rapid economic development in South Korea.
   (b) Modernization has not occurred in many poor countries.
   (c) Rich countries block the paths to development in poor countries.
   (d) Colonialism held many countries back.
   (e) The "Western" idea of progress uses scarce resources quickly.

10. Which of the following is ***not*** a criticism of modernization theory?

   (a) There has been rapid economic development in South Korea.
   (b) Modernization has not occurred in many poor countries.
   (c) Rich countries block the paths to development in poor countries.
   (d) Colonialism held many countries back.
   (e) The "Western" idea of progress uses scarce resources quickly.

11. Canada's approach to foreign aid for developing countries____________________.

   (a) has started to emphasize self-sufficiency in health care, agriculture, and other areas.
   (b) is still linked to potential for trade.
   (c) involves several universities in overseas research and development.
   (d) (all of the above)
   (f) (a and b above)

Fill in the Blank

1. The less-industrialized, socialist countries used to be referred to as the ________________.

2. The _________ _____________ countries have a high proportion of agrarian workers.

3. According to our authors, poverty in the low-income countries is more ________ and more _______ than it is in Canada.

4. In 2003, ______________ was the country identified by the United Nations as having the lowest quality of life.

5. __________________ is a new form of economic exploitation that does not involve formal political control.

6. ____________________ suggests global inequality reflects differing levels of technological development among societies.

7. According to Rostow's stages of modernization, all societies are gradually converging to one general form: thc ___________ model.

8. ____________________ maintains that global poverty historically stems from the exploitation of poor societies by rich societies.

9. Wallerstein suggests that the dependency of low-income countries is related to narrow, export-oriented economies, a lack of industrial capacity, and ______________________.

10. The greatest reduction in poverty has taken place globally in _____________.

Definition and Short Answer

1. Define high-income, middle-income, and low-income countries.

2. How do the economies in each of these categories differ from one another?

3. What factors create the condition of women and children being overrepresented in poverty around the world?

4. What are the different kinds of slavery that exist today?

5. What are the explanations of global poverty?

6. What is neocolonialism? Provide an illustration.

7. What are the four stages of modernization in Rostow's model of societal change and development?

8. Why is there "happy poverty" in India and "angry poverty" in the United States?

9. According to dependency theory, how do rich nations contribute to continued poverty in poor nations?

10. What are the prospects for solving the problems of global stratification?

Answers to Study Questions

True-False

1. T (p. 293)
2. T (p. 293)
3. F (p. 294)
4. F (p. 299)
5. T (p. 302)
6. T (p. 303)
7. T (p. 304)
8. T (p. 306)
9. T (p. 308)
10. T (p. 312)
11. F (p. 312)
12. T (p. 313)

Multiple Choice

1. d (p. 294)
2. a (p. 296)
3. d (p. 298)
4. d (p. 301)
5. e (p. 303)
6. c (p. 303)
7. e (p. 305)
8. b (p. 305)
9. a (pp. 306-307)
10. d (p. 308)
11. d (pp. 310-311)

Fill in the Blank

1. Second World (p. 293)
2. low-income (p. 296)
3. severe; widespread (pp. 298-299)
4. Niger (p. 298)
5. neocolonialism (p. 304)
6. modernization theory (p. 305)
7. industrial (p. 305)
8. dependency theory (p. 307)
9. foreign debt (p. 308)
10. Asia (p. 312)

ANALYSIS AND COMMENT

Go back through the chapter and write down in the spaces below key points from each of the following boxes.

THINKING ABOUT DIVERSITY

"*Las Colonias:* 'America's Third World'"
Key Points:

MEDIA PERSPECTIVES

"Experts Wonder How To Measure Poverty"
Key Points

THINKING GLOBALLY

"God Made Me To Be a Slave"
Key Points:

APPLYING SOCIOLOGY

"'Happy Poverty' in India: Making Sense of a Strange Idea"
Key Points:

THINKING IT THROUGH

"Seeking Livelihood Sustainability for Yucatán Farmers"

Key Points:

SUGGESTED READINGS

Classic Sources

W.W. Rostow. 1960. *The Stages of Economic Growth: A Non-Communist Manifesto.* Cambridge, UK: Cambridge University Press.
Although this book draws on the thinking of several classic sociologists (including Emile Durkheim and Max Weber), it represents the first systematic statement of modernization theory.

Frantz Fanon. 1963. *The Wretched of the Earth.* New York: Grove Press.
This classic analysis highlights the role of colonization, nationalism, and violence in the Algerian struggle for independence.

Contemporary Sources

United Nations Development Programme. 1995. *Human Development Report, 1995.* New York: Oxford University Press.
The World Bank. 1995. *World Development Report 1995: Workers in an Integrating World.* New York: Oxford University Press.
These two annual publications provide a wide range of data on the comparative economic development of the world's nations.

Frances Moore Lappe and Joseph Collins. 1986. *World Hunger: Twelve Myths.* New York: Grove Press/ Food First Books.
Peter Berger. 1986. *The Capitalist Revolution: Fifty Propositions About Prosperity, Equality, and Liberty.* New York: Basic Books.
The first of these two books, by two longtime hunger activists, is guided by dependency theory. The second, written by a well-known contemporary sociologist, argues the merits of modernization theory.

Global Sources

Nancy Scheper-Hughes. 1992. *Death Without Weeping: The Violence of Everyday Life in Brazil.* Berkeley, CA: University of California Press.
Offering a moving portrait of suffering in the shantytowns of Brazil, this researcher identifies strongly with her subjects and makes an outspoken call for change.

Catherin A. Lutz and Jane L. Collins. 1993. *Reading "National Geographic."* Chicago: University of Chicago Press.
Reviewing more than thirty years of popular *National Geographic* magazines, these researchers argue that this prominent publication presents a sugar-coated vision of life in poor countries.

Canadian Sources

Canadian International Development Association (CIDA). 1987. *Sharing our Future: Canadian International Development Assistance.* Ottawa: CIDA.
This policy statement by CIDA makes an attempt to deal with supports for capitalism (economic structural adjustment) and more humanitarian aims, including the involvement of women in development

Jamie Swift and Brian Tomlinson, eds. 1991. *Conflicts of Interest: Canada and the Third World.* Toronto: Between the Lines Press.
This collection of essays provides an overview of Canada's perspective on Third-World issues as well as the nature of its involvement. Among the topics covered are the debt crisis, women in development, environment, and mass media.

CHAPTER 13

Gender Stratification

CHAPTER OUTLINE

- I. **Gender and Inequality**
  - A. Male/Female Differences
  - B. Gender in Global Perspective
    - 1. The Israeli Kibbutz
    - 2. Margaret Mead's Research
    - 3. George Murdock's Research
  - C. In Sum: Gender and Culture
  - D. Patriarchy and Sexism
    - 1. The Costs of Sexism
    - 2. Is Patriarchy Inevitable?
- II. **Gender and Socialization**
  - A. Gender and the Family
  - B. Gender and the Peer Group
  - C. Gender and Schooling
  - D. Gender and the Mass Media
- III. **Gender and Social Stratification**
  - A. Working Women and Men
  - B. Gender, Occupations, and Income
  - C. Housework: Women's "Second Shift"
  - D. Gender and Education
  - E. Gender and Politics
  - F. Are Women a Minority?
  - G. Minority Women: Intersection Theory
  - H. Violence against Women
    - 1. Violence by Women
    - 2. Violence against Men
  - I. Sexual Harassment
  - J. Pornography
- IV. **Theoretical Analysis of Gender**
  - A. Structural-Functional Analysis
    - 1. Talcott Parsons: Gender and Complementarity
  - B. Social-Conflict Analysis
    - 1. Friedrich Engels: Gender and Class
- V. **Feminism**
  - 1. Basic Feminist Ideas
  - 2. Types of Feminism
  - 3. Liberal Feminism
  - 4. Socialist Feminism
  - 5. Radical Feminism
  - 6. Cultural and Postmodern Feminism
- VI. **Gender: Looking Ahead**
- VII. **Making the Grade**
- VIII. **Key Points**
- IX. **Key Concepts**
- X. **Applications and Exercises**
- XI. **MySocLab**

LEARNING OBJECTIVES

- To understand the relationship between gender and inequality
- To describe how culture defines gender relationships
- To describe the link between patriarchy and sexism
- To know the arguments in the debate over whether patriarchy is inevitable
- To describe the role that gender plays in socialization in the family, the peer group, schooling, and the mass media
- To explain how gender stratification occurs in the work-world, housework, economics, education, and politics
- To understand the gender gap in income
- To identify the key arguments in the debate over whether women constitute a minority
- To understand how the intersection of race, class, and gender contributes to multiple levels of disadvantage
- To understand the sources of the expression of violence against women and by women
- To compare and contrast the two sociological analyses of gender: structural-functional analysis and social-conflict analysis
- To define and explain the central ideas of feminism, variations of feminism, and opposition to feminism
- To project the future of male and female roles in Canadian society

CHAPTER REVIEW

The chapter opens with a description of how Canadian women fought to have women recognized as "persons" in 1929 and how they managed to have sexual equality included in the Charter of Rights and Freedoms in 1982.

Much has changed, but gender remains a major dimension of social stratification.

GENDER AND INEQUALITY

Gender refers to the personal traits and social position that members of a society attach to being male and female. Gender involves hierarchy, causing sociologists to talk of ***gender stratification***, the unequal distribution of wealth, power, and privilege between men and women.

Male/Female Differences

There are certainly physical differences between males and females, but many of the social differences have nothing to do with biology and everything to do with cultural conventions. As **Figure 13-1** (p. 319) indicates, even some of the physical differences attributed to the natural inferiority of females have begun to disappear.

Gender in Global Perspective

➢The Israeli Kibbutz

The significance of culture is revealed using studies that focus on egalitarian gender role patterns in Israeli *kibbutzim*. Although social equality is not complete, the effort to share roles equally is noteworthy.

➢Margaret Mead's and George Murdock's Research and Conclusions to be Drawn

Research by Mead and Murdock indicates that what is defined as feminine or masculine varies widely across different cultures. Behaviour by males and females is clearly more a matter of social definition than biological imperative.

Patriarchy and Sexism

While conceptions of gender vary cross-culturally and historically, there is an apparent universal pattern of ***patriarchy***, a form of social organization in which males dominant females. ***Matriarchy***, defined as a form of social organization in which females dominate males has never been documented. The relative power of males over females does however vary significantly between societies. **Global Map 13-1** (p. 322) shows that variation. Patriarchy is based upon ***sexism***, the belief that one sex is innately superior to the other. ***Institutionalized sexism***, or sexism built into the various institutions of our society, is evident in the lack of attention historically to violence against women and their concentration in low-paying jobs.

➢The Costs of Sexism

The costs to women who are denied opportunities and the cost to society of loss of talent are clear. There are also costs to men, as masculinity is related to accidents, suicide, violence, stress, and a loss of intimacy and trust.

➢Is Patriarchy Inevitable?

This discussion illustrates that patriarchy in societies with simple technology tends to reflect biological sex differences. In industrialized societies, technology minimizes the significance of any biological differences.

Generally, the opinion of sociologists is that gender is principally a social construction and patriarchy is therefore subject to change.

GENDER AND SOCIALIZATION

Males and females are encouraged through the socialization process to incorporate gender into their personal identities. Emotional, passive, co-operative females are juxtaposed against rational, active, competitive males, although most young people develop personalities that are a mix of feminine and masculine traits.

Gender roles are attitudes and activities that a society links to each sex. Males are expected to be ambitious and competitive, while women are expected to be deferential and emotional.

Gender and the Family

In many societies, gender is at work before birth when the preference is to have a male child. At birth, families usher girls and boys into different "pink" and "blue" worlds. These differences are accentuated over time as parents stress independence and action for their boys and co-operation and emotion for their girls.

Gender and the Peer Group

Children tend to form single-sex playgroups.

Gender and Schooling

Historically, school texts have shown males doing more interesting things than females. This has begun to change, but sex stereotyping persists.

At the high school and university levels females and males still tend to choose different majors and new areas of study are often sex-linked with males studying computer science and females taking gender studies.

Gender and the Mass Media

The mass media has placed males at centre stage. Women have been shown as less competent than men, and often as sex objects. Changes are occurring, but very slowly. This is particularly true in advertising, which has clung to traditional cultural views of women and men.

The **Thinking About Diversity Box** (p. 344) indicates that the "soft and emotional" image of women changes as the Canadian women's hockey team is successful on the international stage.

GENDER AND SOCIAL STRATIFICATION

Gender helps to determine one's place in the social hierarchy.

Working Women and Men

Women have increased their participation rates in the labour force dramatically in a thirty-year period. In 1971 the majority of women were not in the labour force, even in the prime working years between 35 and 44 years of age. By 2001, almost four in five women of that age were in the working force, so that women now make up 47% of the Canadian labour force. **Figures 13-2** and **13-3** (p. 325) show the participation rates for men and women between 1971 and 2001.

Gender, Occupations, and Income

In the past there was a high gender division in occupations. Women dominated in service and clerical jobs, while men did almost everything else. This distinction has changed quite remarkably as women are now found in business, engineering, medicine, and senior management. Men still tend to hold the power positions, but this is slowly changing. The **Thinking It Through Box** (pp. 328-331) outlines the continuing gender gap in occupation and income and evaluates some of the usual explanations for this fact. As well, the **Media Perspectives Box** (p. 334) shows that some Canadian women exercise immense power.

Housework: Women's "Second Shift"

Despite women's rapid entry into the labour force, they continue to do most of the shopping, cooking, and cleaning, amounting to what sociologists call a "second shift." **Figure 13-4** (p. 327) outlines male and female participation in housework.

Gender and Education

Women were traditionally discouraged from participating in higher education. Recently, however, more than half of all university qualifications were earned by women. More of these have been in fine arts, education, and the humanities, but a growing number of women are entering the fields of medicine, engineering, and science. Men still predominate in engineering and the hard sciences, but women are moving to equality in the professional fields, such as business, law, and medicine. They will likely soon earn more advanced degrees (M.A.s and Ph.Ds) than men. **Table 13-3** (p. 332) outlines educational attainment by gender.

Gender and Politics

Before 1918 women could not vote in federal elections, but by 1940 all eligible women could vote in both federal and provincial elections. **Table 13-4** (p. 333) cites the benchmarks in the women's movement in Canadian political life.

Today women are involved in politics at all levels, but primarily at the municipal level.

Change is slowly occurring, however; currently 20% of M.P.s are women, and many women have taken dominant roles in both federal and provincial cabinets. The 20% share, however, has been unchanged since 1997.

Are Women a Minority?

As a category, women can be viewed as a minority group because of being socially disadvantaged. However, subjectively, most white women in Canada do not perceive themselves as such.

Minority Women: Intersection Theory

Minority women, especially Aboriginals, face a double disadvantage of gender and race or ethnicity. ***Intersection Theory*** suggests that the multiple contributions of race, class, and gender leave people especially disadvantaged.

Violence against Women

Because violence is commonplace in our society, and closely linked to gender, it is often found where men and women interact most intensively (i.e., dating and the family). Sexual violence, it is argued, is mostly about ***power***. From a global viewpoint, the practice of female genital mutilation is notable. The **Thinking About Diversity Box** (p. 338) highlights a case in the U.S. and the **Global Map 13-2** (p. 337) highlights its global distribution.

➢Violence by Women

Generally speaking, we do not link females with violence. Recent studies indicate, however, that girls are involved with violent gangs and violent delinquent acts.

➢Violence against Men

Men are more likely than women to suffer serious assault and murder, usually at the hands of other men.

Sexual Harassment

Sexual harassment is defined as comments, gestures, or physical contact of a sexual nature that is deliberate, repeated, and unwelcome. Most victims of sexual harassment are women, probably because men are socialized to be sexually assertive and are more likely to be in positions of power. While some of it is blatant, some harassment is subtle and seen as creating a ***hostile environment***.

Pornography

The definition of pornography is very ambiguous as well. Current law requires different jurisdictions to decide for themselves what violates "community standards" of decency and lacks any redeeming social value. There seems to be a pattern in our society of now seeing pornography as a ***power*** issue as well as a ***moral*** one. Like sexual harassment, pornography raises complex and conflicting concerns including discrimination against women and the exercise of freedom of expression.

THEORETICAL ANALYSIS OF GENDER

The **Applying Theory Table** (p. 341) summarizes the two major theoretical approaches to gender.

Structural-Functional Analysis

Theorists using this perspective understand gender role patterns over history to be the result of the functional contributions these patterns make to social organization. Although industrial technology has allowed greater variation in gender roles, they still reflect long-standing social mores.

➢Talcott Parsons: Gender and Complementarity

Talcott Parsons theorized that gender plays a part in integrating society by providing men and women with a set of complementary roles (***instrumental*** and ***expressive***), which they learn through the socialization process. The primary societal responsibility of women, in this view, is child rearing. Thus, they are socialized to display expressive qualities. Men are responsible for achievement in the labour force and therefore are socialized to exhibit instrumental traits.

Criticisms of this approach include the lack of recognition that many women have traditionally worked outside the home, the neglect of the personal strains associated with such a family orientation, and the fact that what is reinforced is simply male domination.

Social-Conflict Analysis

Social-conflict analysis of gender stratification focuses on the inequality of men and women. This theoretical view holds that women are disadvantaged while men benefit by the distinction of gender.

➢Friedrich Engels: Gender and Class

Friedrich Engels saw technology leading to a productive surplus and a class system that would dispose of the surplus wealth. With agricultural surplus, gender inequality was created as monogamous marriage and progeny were necessary to maintain control of private property and women built their lives around husbands and children. Engels contended that capitalism intensified this male domination.

Criticisms of this approach suggest that co-operative, happy families are ignored and that gender stratification exists everywhere not just in capitalist societies.

Feminism

Feminism is defined as the advocacy of social equality for the sexes in opposition to patriarchy and sexism. Its first wave in this country occurred in the nineteenth century, culminating with the right to vote for women.

➢Basic Feminist Ideas

Feminists suggest that personal experiences are linked to gender. How we think of ourselves, how we act, and how we are stratified in society relative to the opposite sex are seen as products of how our society attaches meaning to gender. There are five ideas considered central to feminism:

1. Working to increase equality
2. Expanding human choice
3. Eliminating gender stratification
4. Ending sexual violence
5. Promoting sexual freedom

Figure 13-5 (p. 342) provides a snapshot of the global use of contraception by married women of childbearing age.

Variations within Feminism

Four distinct forms of feminism are identified.

➢ Liberal Feminism

Liberal feminism accepts the basic organization of society, but seeks the same rights and opportunities for women and men.

➢ Socialist Feminism

Socialist feminism supports the reforms of liberal feminists, but believes they can be gained only by replacing the traditional family with some collective means of carrying out housework and caring for children.

➢ Radical Feminism

Radical feminism advocates the elimination of patriarchy altogether by organizing a gender-free society, by using new reproductive technology to separate women's bodies from the process of child-rearing.

➤Cultural and Postmodern Feminism

Several other variants of feminism exist, namely, marxist—the system of economic production must change, cultural—cannot ignore the experiences of disadvantaged females, and postmodern—reject all other feminist theories

Feminism has encountered resistance from both men and women. Some men do not wish to lose their privilege. Others are concerned about the traditions of marriage and family life. Still others see feminism as a threat to their masculinity. Women who centre their lives in their families see feminism as a threat to their values and others see women as losing rather than gaining identity. Some academics are also concerned that feminism ignores any evidence that men and women are innately different and ignores the contribution of women to child-rearing. Generally speaking, there is broad support in Canada for the ideals of liberal feminism, but not for socialist and radical feminism.

GENDER: LOOKING AHEAD

There has been a trend over the past century to greater gender equality. Industrialization has reduced the necessity for strength in most occupations and medical technology allows people to control reproduction. As well more men and women are deliberately pursuing equality. While opposition to this shift persists, the trend to greater equality for women is likely to grow.

KEY CONCEPTS

Define each of the following concepts on a separate sheet of paper. Check the accuracy of your answers by referring to the text, as well as by referring to italicized definitions located throughout the chapter.

feminism
gender
gender roles
gender stratification
intersection theory
matriarchy
minority
patriarchy
sexism
sexual harassment

STUDY QUESTIONS

True-False

1. T F The Privy Council ruled in 1929 that women are "persons" and could therefore be appointed to the Senate.

2. T F Personal traits and social positions that members of society attach to being male and female are called sex.

3. T F The performance gap between males and females in the marathon event have widened in the last twenty-five years.

4. T F There is some evidence to indicate that Margaret Mead's "reversal hypothesis" about the Tchambuli was incorrect.

5. T F In a global perspective, the vast majority of activities are consistently defined as feminine or masculine.

6. T F One advantage of the emphasis on masculinity is the opportunity to establish intimacy and trust in a relationship.

7. T F With respect to power, women generally fare better in rich countries than in poor ones.

8. T F Men are still disproportionately represented in math and physics at university.

9. T F In 2001, over 60% of women were active in the Canadian labour force.

10. T F Today, women average 16.5 hours of housework per week, while men average 5 hours.

11. T F The female/male ratio of nurses between 1995 and 2000 declined.

12. T F It is estimated that approximately 50% of women are subject to violence at the hands of an intimate partner.

Multiple Choice

1. Which of the following statements are correct with respect to gender?

   (a) It refers to social positions society attached to being male and female.
   (b) It is a dimension of social organization
   (c) It involves hierarchy
   (d) All of the above
   (e) None of the above

2. With respect to physical characteristics and intellectual skills, which of the following statements is accurate?

   (a) Adolescent males have better verbal skills than females.
   (b) Life expectancy is longer for males
   (c) Women have superior upper body strength
   (d) Adolescent females have superior mathematical skills.
   (e) None of the above is accurate.

3. In which of the following countries do women come closest to social equality with men?

   (a) United States
   (b) Canada
   (c) Brazil
   (d) Norway
   (e) Italy

4. The social inequality of men and women has been shown to be culturally based rather than exclusively biological by which of the following studies?

   (a) George Murdock's research
   (b) Israeli kibbutz
   (c) New Guinea studies by Margaret Mead
   (d) all of the above
   (e) none of the above

5. A form of social organization in which females are dominated by males is termed ________________.

   (a) matriarchy
   (b) oligarchy
   (c) patriarchy
   (d) egalitarian

6. The mass media reinforce gender stratification by ___________________.

   (a) using females in "voice overs"
   (b) photographing men to appear taller than women
   (c) having women appear in childlike poses
   (d) (all of the above)
   (e) (b and c above)

7. In 1901, women made up ________ % of Canada's paid workforce.

   (a) 2
   (b) 7
   (c) 13
   (d) 28
   (e) 35

8. In the year 2000, the occupation with the highest female proportion was __________.

   (a) registered nurses
   (b) cashiers
   (c) secretaries
   (d) early childhood educators
   (e) elementary school teachers

9. The first major party to elect a woman leader was the _____________________.

   (a) Progressive Conservatives
   (b) Alliance
   (c) Liberals
   (d) Green
   (e) N.D.P.

10. Pornography in Canada is defined as ______________________________________.

    (a) erotic, lascivious material
    (b) material that violates community standards of decency and lacks any redeeming social value
    (c) any graphic presentation of male and female genitals in contact with each other
    (d) any material that has graphic presentations of homosexual sexuality

11. Talcott Parsons argues that there exists two complementary role sets that link males and females together within social institutions. He calls these _____________________.

    (a) rational and irrational
    (b) effective and affective
    (c) fundamental and secondary
    (d) residual and basic
    (e) instrumental and expressive

12. The kind of feminism that suggests that gender equality can be realized only by eliminating the cultural notion of gender itself is ___________________________.

    (a) socialist feminism
    (b) liberal feminism
    (c) oppressive feminism
    (d) politically correct feminism
    (e) radical feminism

Fill in the Blank

1. The unequal distribution of wealth, power and privilege between men and women is called ___________ _____________.

2. ______________ refers to personal traits and social positions that members of a society attach to being male and female.

3. ____________________ is the belief that one sex is innately superior to the other.

4. __________________ are attitudes and activities that a culture links to each sex.

5. When women return to the home after working in the occupational world and they begin the tasks of cooking, cleaning, and child care, they are said to be performing a ______________.

6. Before __________, women could not vote in federal elections.

7. The interplay of race, class, and gender, often resulting in multiple levels of disadvantage, is at the heart of ________________.

8. In Melfort, Saskatchewan, it was found that _______________ _________ started the majority of swarmings and beatings.

9. ______________ is defined as the advocacy for social equality of the sexes, in opposition to patriarchy and sexism.

10. By 1995 the idea in Canada of equal pay for equal work was supported by _________ % of a representative sample.

Definition and Short Answer

1. Compare the research by Margaret Mead in New Guinea with the research done at the Israeli kibbutz in terms of the cultural variability concerning gender.

2. What generalizations about the linkage between sex and gender can be made based on the

cross-cultural research of George Murdock?

3. Is patriarchy inevitable?

4. In what ways do the family, peer group, and educational institution affect how women and men come to perceive themselves?

5. How have women changed their participation in the Canadian labour force in the last thirty years?

6. What is the impact of "second shift" on women?

7. Discuss the issue of sexual harassment against women in our society. What needs to be done to help solve this problem?

8. In what ways is pornography an underlying factor for violence against women in our society? Explain.

9. What are the consequences of female genital mutilation?

10. Identify five important demographic facts about gender stratification within the occupational domain of our society.

11. Are women a minority group? What are the arguments for and against this idea?

12. Compare and contrast the analyses of gender stratification as provided by structural-functionalists and social-conflict theorists.

13. What are the major feminist approaches? Briefly differentiate between them in terms of the arguments being made about gender roles in our society.

14. What is Friedrich Engels' argument about gender and class?

Answers to Study Questions

True-False

1. T (p. 318)
2. F (p. 319)
3. F (p. 319)
4. T (p. 320)
5. F (p. 321)
6. F (p. 321)
7. T (p. 322)
8. T (p. 323)
9. T (p. 324)
10. F (p. 327)
11. T (p. 330)
12. F (p. 334)

Multiple Choice

1. d (p. 319)
2. e (p. 319)
3. d (p. 322)
4. d (pp. 320-321)
5. c (p. 321)
6. e (p. 324)
7. c (p. 324)
8. c (p. 329)
9. e (p. 332)
10. b (p. 338)
11. e (p. 340)
12. e (p. 342)

Fill in the Blank

1. gender stratification (p.319)
2. gender (p. 319)
3. sexism (p. 321)
4. gender roles (p. 322)
5. second shift (p. 326)
6. 1918 (p. 332)
7. interaction theory (p.333)
8. teenaged girls (p. 337)
9. feminism (p. 341)
10. 98 (p. 343)

ANALYSIS AND COMMENT

Go back through the chapter and write down in the spaces below key points from each of the following boxes.

THINKING IT THROUGH

"Understanding the Gender Gap in Occupation and Income"
Key Points:

____

____

____

____

____

MEDIA PERSPECTIVES

"Powerful Canadian Women"
Key Points:

THINKING ABOUT DIVERSITY

"Female Genital Mutilation: Violence in the Name of Morality"
Key Points:

THINKING ABOUT DIVERSITY

"Canadian Women In Hockey: Going for Gold"
Key Points:

SUGGESTED READINGS

Classic Sources

Margaret Mead. 1963; orig. 1935. *Sex and Temperament in Three Primitive Societies.* New York: William Morrow.
This comparative study carried out in New Guinea was an early effort to advance the social equality of the sexes.

Jessie Bernard. 1981. *The Female World.* New York: The Free Press.
This more recent classic explores how females and males live in different, socially constructed worlds.

Global Sources

Marnia Lazreg. 1994. *The Eloquence of Silence: Algerian Women in Question.* New York: Routledge.
This historical survey of the lives of women in a North African nation suggests that women everywhere—
despite profound cultural differences—confront many of the same basic problems.

Cynthia Enloe. 1990. *Bananas, Beaches, and Bases: Making Feminist Sense of International Politics.* Berkeley, CA: University of California
Anita Fochs Heller. 1986. *Health and Home: Women as Health Guardians.* Ottawa: Canadian Advisory Council on the Status of Women.
M. Janine Brodie and Jill M. Vickers. 1982. *Canadian Women in Politics: An Overview.* Ottawa: Canadian Research Institute for the Advancement of Women.
Statistics Canada. 1990. *Women in Canada: A Statistical Report.* Ottawa: Statistics Canada.
Morley Gunderson, Leon Muszynski, and Jennifer Keck. 1990. *Women and Labour Market Poverty.* Ottawa: Canadian Advisory Council on the Status of Women.
L. MacLeod. 1980. *Wife Battering in Canada: The Vicious Circle.* Ottawa: Advisory Council on the Status of Women.
The above books are publications of the Canadian Research Institute for the Advancement of Women, Statistics Canada, or the Advisory Council on the Status of Women. The first documents the nature and extent of women's health work in the home. The second is a description of the political participation of Canadian women both today and in historical context. The third publication provides a review of the status and role of women in Canada today and in a historical
context. The fourth describes women's labour force participation. The fifth and sixth books document the extent of wife abuse and the various "prevention" policies and programs associated with wife abuse. This book pushes the issue of gender into the international arena, arguing that gender (along with race and class) are important dimensions of the geopolitical system.

Canadian Sources

Walter DeKeseredy and Ronald Hinch. 1991. *Woman Abuse: Sociological Perspective.* Toronto: Thompson Educational Pub. Inc.
This book describes the abuse of women in the home, in the streets, and in the corporate sector.

Susanna J. Wilson. 1986. *Women, the Family and the Economy.* Toronto: Prentice Hall Canada.
This is an overview of sociological data and interpretations of Canadian women in the family and in the economy.

Hugh Armstrong and Pat Armstrong. 1978. *The Double Ghetto: Canadian Women and their Segregated Work.* Toronto: McClelland & Stewart.
This book provides an overview of the gendered basis of the labour force.

Contemporary Sources

Margrit Eichler. 1980. *The Double Standard: A Feminist Critique of Feminist Social Science.* New York: St. Martin's Press.
This is a critique of social science from the perspective of a feminist.

Mary O'Brien. 1981. *The Politics of Reproduction.* Boston: Routledge and Kegan Paul.
This book examines the thesis that gender inequity is based on the alienation of men from reproduction.

Dawn H. Currie and Valerie Raoul. 1992. *Anatomy of Gender: Women's Struggle for the Body.* Ottawa: University of Ottawa Press.
This is a collection of various interpretations of women's bodies.

Dorothy Smith. 1987. *The Everyday World as Problematic: A Feminist Sociology.* Toronto: University of Toronto Press.
This is a description and analysis of Smith's methodology of and for women.

Meg Luxton. 1980. *More Than a Labour of Love: Three Generations of Women's Work in the Home.* Toronto: The Women's Press.
This is an examination of women's lives over three generations in the company town of Flin Flon, Manitoba.

CHAPTER 14

Race and Ethnicity

CHAPTER OUTLINE

I. **The Social Meaning of Race and Ethnicity**
   - A. Race
     - 1. Racial and Ethnic Categories
     - 2. A Trend Toward Mixture
   - B. Ethnicity
   - C. Minorities

II. **Prejudice**
   - A. Stereotypes
     - 1. Racism
   - B. Theories of Prejudice
     - 1. Scapegoat Theory
     - 2. Authoritarian Personality Theory
     - 3. Culture Theory
     - 4. Conflict Theory

III. **Discrimination**
   - A. Institutional Prejudice and Discrimination
   - B. Prejudice and Discrimination: The Vicious Circle

IV. **Majority and Minority: Patterns of Interaction**
   - A. Pluralism and Multiculturalism
   - B. Assimilation
   - C. Segregation
   - D. Genocide

V. **Race and Ethnicity in Canada**
   - A. Social Standing
   - B. Special Status Societies
     - 1. Aboriginal Peoples
     - 2. The Québécois: From New France to the Quiet Revolution and Beyond
   - C. The Growing Demand for Sovereignty
   - D. Immigration to Canada: A Hundred-Year Perspective

VI. **Race and Ethnicity: Looking Ahead**

VII. **Making the Grade**

VIII. **Key Points**

IX. **Key Concepts**

X. **Applications and Exercises**

XI. **MySocLab**

LEARNING OBJECTIVES

- To understand the biological basis for definitions of race
- To distinguish between the biological concept of race and the cultural concept of ethnicity
- To identify the two major characteristics of any minority group
- To describe the two forms of prejudice: stereotyping and racism
- To identify and explain the four theories of prejudice
- To distinguish between prejudice and discrimination
- To provide examples of institutional prejudice and discrimination
- To explain how prejudice and discrimination combine to create a vicious cycle of persistent beliefs and practices
- To compare and contrast the patterns of interaction between minorities and the majority identifying the four major models
- To describe the history and relative status of each of the racial and ethnic groups in Canada
- To understand the position of special status societies
- To understand the changes in immigration policy in Canada and the likely future of race and ethnic relations in this country

CHAPTER SUMMARY

Being Black in Canada in the 1940s sometimes meant being treated less civilly than a German prisoner of war. While segregation has ended today and race relations in other portions of the world are far worse, racial discrimination is not unknown. The **Thinking About Diversity Box** (p. 362) outlines a history of racism in this country.

Ethnicity and race can be sources of group unity, but they are sources also of conflict and violence. This chapter investigates the meanings and consequences of race and ethnicity.

THE SOCIAL MEANING OF RACE AND ETHNICITY

Race

A ***race*** is a socially constructed category of people who share biologically transmitted traits that are defined as important. Common distinguishing characteristics include skin colour, hair texture, shape of facial features, and body shape. Over thousands of generations, the physical environments that humans lived in created physical variability. In addition, migration and intermarriage spread genetic characteristics throughout the world. Race is a very much a socially constructed concept, as it varies across time and cultural circumstance.

➢Racial and Ethnic Categories

During the nineteenth century, scientists developed a three-part scheme of racial classification, including ***Caucasian, Negroid,*** and ***Mongoloid***. Although research confirms that no pure races exist, cultural definitions still operate as if the differences are meaningful, especially if they support a system of social inequality. The **Thinking Critically Box** (p. 356) outlines how I.Q. tests have been used to justify systems of social inequality. Recently in Canada we have attempted to measure our racial composition, but because of biological mixing the attempt is, at best, an approximation.

➢A Trend towards Mixture

Over the generations, a great deal of racial mixing has occurred in the world. In Canada where we blend racial and ethnic categories, 38% claim multiple origins.

Ethnicity

Ethnicity is a cultural heritage shared by a category of people. Objective criteria are those of ancestry, cultural practices, language, religion, and dress while subjective criteria are those involving the internalization of a distinctive identity. Sometimes the objective components may be lost through assimilation, but the subjective identification remains. While ethnicity is cultural, race is biological. The two often go hand in hand. Ethnicity is also sometimes lost; people simply lose touch with their ethnic origins, but ethnicity can also be regained as people attempt to return to their roots.

Minorities

A racial or ethnic ***minority*** is a category of people, distinguished by physical or cultural traits, that a society subordinates. Minority groups have two distinctive characteristics, they maintain a distinctive identity, and are subordinated through the social stratification system. While usually a relatively small segment of a society, there are exceptions, for example blacks in South Africa and women in Canada.

PREJUDICE

Prejudice is a rigid and irrational generalization about an entire category of people, which can be positive or negative in nature, and vary in intensity.

Stereotypes

Stereotypes are prejudicial views or descriptions of some categories of people. They involve inaccurate descriptions of a category of people even when evidence would contradict the description. They can grossly distort reality.

➢Racism

A powerful form of prejudice is ***racism***, the belief that one racial category is superior or inferior to another. There is a long history of racism globally and in Canada. From colonialism to the Nazi horrors to the current racial conflicts in European cities and finally to the treatment of Aboriginals in Canada, there are ample examples of systematic mistreatment of racial groups. Although racism appears to have declined in Canada, it persists in more covert ways.

Theories of Prejudice

➢Scapegoat Theory

Scapegoat theory suggests that frustration leads to prejudice, especially on the part of people who themselves are disadvantaged. A ***scapegoat*** is a person or category of people unfairly blamed for the troubles of others.

➢Authoritarian Personality Theory

The ***authoritarian personality*** notion, first suggested by T.W. Adorno, holds that extreme prejudice is a personality trait linked to people who conform rigidly to cultural norms and values. Such people typically have little education and were raised by cold and demanding parents.

➢Culture Theory

This view suggests that some prejudice is embedded in cultural values. Emory Bogardus developed the concept of social distance to measure the attitudes of Americans toward different racial and ethnic groups. His findings conclude that prejudice is operative throughout American society. Research using the Bogardus scale finds the same thing in Canada.

➢Conflict Theory

This approach argues that prejudice results from social conflict among categories of people. Prejudice is used as an ideology to legitimate the oppression of certain groups or categories of people. A different argument is also presented in this context, which focuses on the climate of ***race consciousness*** being created by minorities themselves as a political strategy to gain power and privilege.

DISCRIMINATION

Discrimination involves treating various categories of people unequally. While prejudice concerns attitudes and beliefs, discrimination involves behaviour.

Institutional Prejudice and Discrimination

Institutional prejudice and discrimination refers to bias built into the operation of society's institutions. Notions about a persons "place" are sometimes deeply entrenched, as Aboriginal peoples in the past have discovered when seeking employment at the Department of Indian Affairs. They are now encouraged to apply.

Prejudice and Discrimination: The Vicious Circle

It is argued that these characteristics in our society persist because they are mutually reinforcing. The Thomas Theorem, discussed in Chapter 6, relates to this situation. The stages of the ***vicious circle*** of prejudice and discrimination are outlined in **Figure 14-1** (p. 359).

MAJORITY AND MINORITY: PATTERNS OF INTERACTION

Four models can be used to describe patterns of interaction between minorities and the majority.

Pluralism and Multiculturalism

Pluralism is a state in which racial and ethnic minorities are distinct but have social parity. Social diversity has been a source of pride in Canada and multiculturalism is officially adopted as government policy. To the extent that an ethnic community has ***institutional completeness,*** the needs of its members can be met within the boundaries of the group. While various heritage programs support and celebrate the multicultural ideal, some critics suggest that the policy is detrimental to the development of a shared and coherent Canadian identity and a strong social fabric. Recently, the province of Ontario was considering the adoption of *sharia*, a body of Muslim laws, to deal with matters of family law in the Muslim community. It was passionately opposed and ultimately not adopted because multiculturalism, in this instance, might be authorizing discrimination.

Assimilation

Assimilation is the process by which minorities gradually adopt patterns of the dominant culture.

Some minority groups have maintained separate patterns despite the assimilation ideal in the U.S. and in Canada. While we officially encourage distinctive patterns, assimilation, in fact, occurs.

The process of assimilation involves changes in ethnicity, but not race. However, racial traits may diminish over the generations through ***miscegenation***, or the biological process of reproduction among racial categories.

Segregation

Segregation is the physical and social separation of categories of people. It is generally an involuntary separation of the minority groups, although voluntary segregation occurs occasionally, such as in the case of the Hutterites. Racial segregation has a long history in the U.S. ***De jure*** segregation, or "by law" has ended, however ***de facto***, or "by fact" segregation continues. Residential segregation is a particularly crucial problem in American society, and has declined only slightly in recent decades. Canadians do not wish to view themselves as a society that practises segregation, but the examples of Africville in Halifax, Buxton in Southern Ontario, and reservations and residential schools indicate otherwise.

Genocide

Genocide is the systematic annihilation of one category of people by another. While being contrary to virtually every moral standard, genocide has existed throughout history. As recently as 2002, 800 000 Tutsis were slaughtered in Rwanda.

RACE AND ETHNICITY IN CANADA

Canada truly is a land of immigrants, starting with the Aboriginal peoples crossing the Bering Strait from Siberia to Alaska several thousand years ago. The French and English came in the 1600s and 1700s, ignored the Aboriginal peoples and declared themselves the founding nations. They were followed primarily by Europeans and finally, the newest of Canadians have come from Asia, Africa, the Caribbean, and Latin America. Immigrants from many other countries arrive under stress, by way of refugee status.

While the largest categories used to be English and French, **Table 14-1** (p. 361) tells us that more than a third of Canadians now claim "Canadian" ethnicity. It should be noted that the use of "Canadian" in Quebec does not imply some solidarity with those who use "Canadian" in other provinces. After Canadian, the largest group are English and French. The rest of Canada is made up of a remarkable ethnic diversity**.** **Table 14-2** (p. 364) indicates diversity of ethnicity by region of Canada and **Table 14-3** (p. 365), using 2001 Census data, shows that education, employment, and income are differently allocated by ethnic and racial categories.

Social Standing

There appears to be a system of social inequality based on race and ethnicity in Canada. While **Table 14-3** (p. 365) is not absolutely clear with respect to what is operative, it would seem that Chinese and Blacks in Canada must be facing some employment and income discrimination in that their occupational success with respect to income is not matched with their educational achievement.

Special Status Societies

Two categories of people have unique relationships in Canada with the federal government.

➢Aboriginal Peoples

There were fifty-five or more sovereign peoples who established themselves on the North American continent thousands of years before the Europeans arrived. Included are the major groupings, Indian, Inuit, and Métis, a category of biracial descent, usually French and Indian.

Registered or status Indians can be registered under the Indian Act, treaty or non-treaty depending on whether their ancestors signed treaties. There is also an undetermined group who may be biologically or culturally Indian, but are not officially declared as such. There are perhaps 1.5 million people of Aboriginal ancestry. Registered Indians who live on reserves are the special responsibility of the Department of Indian and Northern Affairs. The relationship with Ottawa has been paternalistic and has led to a severe erosion of their cultural fabric and community life. Residential schools for Aboriginal children were a devastating blow to their culture. Non-status Indians, the Métis, and the Inuit were never confined to reservations, but their cultural integrity is certainly diminished. There are many Aboriginal communities that are solving their problems, but many others are in a process of social disintegration. Contemporary leaders point the way to a brighter future of self-government, which was punctuated in 1999 with the creation of Nunavut, a new territorial government carved out of the Northwest Territories and controlled by an Inuit majority. The **Media Perspectives Box** (p. 369) describes the Aboriginal Peoples Television Network, which empowers the Aboriginal community.

➢The Québécois

The French presence in Canada goes back to 1608, the first permanent settlement being established at Québec City. New France at first grew slowly, but two centuries later at Confederation, Canada's population was 31% French. The B.N.A. Act of 1867 recognized the province's civil law, language, and Catholic schools. The French and English communities co-existed and bilingualism was eventually strengthened by the *Official Languages Act* of 1969.

Quebec at the time of Confederation was a traditional society and was ineffectively governed. The church took responsibility for education, health care, and social welfare, but was more concerned with maintaining its position than helping people adjust to changing circumstances. The economic institution was controlled by the minority English in Montreal. Not until the Quiet Revolution of the 1960s was the power of the church diminished. The government of Jean Lesage focused on education, attracting industry, and integrating Quebec into the North American economic structure.

The Growing Demand for Sovereignty

Quebecers eventually reached the conclusion that their language and culture needed protection in the sea of English North America. Their demand for institutional dominance led to a demand for sovereignty. Although they voted not to seek independence in a 1960 referendum, the failure of the Meech Lake Accord, which would have given Quebec a "distinct society" status, and the more recent rejection almost everywhere in Canada of the Charlottetown Accord has left Canada uncertain of the future of Quebec in Canada.

In October 1995, a razor-thin victory for the "No" side in the separation referendum continued the uncertainty about the future of Quebec in Canada. (See the **Thinking It Through Box**, p. 374, for a discussion of national unity.)

Immigration to Canada: A Hundred-Year Perspective

Canada has been, and will probably remain, a land of immigrants. Two-and-a half million people arrived between 1905 and 1914, so that in 1913, one in every seventeen Canadians was a newcomer. Most of the migrants were from Britain and were expected to maintain the British character of the country. A trickle of Ukrainians and other Europeans arrived to settle farming areas in the West. By 1931, Canada closed the doors, especially to Jewish refugees because of substantial anti-Semitism across the country. After WW II, the doors opened again to meet Canada's labour needs and although Europeans were preferred, more Asians were permitted entry along with Palestinians and Hungarians in the 1950s. Not until 1962, however, was an official end put to the "White Canada" immigration policy. Educational, occupational, and language skills were the criteria, which were formalized in a points system in 1965 in order to meet the needs of the labour market. These changes were followed by waves of immigration from the West Indies and Asia in the 1990s. The *Immigration Act* of 1976 recognized three classes of people for landed immigrant status: ***family class*** (immediate family, parents, and grandparents), ***humanitarian class*** (refugees or persecuted and displaced persons), and ***independent class*** (those admitted on the point system). This stimulated a huge number of refugees and family applicants and they have settled primarily in Ontario and British Columbia, in the cities of Toronto and Vancouver. The **Applying Sociology Box** (p. 366) describes the impact on those cities. **Tables 14-4 and 14-5** (p. 373) and **Canada Map 14-1** (p. 372) outline the immigration picture for Canada in 2001.

RACE AND ETHNICITY: LOOKING AHEAD

Canada's future will depend upon forging an identity out of diversity.

KEY CONCEPTS

Define each of the following concepts on a separate sheet of paper. Check the accuracy of your answers by referring to the text, as well as by referring to italicized definitions located throughout the chapter.

assimilation
discrimination
ethnicity
genocide
institutional completeness
institutional prejudice and discrimination
miscegenation
minority
pluralism
prejudice
racism
scapegoat
segregation
stereotype

STUDY QUESTIONS

True-False

1. T F Cultural practices, dress, ancestry, and language are referred to as objective criteria of ethnicity.

2. T F A racial or ethnic minority is a category of people distinguished by physical or cultural differences that society subordinates.

3. T F Prejudice is a rigid and irrational generalization about an entire category of people.

4. T F The research by Sowell on intelligence tests found that cultural patterns were a better explanation for I.Q. scores than racial or ethnic differences.

5. T F Emory Bogardus suggests that those who display prejudice exhibit authoritarian personalities.

6. T F The viability of ethnic communities in Canada is affected by their level of institutional completeness.

7. T F Ontario recently accepted that *sharia* law could be used by the Muslim community to handle matters of family law.

8. T F Among the provinces, the ones east of Ontario are more likely than the others to report their ethnic origins as "Canadian."

9. T F It is likely that more than 1.5 million Canadians have Aboriginal roots.

10. T F Unlike Aboriginal peoples elsewhere, Canadian Aboriginal peoples do not have their own television network.

11. T F Between 1991 and 2001, the largest immigrant group to Canada was Chinese.

Multiple Choice

1. Although no society or region of the world lacks genetic mixture, there is especially pronounced racial mixing in _____________.

   (a) Africa
   (b) North America
   (c) Oceania
   (d) the Middle East
   (e) Japan

2. Race is _____________, while ethnicity is ___________.

   (a) objective, subjective
   (b) extrinsic, intrinsic
   (c) biological, cultural
   (d) deductive, inductive
   (e) Caucasian, Mongoloid

3. Minority groups have which two major characteristics?

   (a) race and ethnicity
   (b) religion and ethnicity
   (c) physical traits and political orientation
   (d) sexual orientation and race
   (e) distinctive identity and subordination

4. Which theory of prejudice suggests that prejudice springs from frustration?

   (a) Scapegoat Theory
   (b) Authoritarian Personality Theory
   (c) Cultural Theory
   (d) Conflict Theory
   (e) Social Distance Theory

5. When bias is built into the operation of society's institutions, we call it _____________.

   (a) racism
   (b) discrimination
   (c) race consciousness
   (d) institutional prejudice and discrimination
   (e) complex institutional completeness

6. According to the work of W.I. Thomas, a "vicious circle" is formed by which variables?

   (a) miscegenation and authoritarianism
   (b) race and ethnicity
   (c) pluralism and assimilation
   (d) segregation and integration
   (e) prejudice and discrimination

7. Which pattern of minority/majority interaction is characterized by distinct racial and ethnic minorities who have social parity?

   (a) pluralism
   (b) assimilation
   (c) segregation
   (d) genocide
   (e) completeness

8. Biological reproduction by partners of different racial categories is called _____________.

   (a) miscegenation
   (b) multiple origin
   (c) racial mixing
   (d) assimilation
   (e) racial pollution

9 Which city in Canada has the most diverse visible minority population?

   (a) Toronto
   (b) Montreal
   (c) Vancouver
   (d) Hamilton
   (e) Windsor

10 Between 1991 and 2001, the largest percentage of immigrants to Canada were from ___________.

   (a) Europe
   (b) the Caribbean
   (c) Africa
   (d) Asia
   (e) South America

Fill in the Blank

1. The term __________ refers to a socially constructed category of people who share biologically transmitted traits deemed important.

2. The three-part scheme of racial classification developed by scientists during the nineteenth century included ________________, _______________, and _________________.

3. In Canada, _________ form a numerical majority but are regarded as minority.

4. Contrary to stereotype, most poor people in Canada are ___________.

5. Adorno discovered extreme prejudice in _____________ .

6. According to ______________, powerful people use prejudice to justify their oppression of minorities.

7. ________________ is a process by which minorities gradually adopt patterns of the dominant culture.

8. The Underground Railroad brought escaped slaves to freedom in the province of ________.

9. The ethnic or racial category in Canada with the highest percentage of university degree completion is the ____________.

10. The *Immigration Act* of 1976 recognized three classes of people eligible for landed immigrant status. They are ____________, ___________, and ___________.

Definition and Short Answer

1. Identify the four explanations of why prejudice exists.

2. Differentiate between the concepts prejudice and discrimination.

3. Discuss Sowell's work on I.Q. scores and racial intelligence.

4. What is institutional prejudice and discrimination? Provide an example.

5. What are the four models representing the patterns of interaction between minority groups and the majority group?

6. In what ways have Aboriginal peoples lost their cultural identity?

7. Identify the various waves of immigration to Canada and the reasons for them.

8. Differentiate the concepts of race and ethnicity.

9. What are the major characteristics of minority groups?

10. minority groups ever a majority in society?

11. What might the consequences be of enshrining in the Canadian constitution "distinct society" status for Quebec?

Answers to Study Questions

True-False

1. T (p. 352)
2. T (p. 353)
3. T (p. 354)
4. T (p. 356)
5. F (p. 357)
6. T (p. 359)
7. F (p. 360)
8. T (p. 364)
9. T (p. 367)
10. F (p. 369)
11. T (p. 373)

Multiple Choice

1. d (p. 350)
2. c (p. 353)
3. e (pp. 353-354)
4. a (p. 357)
5. d (p. 358)
6. e (pp. 358-359)
7. a (p. 359)
8. a (p. 360)
9. a (p. 366)
10. d (p. 373)

Fill in the Blank

1. race (p. 350)
2. Caucasoid, Negroid, Mongoloid (p. 351)
3. women (p. 353)
4. White (p. 354)
5. authoritarian personalities (p. 357)
6. conflict theory (p. 357)
7. assimilation (p. 360)
8. Ontario (p. 361)
9. Japanese (p. 365)
10. family, humanitarian, independent (p. 373)

ANALYSIS AND COMMENT

Go back through the chapter and write down in the spaces below key points from each of the following boxes.

THINKING CRITICALLY

"Does Race Affect Intelligence?"
Key Points:

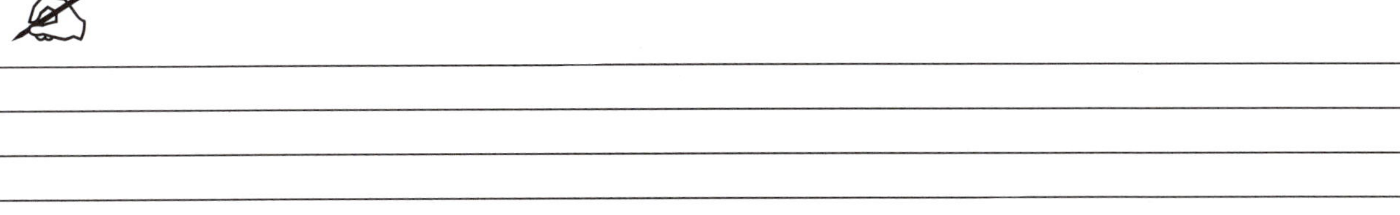

THINKING ABOUT DIVERSITY

"Black Citizens of Canada: A History Ignored"
Key Points:

APPLYING SOCIOLOGY

"Visible Minorities: Toronto, Vancouver, and Montreal"
Key Points:

MEDIA PERSPECTIVES

"The Aboriginal Peoples Television Network"
Key Points:

THINKING IT THROUGH

"Distinct Societies and National Unity"
Key Points:

SUGGESTED READINGS

Contemporary Sources

Harry H.L. Kitano. 1990. *Race Relations.* 4th Ed. Englewood Cliffs, NJ: Prentice Hall.
This paperback text delves into the issues raised in this chapter.

George J. Borgas. *Friends or Strangers: The Impact of Immigrants on the U.S. Economy.* New York: Basic Books.
Do immigrants bring innovation and economic vitality to a society or merely raise unemployment? This book paints a multidimensional portrait of newcomers to the United States and assesses the economic consequences of immigration.

Herman Belz. 1991. *Equality Transformed: A Quarter-Century of Affirmative Action.* New Brunswick, NJ: Transaction.
This history of racial preferences examines the complex consequences of affirmative action with regard to race relations.

Canadian Sources

Peter S. Li. 1988. *Ethnic Inequality in a Class Society.* Toronto: Wall and Thompson.
Christopher McAll. 1990. *Class, Ethnicity, and Social Inequality.* Montreal & Kingston: McGill-Queen's University Press.
These two books spotlight the centrality of race and ethnicity to social stratification in Canada.

Valerie Knowles. 1992. *Strangers at Our Gates: Canadian Immigration and Immigration Policy, 1540-1990.* Toronto: Dundurn Press.
This book explores Canada's immigration policy and details its consequences.

Bissoondath, Neil. 1994. *Selling Illusions: The Cult of Multiculturalism in Canada.* Toronto: Penguin Books.
Jeffrey S. Reitz, and Raymond Breton. 1994. *The Illusion of Difference: Realities of Ethnicity in Canada and the United States.* Toronto: C. D. Howe Institute.
These two books deal with "illusions" relating to ethnicity and multiculturalism. The first, by Bissoondath, questions the goal of preserving cultural differences at the expense of a Canadian identity. The second, by Reitz and Breton, looks at multiculturalism and the American "melting pot" and asks if these policy thrusts have any impact on the economic and social incorporation of minorities.

Stanley R. Barrett. 1987. *Is God Racist: The Right Wing in Canada.* Toronto: University of Toronto Press.
This fascinating account of White, racist, right-wing organizations in Canada is based upon extensive interviews.

Mordecai Richler. 1991. *Oh Canada! Oh Quebec! Requiem for a Divided Country.* Toronto: Penguin Books.
Novelist and essayist Mordecai Richler details the experience of being Jewish and anglophone in Quebec.

Edward N. Herberg. 1989. *Ethnic Groups in Canada: Adaptations and Transitions.* Scarborough, ON: Nelson Canada.
This book investigates the social dynamics of race and ethnicity in Canada.

Frank Cassidy, ed. 1991. *Aboriginal Self-Determination.* Montreal: The Institute for Research on Public Policy.
This book, the edited proceedings of a conference on Aboriginal self-government, contains contributions from a wide range of Aboriginal leaders, as well as politicians and academics.

Global Sources

Milton J. Esman and Itamar Rabinovich, eds. 1988. *Ethnicity, Pluralism, and the State in the Middle East.* Ithaca, NY and London: Cornell University Press.
David K. Shipler. 1986. *Arab and Jew: Wounded Spirits in a Promised Land.* New York: Times Books
This investigation of the resurgence of ethnicity in Israel also demonstrates how ethnicity interacts with social class. If cultural patterns can build community, they can also turn people against one another. Nowhere has this been truer than in the Middle East. The first book examines how ethnicity stands at the core of Middle Eastern social structure. The second book, by a noted foreign correspondent who lived in Jerusalem for five years, explores how stereotypes carry hatred into the lives of each new generation.

Eliezer Ben-Raphael and Stephen Sharot. 1991. *Ethnicity, Religion, and Class in Israeli Society.* Cambridge, UK: Cambridge University Press.
John Solomos. 1989. *Race and Racism in Contemporary Britain.* London: Macmillan.
Walter P. Zenner. 1991. *Minorities in the Middle: A Cross-Cultural Analysis.* Albany, NY: SUNY Press.
These global analyses explore the experiences of Jews, Scots, Chinese, and other ethnic categories that have marginal standing in various societies.

CHAPTER 15

Aging and the Elderly

CHAPTER OUTLINE

I. **The Greying of Canada**
   - A. Canada's Birth Rate: Going Down
   - B. Life Expectancy: Going Up
   - C. An Aging Society: Cultural Change
   - D. The "Young" Old and the "Old" Old

II. **Growing Old: Biology and Culture**
   - A. Biological Changes
   - B. Psychological Changes
   - C. Aging and Culture
   - D. Age Stratification: A Global Survey
     1. Hunter/ Gatherer Societies
     2. Pastoral, Horticultural, and Agrarian Societies
     3. Industrial and Post-industrial Societies

III. **Transitions and Challenges of Aging**
   - A. Finding Meaning
   - B. Social Isolation
   - C. Retirement
   - D. Aging and Income
   - E. Care Giving
     1. The Care Givers
     2. Elder Abuse
   - F. Ageism
   - G. The Elderly: A Minority?

IV. **Theoretical Analysis of Aging**
   - A. Structural-Functional Analysis: Aging and Disengagement
   - B. Symbolic-Interaction Analysis: Aging and Activity
   - C. Social-Conflict Analysis: Aging and Inequality

V. **Death and Dying**
   - A. Historical Patterns of Death
   - B. The Modern Separation of Life and Death
   - C. Ethical Issues: Confronting Death
     1. When Does Death Occur?
     2. The Right to Die Debate
   - D. Bereavement

VI. **Aging: Looking Ahead**

VII. **Making the Grade**

VIII. **Key Points**

IX. **Key Concepts**

X. **Applications and Exercises**

XI. **MySocLab**

LEARNING OBJECTIVES

- To define and explain the development of the greying of Canada
- To describe the interrelationship and respective roles of biology and culture in growing old
- To describe the life changes in growing old
- To explain the role of the elderly in cross-cultural and historical perspectives
- To describe the problems and challenges involved in growing old
- To describe the role of caregivers
- To explain ageism and its impact on the elderly
- To understand that some cultures are not characterized by ageism
- To identify the key arguments in the debate over whether the elderly constitute a minority group
- To describe, compare, and contrast the three sociological explanations of aging
- To describe the changing character of death throughout history and into modern times
- To understand the ethical issues associated with death
- To describe the process of bereavement
- To project the future of a greying society

CHAPTER REVIEW

The chapter opens with the description of the life of an elder who is 107 years "young." She, like most elders, describes her life as happy, but seniors often face lower income, prejudice, and abuse, along with deteriorating health.

THE GREYING OF CANADA

A powerful revolution is reshaping Canada. It is referred to as the greying of Canada. In just over a century, life expectancy has doubled and the average number of children has declined by half. **Figure 15-1** (p.381) shows the changing population pyramid of Canada. In 2001 the population over 65 made up 13% of the whole, but by 2041 the percentage will be 23.8%. The two causes of this shift are the tremendous post-WW II baby boom, followed by a sharp decline in birth rates. **Canada Map 15-1** (p. 382) shows the distribution of the over-65 population across Canada. The industrialized societies, along with the countries of the old Soviet Union, will experience population decline.

Canada's Birth Rate: Going Down

In industrialized societies, children are a major expense rather than an economic asset and women are choosing careers. The birth rate typically goes down.

Life Expectancy: Going Up

Women can expect to live to 83.4 years of age, and men to 76.4 years. The possible consequences of the massive increase in the elderly population are immense. The old-age dependency ratio will double in the next fifty years as the proportion of non-employed adults soars and the costs of health care also rise. There are those, however, who suggest today's seniors are healthier than previous generations.

An Aging Society: Cultural Change

Age segregation will decline but a "culture of aging" is unlikely in such a diverse society.

The "Young" Old and the "Old" Old

The "young" old are between 65 and 75 years of age and are living in reasonable health and financial security, while the "old" old, those over 75, are increasingly dependent on others. This total older segment of the population, however, will not be growing rapidly until the boomers reach 65 around 2010.

GROWING OLD: BIOLOGY AND CULTURE

Gerontology is the study of aging and the elderly. This field examines biological processes, personality changes, and the impact of culture and social definitions in different societies as people age.

Biological Changes

While aging does lead to some bodily deterioration, cultural labels have a major impact on how we perceive these changes. In Canada's youth-oriented society, growing old is seen as growing down. Older people do suffer more chronic illnesses and life-threatening diseases such as cancer and heart disease and experience some decline in sensory abilities. Dementia, progressive cognitive impairment, affects 5% to 10% of those over 65 years of age and 20% of those over 80, but the vast majority of the elderly population are neither discouraged nor disabled by their physical or mental condition. Patterns of aging vary greatly, however, between social groups. Because women live longer, they suffer more chronic illness and income is positively related to preventative care and perceptions of happiness.

Psychological Changes

Most elderly people do not suffer from mental or psychological problems. While research suggests that measures of intelligence focusing on sensorimotor coordination do show decline in aged persons, intelligence tests focusing on knowledge show no decline. The capacity for thoughtful reflection and spiritual growth actually increases. Psychological research has also shown that personality changes little as we grow old.

Aging and Culture

The significance of growing old is a matter of cultural definition. Old is a relative term as **Global Map 15-1** (p.386) illustrates. In many of the poorer countries the average lifespan is fifty years, while a Canadian of sixty years is not identified as old. Advances in medicine and health have made a difference, but cultural definition is just as important, as shown in the **Applying Sociology Box** (p. 387).

Age Stratification: A Global Survey

Age stratification is defined as the unequal distribution of wealth, power, and privileges among people at different stages of the life course. This varies by societal development and the old seem to generally have more power in societies in which they can accumulate wealth. In ***hunter/gatherer*** societies age is seen as a burden. ***Pastoral, horticultural***, and ***agrarian*** societies, on the other hand, have the technological capabilities to produce surpluses to enable accumulation to occur. Such societies tend toward ***gerontocracy***, a form of social organization in which the elderly have the most wealth, power, and prestige. ***Industrialization*** tends to create a decline in the relative power and prestige of the aged, as the prime source of wealth shifts away from the land and geographical mobility undermines the strength of families. The rapid change in technology also diminishes the expertise of the elderly and they are pushed toward nonproductive roles. Japan is a culture in which the productive role and status of the elderly in the family and labour force has remained intact, providing the aged with greater prestige. But even Japan is becoming more like other industrial societies where age means giving up a measure of social importance.

TRANSITIONS AND CHALLENGES OF AGING

Of all life stages, old age presents the greatest personal challenges. The body is in some measure of decline and lives are nearing an end.

Finding Meaning

Although some face the end with despair, those who learn to accept their past mistakes and successes fare well. There are illnesses to face but as **Table 15-1** (p. 389) indicates, most elderly people are at least somewhat happy with life, especially those who are healthy and who have spouses who are healthy. People who were well adjusted earlier in life tend to be well adjusted as they age.

Social Isolation

Central among the adjustments an individual must make during old age is the accommodation to increased social isolation. Negative stereotypes, retirement, and physical problems diminish social interaction. The most profound social isolation occurs, however, with the death of a significant other, particularly a spouse.

Almost three-quarters of widows and widowers cite loneliness as their most serious problem. The problem of social isolation falls mostly on women as **Table 15-2** (p. 390), on living arrangements of the elderly, shows. Spouses provide emotional support for men but women rely on more varied support, particularly daughters, after their husbands die. (See **Figure 15-2,** p. 390.) Women who are widowed later in life (65-74) are less likely to move in with their children, perhaps because grandchildren have reached adulthood. Many elderly choose to live in retirement residences or communities. The **Media Perspectives Box** (p. 392) looks at issues related to these residence options.

Retirement

Work figures prominently in personal identity. The loss of work, therefore, generally entails less income, less prestige, and loss of purpose. Some organizations, like universities, ease the transition and for many older people new challenges like volunteer activities fill the void. Retirement is a recent phenomenon prompted by the need to use fewer workers and to bring in younger workers in a rapidly changing society.

Pension plans have eased the financial burdens in Canada where the aged are now less likely to be poor. While there is a debate about the constitutionality of mandatory retirement, and in many provinces, it has been eliminated, only about 1% of the workforce would continue past 65 if given the choice. Recently, global restructuring and government downsizing has led to many early retirements and the launching of new careers.

Aging and Income

The image of the elderly as poverty stricken is somewhat unfounded. While retirement leads to a decline in income, expenses also decline. But women and visible minorities suffer proportionately greater deprivation. The pride of many older citizens leads them to hide even from their families their economic difficulties.

Care Giving

Care giving refers to informal and unpaid care provided to a dependent person by family members, other relatives, or friends. Current middle-aged adults are often referred to as the "sandwich generation," as they care for their aging parents while still caring for their children.

➤The Care Givers

Family members provide 80% of care to elders, and 75% of it is provided by women. Daughters-in-law are more likely to provide the care than sons. These are people (daughters and daughters-in-law) who are likely working as well.

➤Elder Abuse

Three to five percent of the elderly suffer from abuse at the hands of relatives or care givers in the home or institutions. Abuse is most likely to occur if the care giving is difficult.

Ageism

Ageism refers to prejudice and discrimination against the elderly. While old people are more likely to be mentally and physically impaired, the majority are not. Unwarranted generalizations lead to stereotypes that result in overt (e.g., loss of job) and subtle (condescending tones) discrimination. Betty Friedan suggests that older people have much to contribute and would, if negative definitions in the media and elsewhere were to disappear.

The Elderly: A Minority?

Sociologists vary in their opinion concerning the classification of the aged as a minority group. Certain general characteristics of the aged population seem consistent with such a status, however, the social disadvantages faced by the elderly are less substantial than those experienced by other categories of people labelled as minorities. Their situation is labelled as an open status, not permanent or exclusive. The old are simply a part of the Canadian population who face challenges based on age.

THEORETICAL ANALYSIS OF AGING

Structural-Functional Analysis: Aging and Disengagement

Disengagement theory links the disengagement by elderly people from positions of social responsibility to the orderly operation of society. This theory, based on Talcott Parson's structural-functional analysis, suggests that the orderly transfer of various statuses and roles from the old to the young provides benefits for both society and individuals with diminished capacity. A problem with this view is that many older people do not want to relinquish their statuses and roles and are quite capably functioning within them. As well, workers cannot freely disengage unless they have financial security and the costs of loss of independence are considerable. Finally, with a low birth rate, society needs their older workers in the workforce.

Symbolic-Interaction Analysis: Aging and Activity

Activity theory links personal satisfaction in old age to a high level of activity. Disengagement is viewed as diminishing satisfaction and meaning in life. While disengaging from certain statuses and roles, the elderly shift to new ones based on their own distinctive needs, interests, talents, and capabilities. This approach may, however, underestimate the loss of competency among the aged.

Social-Conflict Analysis: Aging and Inequality

This approach sees different age categories across the life cycle competing for scarce resources. The status of the elderly relative to younger people is viewed as being disadvantaged as a result of the emphasis in capitalist societies on keeping costs down. While focusing our attention on the age stratification that does exist in society, this approach tends to ignore the improvement in social standing of the elderly in recent decades, and focuses upon capitalism when industrialization may be the major culprit.

DEATH AND DYING

There are two certainties: the fact of birth and the inevitability of death. The changing character of death is discussed in this section.

Historical Patterns of Death

Throughout much of human history death was a natural part of everyday life. Disease and catastrophes were widespread. In pre-industrial societies, less productive people (infants and the aged) were sometimes put to death (infanticide/geronticide) for the sake of preserving the group. As societies began to gain some measure of control over death through technological advances, attitudes about death changed. It was no longer an everyday experience in the lives of people. Now old age and death have become fused.

The Modern Separation of Life and Death

Death is now looked at as something unnatural, separate from life. Death and dying are now physically removed from everyday activities and typically occur away from the family, in a hospital.

Ethical Issues: Confronting Death

As the capacity to extend life through "heroic measures" and artificial means increases, the question about when life ceases becomes ever more problematic.

Many individuals would like the capacity to choose when their life should end, sometimes as a release from suffering. The **Thinking Critically Box** (p. 398) indicates that the Dutch provide people the opportunity of ***euthanasia***, but it remains illegal in Canada. Should we allow people the right to end their suffering or is this the "slippery slope" towards forcing death on those who are becoming medically expensive? The Sue Rodriguez case (she had ALS) was our own confrontation with the ethical issue of euthanasia, which was resolved by the Supreme Court by denying her the opportunity of assisted suicide.

Bereavement

It can be argued that Kübler-Ross's stages of death can be applied to the bereavement process. Hospice is a program that helps people, through palliative care, to have better deaths. Bereavement, however, may last a long time and cause profound grief, unless a satisfactory closure to a relationship is attained.

AGING: LOOKING AHEAD

There are reasons for both concern and optimism as we look ahead. Within the next fifty years, one in four Canadians will be over 85. They will require support services that a smaller working population will be hard-pressed to provide (See the **Thinking It Through Box** (pp. 399-400). On the positive side, those seniors will be more healthy and wealthy than previous generations and medical technology will continue to improve.

On balance we will have mounting responsibilities to care for the aged but death will perhaps become again, a natural part of the life course.

KEY CONCEPTS

Define each of the following concepts on a separate sheet of paper. Check the accuracy of your answers by referring to the text, as well as by referring to italicized definitions located throughout the chapter.

activity theory
ageism
age stratification
care giving
disengagement theory
euthanasia
gerontocracy
gerontology

STUDY QUESTIONS

True-False

1. T F Presently men can expect to live to be about 76 years of age.

2. T F Health care spending is 6.5 times greater for those over 75 years than for those under 65 years.

3. T F Among the "older" elderly, about 90% are women.

4. T F The elderly are in better health than in previous generations and are spending fewer days in the hospital.

5. T F Aboriginal peoples in Canada strive to maintain cultural traditions, where elders are held in high esteem.

6. T F Older people are dominant in the occupation of farming.

7. T F The most likely source of emotional support for elderly women living without their spouses is a son.

8. T F Over 80% of the elderly live above the low income level cutoff.

9. T F Over 75% of all care giving is provided by women.

10. T F Death in Canada is physically removed from everyday activities.

Multiple Choice

1. Census figures for 2001 revealed that ______% of the Canadian population were people older than 65 years.

   (a) 8
   (b) 13
   (c) 20
   (d) 26
   (e) 32

2. By 2041 the percentage of the Canadian population that will be over 65 years of age will be ____________.

   (a) 11.6% (b) 17.8% (c) 21.2% (d) 23.8%

3. Life expectancy for females in Canada is currently ______________.

   (a) 64 years (b) 70 years (c) 75 years (d) 83 years

4. Which of the following is a reason that patterns of well-being vary greatly within the elderly population?

   (a) People with higher incomes are likely to work in a healthful and safe environment, which pays benefits into old age.
   (b) Richer people can afford much more preventive medical care.
   (c) Women, because they typically live longer than men, suffer more from chronic disabilities than men.
   (d) a and b above
   (e) all of the above

5. In most industrial societies, the power and prestige of the elderly is severely eroded. What country is an exception?

   (a) Canada
   (b) Japan
   (c) United States
   (d) The Netherlands
   (e) France

6. Most elderly males ________________________.

   (a) live alone
   (b) live in nursing homes
   (c) live with extended family members
   (d) live with their spouse

7. What percentage of the Canadian workforce would work past the age of 65 if given the choice?

   (a) 1% (b) 5% (c) 15% (d) 20% (e) 50%

8. _______ % of all care giving is provided by women.

   (a) 40 (b) 60 (c) 75 (d) 85 (e) 100

9. Which of the following would a social-conflict analysis identify as problems for the aged?

   (a) Employers replace older workers with younger ones in order to keep wages down.
   (b) When a society is concerned with profit, it will devalue those who are less productive.
   (c) There is a lack of diversity in the elderly population.
   (d) a and b above
   (e) a and c above

10. The future of aging in our country is likely to include which of the following?

    (a) By 2050, one in four seniors will be over 85.
    (b) The elderly of the next century will be more vigorous and independent than the elderly today.
    (c) The elderly of the next century will have more affluence than the elderly today.
    (d) all of the above
    (e) b and c above

Fill in the Blank

1. The period after 1965, during which the birth rate took a sharp turn downward, is often called the ____________________.
2. The ratio of elderly people to working-age adults is called the ______________.
3. Erik Erikson suggests that elderly people must resolve a tension of __________ versus __________.
4. The primary source of emotional support for elderly women is ______________.
5. Today's middle-aged adults represent a ____________ generation who may spend as much time caring for their aging parents as for their own children.
6. ____________ refers to prejudice and discrimination against older people.
7. As Gordon Streib sees it, it is not so much that the old grow poor as that the __________ __________ ____________.
8. In 1900, about ______ of all deaths in Canada occurred before the age of five.
9. ______________ has gone further than any nation in allowing euthanasia.
10. Currently about ___________ of the total lifetime medical costs of care for an individual are incurred during the last years of his or her life.

Definition and Short Answer

1. Why is the old-age dependency ratio increasing?
2. Discuss the role of elders in Aboriginal cultures.

3. Define age stratification. How does it vary between hunter/gatherer, horticultural, agrarian, and industrial societies?

4. In what ways can a person adjust to old age?

5. Differentiate between activity theory and disengagement theory in terms of how each helps us understand the changing status of the aged in society.

6. Who are the care givers in Canadian society?

7. Discuss the relative economic condition of the aged in our society today.

8. According to social-conflict theorists, why is the status of the aged diminished in capitalist societies?

9. What are the arguments in the debate concerning whether the aged are a minority group?

10. What are the problems facing Canada as the proportion of aged citizens grows?

Answers to Study Questions

True-False

1. T (p. 381)
2. T (p. 382)
3. F (p. 383)
4. T (p. 384)
5. T (p. 385)
6. T (p. 388)
7. F (p. 390)
8. T (p. 391)
9. T (p. 392)
10. T (p. 396)

Multiple Choice

1. b (p. 380)
2. d (p. 380)
3. d (p. 381)
4. e (pp. 384-385)
5. b (p. 388)
6. d (p.390)
7. a (p. 391)
8. c (p. 392)
9. d (p. 396)
10. d (p. 399)

Fill in the Blank

1. baby bust (p. 381)
2. old-age dependency (p. 382)
3. integrity, despair (p. 389)
4. daughter (p. 390)
5. sandwich (p. 391)
6. ageism (p. 394)
7. poor grow old (p. 394)
8. one-third (p. 396)
9. The Netherlands (p. 398)
10. half (p. 399)

ANALYSIS AND COMMENT

Go back through the chapter and write down in the space below key points from each of the following boxes.

THINKING GLOBALLY

"Can Too Many Be Too Old? A Report from Japan"
Key Points:

APPLYING SOCIOLOGY

"Aboriginal Elders: Cultural Custodians"
Key Points:

MEDIA PERSPECTIVES

"Aging in Retirement Residences and Nursing Homes"
Key Points:

THINKING CRITICALLY

"Death on Demand: A Report from the Netherlands"
Key Points:

THINKING IT THROUGH

"Setting Limits: Must We 'Pull the Plug' on Old Age?"
Key Points:

SUGGESTED READINGS

Classic Source

Robert N. Butler. 1975. *Why Survive? Being Old in America.* New York: Harper and Row.
This Pulitzer Prize-winning book launched a growing social movement critical of our society's approach to aging.

Contemporary and Canadian Sources

Robert O. Hansson and Bruce N. Carpenter. 1994. *Relationships in Old Age: Coping with the Challenge of Transition.* New York: Guilford.
This book explores one of the most challenging aspects of growing old: maintaining relationships during a time of transition.

E. Gee and M. Kimball. 1987. *Women and Aging.* Toronto: Butterworths.
A. Martin-Matthews. 1989. "Widowhood as an Expectable Life Event," in V. Marshall, ed., *Aging in Canada: Social Perspectives,* 2nd. ed., pp. 343-66. Markham, ON: Fitzhenry and Whiteside.
This article and book examine some of the issues facing women as they grow older.

N. Chappell, L. Strain, and A. Blandford. 1986. *Aging and Health Care: A Social Perspective.* Toronto: Holt, Rinehart, and Winston.
This is an overview of the health and health services issues confronting the elderly in Canada.

I. Connidis. 1989. *Family Ties and Aging.* Toronto: Butterworths.
This book examines the social and familial relationships of elderly Canadians.

W. Forbes, J. Jackson, and A. Kraus. 1987. *Institutionalization of the Elderly in Canada.* Toronto: Butterworths.
This provides an overview of the living arrangements and institutionalization of elderly Canadians.

S. McDaniel. 1986. *Canada's Aging Population.* Toronto: Butterworths.
This book focuses on the demographic description of Canadian elders.

B. McPherson. 1991. *Aging as a Social Process: An Introduction to Individual and Population Aging,* 2nd Ed. Toronto: Butterworths.
This is a comprehensive text on aging in Canada.

Canada. 1988. *Canada's Seniors—A Dynamic Force.* Ottawa: Seniors Secretariat.
This government publication describes the status and role of aging Canadians.

CHAPTER 16 The Economy and Work

CHAPTER OUTLINE

I. The Economy: Historical Overview
- A. The Agricultural Revolution
- B. The Industrial Revolution
- C. The Information Revolution and Post-industrial Society
- D. Sectors of the Economy
- E. The Global Economy

II. Economic Systems: Paths to Justice
- A. Capitalism
- B. Socialism
- C. Welfare Capitalism and State Capitalism
- D. Relative Advantages of Capitalism and Socialism
  - 1. Personal Freedom
- E. Changes in Socialist Countries

III. Work in the Post-industrial Economy
- A. The Decline of Agricultural Work
- B. From Factory Work to Service Work
- C. The Dual Labour Market
- D. Labour Unions
- E. Professions
- F. Self-Employment
- G. Underemployment
- H. Unemployment
- I. The Underground Economy
- J. New Information Technology and Work

IV. Corporations
- A. Economic Concentration
- B. Conglomerates and Corporate Linkages
- C. Corporations and the Global Economy

V. The Economy: Looking Ahead

VI. Making the Grade

VII. Key Points

VIII. Key Concepts

IX. Applications and Exercises

X. MySocLab

LEARNING OBJECTIVES

- To explain the history and development of economic activity from the agricultural revolution through the industrial revolution to the post-industrial society
- To identify and describe the primary, secondary, and tertiary sectors of the economy
- To understand regional economic disparities
- To compare and contrast the economic systems of capitalism and socialism
- To identify the differences between welfare capitalism and state capitalism
- To identify the changes in socialist countries
- To identify the advantages and disadvantages of capitalism and socialism
- To describe the general characteristics and trends of work in Canadian post-industrial society
- To understand the consequences of the shift in post-industrial societies to service work and the attendant problems of unemployment, underemployment, and lower wages
- To describe the nature of employment in the Canadian economy
- To compare and contrast corporations and conglomerates
- To explain the impact of multinational corporations on the world economy
- To identify the likely changes in the Canadian economy

CHAPTER REVIEW

This chapter focuses on the economy as a social system that is operating within a complex global market. The opening scenario portrays the difficulties Canadians face in the job market as the economy restructures. Seldom do people now work for one employer during a working life.

THE ECONOMY: HISTORICAL OVERVIEW

The ***economy*** is the social institution that organizes production, distribution, and consumption of goods and services. Goods range from basic necessities to luxury items. Services include various activities that benefit others including government services. Modern complex societies are the result of centuries of technological development and social change.

The Agricultural Revolution

Agrarian societies were much more productive than hunter/gatherer societies and the agricultural surplus permitted people to take on specialized tasks. For the first time, there is a distinct economic institution.

The Industrial Revolution

Five revolutionary changes are identified as resulting from the Industrial Revolution of Europe beginning in the mid-eighteenth century. These include new forms of energy, the spread of factories, manufacturing and mass production, specialization, and wage labour. Greater productivity steadily raised the standard of living, although the benefits were unequally distributed. The **Thinking About Diversity Box** (p. 405) describes the migration of poor rural families in Quebec to the textile factories in Manchester, New Hampshire.

The Information Revolution and Post-industrial Society

By 1950, Canada was becoming a post-industrial economy, one based on service work and information technology. Machines reduced human production labour and the service industries expanded as manufacturing declined. Finally, an information revolution is being driven by computer technology where ideas and literacy are important and work is being decentralized.

Sectors of the Economy

Three economic sectors exist and their relative balance shifts over time. The ***primary sector*** is the part of the economy generating raw materials directly from the natural environment. Today in Canada only 3.9% of the labour force is involved in this sector. The ***secondary sector*** is the part of the economy that transforms raw materials into manufactured goods. Only 21.7% of the labour force is involved in such work. The ***tertiary sector*** is the part of the economy that involves services rather than goods. About 74% of our labour force is employed in such work. **Figure 16-1** (p. 407) indicates the different sector activities by a country's level of income. High-income countries such as Canada create most of their jobs in the tertiary sector. **Figure 16-2** (p. 407) shows the shifts in sector activity in Canada from 1871 to 2001. The shift away from the primary sector is quite dramatic. The **Thinking It Through Box** (p. 408) looks at the distribution of secondary jobs through the provinces. Ontario and Quebec remain the manufacturing centres in Canada.

The Global Economy

Global economic activity reduces the concept of nationhood as we have an "expanding economic activity that crosses national borders." As **Global Maps 16-1 and 16-2** (p. 409) indicate, there is specialization in economic activity in various countries. Economic activity is such that products pass through more than one nation. Businesses, rather than nations, make the decisions and the rights of workers may be compromised.

ECONOMIC SYSTEMS: PATHS TO JUSTICE

Capitalism

Capitalism is an economic system in which productive resources are privately owned. This system has three distinctive features: private ownership of property, pursuit of personal profit, and free competition and consumer choice. Although Canada is a capitalist country, the government intervenes in the marketplace by owning resources and making regulatory decisions. Justice is still governed primarily in freedom of the market place.

Socialism

Socialism is an economic system in which productive resources are collectively owned. Its distinguishing characteristics include collective ownership of property, pursuit of collective goals, and government control of the economy. Justice is attempted through meeting everyone's needs equally. Socialism as an economic system is declining globally.

Communism is a hypothetical economic and political system in which all members of society have economic and social equality. Marx viewed socialism as a transitory stage on the way to communism. However, nowhere has this system been achieved and political equality has been achieved nowhere.

Welfare Capitalism and State Capitalism

Several Western European democracies have combined a market-based economy with social welfare programs. ***Welfare capitalism*** is a political and economic system that combines mostly a market-based economy with extensive welfare programs. Sweden and Italy are examples. In Japan and other Pacific Rim countries, ***state capitalism*** exists where government and private industry co-operate to facilitate productivity.

Relative Advantages of Capitalism and Socialism

Since no pure examples of capitalism and socialism exist, precise objective comparisons are not possible. However, certain crude comparisons can be made keeping the following factors in mind. Capitalist societies out-produce socialist societies by a ratio of 2.7 to 1. While socialist societies have lower overall standards of living, they create less income disparity.

➢Personal Freedom

Capitalist societies provide freedom to pursue one's self-interest, while socialist societies provide freedom from want. Socialist societies regulate the behaviour of their citizens more than capitalist societies.

Changes in Socialist Countries

The collapse of the Soviet Union has led to sweeping changes in Eastern Europe and the previous Soviet republics. The market reforms are proceeding unevenly and there is some evidence that improvements in living standards are accompanied by increasing economic disparity.

WORK IN THE POST-INDUSTRIAL ECONOMY

The Canadian labour force is also undergoing dramatic change. In 2001, 16.7 million people were in the labour force, representing two-thirds of those over the age of 15. Male participation is higher than female, but the differences are diminishing. **Figure 16-4** (p. 414) shows that Blacks have the highest participation rate and English the lowest.

The Decline of Agricultural Work

Currently, less than 4% of the Canadian labour force is involved in farming. Yet, Canadian agriculture is more productive now than it was in the past. More and more production is occurring in corporate agribusinesses, as the "family farm" disappears. There is some concern that increased productivity comes hand in hand with pesticides and chemicals. Organic farming is becoming increasingly popular.

From Factory Work to Service Work

The move from manufacturing to service work is significant, but many of the jobs pay less than those in the manufacturing sector that they have replaced.

The Dual Labour Market

One way to describe the change that is occurring in our economy is to divide work into two different labour markets. The ***primary labour market*** includes occupations that provide extensive benefits to workers, while the ***secondary labour market*** includes jobs providing minimal benefits to workers. A growing proportion of new jobs in post-industrial economies fall into the secondary labour market. The workers in these jobs are those most likely to experience dissatisfaction and are sometimes referred to as the ***reserve army of labour***, those last hired during expansion and first fired when the economy contracts.

Labour Unions

Labour unions are organizations of workers that attempt to improve wages and working conditions through strategies including negotiations and strikes. Canadian labour union membership has been remarkably stable, with approximately one-third of the labour force involved for the last twenty years. Women's involvement has increased slightly and the highest level of penetration is in the government or public administration, where 70% belong to unions.

There is considerable variation by industry sector and by region of the country. Globally, those countries with social democratic values have higher levels of union participation than those with pro-capitalist values. Global competition has led to unions in Canada being less concerned with wage increases and more concerned with job security.

Professions

A ***profession*** is a prestigious, white-collar occupation that requires extensive formal education. Professions share the following characteristics: theoretical knowledge, self-regulated training and practice, authority over clients, and community orientation rather than self-interest.

Many new service occupations are seeking professional standing, a process known as professionalization. This process is initiated by members of an occupational category by labelling their work in a new way. This is followed by the development of a professional association, which initiates a code of ethics and perhaps even schools to train members. In marginal cases, paraprofessional status may be obtained, denoting special training, but lacking extensive theoretical education. Because of our proximity to the U.S., we lose much of our possible professional workforce. The **Media Perspectives Box** (pp. 416-417) indicates that we are regaining some of our losses.

Self-Employment

Self-employment refers to earning a living without working for a large organization. In the early nineteenth century, about 80% of the U.S. labour force was self-employed, but this then declined precipitously.

In recent years Canada has experienced increases in self- employment so that in 2001 the self-employed made up 15% of the labour force. Some professionals are involved but most are small business owners. For the most part these are well-educated, relatively affluent individuals. Although women are increasingly joining this category, 65% of the self-employed are men.

While substantial profits are possible, many small businesses go bankrupt during downturns and pension and health care benefits must be self-provided. As well, these individuals are ineligible for government programs like employment insurance.

Underemployment

Underemployment is employment at a task that uses less than one's full talents or abilities. Part-time workers, young university graduates, and immigrants with credentials not recognized in Canada often find themselves doing much less than what their training would indicate they can do. **Table 16-1** (p. 418) would appear to indicate, however, that education is ultimately a good predictor of occupational success.

Unemployment

While unemployment is found in all societies, it is seen as a natural phenomenon in capitalist societies. It is, however, a problem in socialist societies as well. Canada's unemployment rate in 1993 was 11%, but dropped to 6.8% in 2005. While part-time work has been increasingly replacing full-time work, many of these positions are accepted involuntarily.

Unemployment rates vary by region (see **Canada Map 16-1**, p. 420) and by race/ethnicity (see **Figure 16-4**, p. 414). Official unemployment rates, however, understate the problem since "discouraged workers" and the underemployed are not identified.

The Underground Economy

In violation of government law, there exists an ***underground economy***, or economic activity involving income or the exchange of goods and services that is not reported to the government. Such activity ranges from having garage sales and not reporting the money generated, to the illegal drug trade. The single largest segment of this underground economy, however, is legally obtained income unreported on income taxes. Perhaps 15-20% of the economic activity in Canada is unreported. The imposition of the G.S.T. in 1991 has provided the incentive for under-the-table cash payments.

New Information Technology and Work

Computer technology is changing the character of work. The changes include de-skilling labour, making work more abstract, limiting interaction, and enhancing employer's control of workers. The **Thinking Globally Box** (p. 421) shows clearly how information technology is changing the way all work is done and, indeed, what kinds of jobs are created.

CORPORATIONS

A ***corporation*** is an organization with a legal existence including rights and liabilities apart from those of its members. Most large corporations are owned by thousands of shareholders, which theoretically should disperse wealth in society. Sociologists note, however, that major stockholders comprise a small economic elite in Canada, so that the distribution of wealth in Canada has been unchanged by corporate proliferation.

Economic Concentration

Although many Canadian corporations are small, the Canadian economy is dominated by large corporations that, unlike the U.S., include the banks and other financial institutions. Canada's banks are, in fact, involved in attempts to merge in order to be larger global players. Corporate concentration arises in Canada because of the power of a small number of people, interlocking directorships, geographic centralization of investment in Ontario and Quebec, and the tendency of corporations, especially after the Free Trade Agreement, to expand by acquisition or merger. **Table 16-2**, p. 424, shows the top revenue-producing companies in Canada for 2006. Clearly money, finance, oil, and other natural resources dominate, with oil playing an increasingly larger role.

Conglomerates and Corporate Linkages

A ***conglomerate*** is a giant corporation composed of many smaller corporations. Beatrice Foods and the Irving empire are examples. Corporations are also linked by wealthy families, most of whom know each other socially and have business interests in common.

Another type of linkage among corporations is called ***interlocking directorates***, or social networks made up of people who simultaneously serve on the boards of directors of many corporations. It is not necessarily against the public interest, but does tend to concentrate power. Not all the linkages are necessarily formal, but the social circles exchange valuable information.

More recently, Peter C. Newman has suggested that the arrangements described above are outdated. The new establishment is a meritocracy, based on "what one can do" rather than "whom one knows."

Corporations and the Global Economy

The largest corporations, centred in the U.S., Canada, Japan, and Western Europe now span the globe. Access to vast markets and cheaper labour is part of the reason. As was noted in Chapter 12 (Global Stratification), there is a substantial debate on the effects of capitalist expansion to poor countries. Modernization theorists suggest long-term advantages of expanded economies, while dependency theorists suggest expanded inequality with the rich nations benefitting at the expense of the poor. The issue of market versus government economies is discussed in the **Thinking Globally Box** (pp. 426-427).

THE ECONOMY: LOOKING AHEAD

The economy is one of several social institutions designed to meet the needs of societal members. The distribution of resources in Canada is highly unequal and there are two major changes that will impact upon that distribution

The Information Revolution is changing the nature of the labour market, but a high proportion of Canadians lack the language and computer skills to effectively participate.

The globalization of economies means that national decisions are often irrelevant to international market conditions. What will Canada and other countries do to respond to these changes? The **Media Perspectives Box** (pp. 416-417) discusses the loss of Canada's brightest to the U.S. and the recent moves in the other direction.

KEY CONCEPTS

Define each of the following concepts on a separate sheet of paper. Check the accuracy of your answers by referring to the text, as well as by referring to italicized definitions located throughout the chapter.

capitalism
communism
conglomerates
corporation
economy
global economy
labour unions
post-industrial economy
primary labour market
primary sector
profession
reserve army of labour
secondary labour market
secondary sector
self-employment
socialism
state capitalism
tertiary sector
underground economy
welfare capitalism

STUDY QUESTIONS

True-False

1. T F In Canada more than in the United States, governments are involved in the distribution of goods and services.

2. T F Industrialization had the effect of centralizing work in factories.

3. T F Between 1961 and 2001 in Canada, the primary sector labour force declined from 13% to 4%.

4. T F Manufacturing in Canada is now centralized in Alberta and British Columbia.

5. T F One consequence of the global economy is that national governments no longer control the economic activity that takes place within their borders.

6. T F A purely capitalist economy would operate without interference from the government.

7. T F Socialist countries have been successful in eliminating the power of all elites.

8. T F By 2001, 75% of the Canadian labour force worked in the service sector.

9. T F Almost 50% of young university graduates in Canada find themselves in jobs that do not require university-level credentials.

10. T F Canada's banks are much smaller than their American counterparts.

Multiple Choice

1. That part of the economy that transforms raw materials into manufactured goods is termed the ____________________.

   (a) primary sector
   (b) secondary sector
   (c) manifest sector
   (d) competitive sector
   (e) basic sector

2. Which of the following is *not* a feature of a capitalist economy?

   (a) private ownership of property
   (b) free competition
   (c) pursuit of collective goals
   (d) consumer choice
   (e) pursuit of personal profit

3. An economic and political system in which companies are privately owned, but co-operate closely with the government is called ____________________.

   (a) democratic socialism
   (b) utopian capitalism
   (c) capital oligarchy
   (d) state capitalism
   (e) withered communism

4. Which of the following racial/ethnic groups had the highest percentage participation in the labour force in 2001?

   (a) British
   (b) French
   (c) Asian
   (d) Black
   (e) Native

5. By 2001 the proportion of the Canadian labour force engaged in farming had fallen to________.

   (a) 2% (b) 4% (c) 8% (d) 15% (e) 22%

6. The highest level of union membership in Canada is found in which of the following areas?

(a) construction
(b) manufacturing
(c) public administration
(d) mining

7. Which of the following is ***not*** a characteristic of professions?

(a) practical knowledge
(b) self-regulated training
(c) authority over clients
(d) community orientation

8. In which province was the unemployment rate the highest in 2001?

(a) Ontario
(b) Alberta
(c) Newfoundland and Labrador
(d) Quebec
(e) New Brunswick

9. In which of the following ways are computers altering the character of work?

(a) They enhance the skill of managers.
(b) They make work more practical.
(c) They enhance workplace interaction.
(d) They increase employers' control of workers.
(e) They centralize the workforce.

10. Giant corporations that are clusters of many smaller companies are called ____________.

(a) megacorporations
(b) multinational corporations
(c) oligarchies
(d) monopolies
(e) conglomerates

11. Peter C. Newman suggests that the new Canadian "establishment" is based upon ________________________.

(a) an "old boy's" network
(b) long-established family ties
(c) early migration to Canada
(d) social networks
(e) merit

Fill in the Blank

1. ____________________ range from necessities like food, to luxuries like swimming pools, while ____________ include various activities that benefit others.

2. A ____________________________ is an economy based on service work and information

technology.

3. The ________________ is the part of the economy generating services rather than goods.

4. In the poor countries of Africa and Asia, as many as half of all workers are ________.

5. ________________ is an economic system in which productive resources are collectively owned.

6. In Canada the racial or ethnic group most likely to be unemployed is ______________.

7. That part of the labour force that is last hired during expansion and first fired when the economy contracts is called the ______________.

8. ______________ is employment at a task that uses less than one's full talents or abilities.

9. An economic activity involving the exchange of goods and services that is not reported to the government is called the ______________.

10. In 2006, the Canadian company with the highest level of profits was ____________.

11. ________________ theorists claim that multinationals have intensified global inequality.

Definition and Short Answer

1. What were the three technological revolutions that re-organized the means of production?
2. What were the five notable changes brought about by the Industrial Revolution?
3. Define the concept post-industrial economy.
4. What are the basic characteristics of capitalism as reviewed in the text?
5. What are the basic characteristics of socialism as reviewed in the text?
6. What are the relative advantages of capitalism and socialism?
7. What is welfare capitalism? What is state capitalism?
8. Differentiate between the primary and secondary labour markets.
9. What are the basic characteristics of a profession?
10. How is work changed in a post-industrial economy?

11. What impact do conglomerates have on the global economy?

12. What will be the long-term effects for Canada of the globalization of economies?

Answers to Study Questions

True-False

1. T (p. 404)
2. T (p. 406)
3. T (p. 407)
4. F (p. 408)
5. T (p. 410)
6. T (p. 410)
7. F (p. 411)
8. T (p. 414)
9. T (p. 418)
10. F (p. 423)

Multiple Choice

1. b (p. 407)
2. c (p. 410)
3. d (p. 412)
4. d (p. 413)
5. b (p. 413)
6. c (p. 414)
7. a (p. 415)
8. c (p. 420)
9. d (pp. 421-422)
10. e (p. 424)
11. e (p. 425)

Fill in the Blank

1. goods, services (p. 404)
2. postindustrial economy (p. 406)
3. tertiary sector (p. 407)
4. farmers (p. 409)
5. Socialism (p. 411)
6. Aboriginal peoples (p. 413)
7. reserve army of labour (p. 414)
8. underemployment (p. 418)
9. underground economy (p. 419)
10. EnCana Corp. (p. 424)
11. dependency (426)

ANALYSIS AND COMMENT

Go back through the chapter and write down in the spaces below key points from each of the following boxes.

THINKING ABOUT DIVERSITY

"The French-Canadians of Manchester, New Hampshire"
Key Points:

THINKING IT THROUGH

"Regional Economic Disparities"
Key Points:

MEDIA PERSPECTIVES

"Brain Drain: Brain Gain"
Key Points:

THINKING GLOBALLY

"Working Through Cyberspace"
Key Points:

THINKING GLOBALLY

"The Free Market or Government Intervention?"
Key Points:

SUGGESTED READINGS

Classic Sources

Thorstein Veblen. 1953; orig. 1899. *The Theory of the Leisure Class.* New York: New American Library.
One of the earliest U.S. sociologists explains how patterns of consumption confer social status on people in an increasingly affluent and upwardly mobile society.

Daniel Bell. 1976. *The Coming of Post-Industrial Society: A Venture in Social Forecasting.* New York: Harper Collins.
Daniel Bell was among the first sociologists to recognize and analyze the emerging pos-tindustrial society.

Contemporary Sources

Peter L. Berger. 1986. *The Capitalist Revolution: Fifty Propositions About Prosperity, Equality, and Liberty.* New York: Basic Books.
One of sociology's best contemporary thinkers examines the social consequences of capitalism.

James A. Yunker. 1992. *Socialism Revised and Modernized: The Case for Pragmatic Market Socialism.* New York: Praeger.

This author envisions how a fusion of capitalist and socialist models—involving public ownership of larger, profit-seeking corporations—would capitalize on the advantages of both economic systems.

Canadian Sources

Wallace Clement. 1975. *The Canadian Corporate Elite.* Toronto: McClelland & Stewart.
Diane Francis. 1986. *Controlling Interest: Who Owns Canada?* Toronto: Macmillan.
The first title is a Canadian classic dealing with the small group of people who control our economy. The relationships among them are also explored. The second is a highly readable, though disturbing, account of the wealthiest Canadian families and the corporations they control.

Terry Wotherspoon and Vic Satzewich. 1993. *First Nations: Race, Class and Gender Relations,* Scarborough, ON: Nelson.
Jennifer Wells. 1996. "Jobs." *Maclean's,* March 11, 1996: 12-16.

Ralph Matthews. 1983. *The Creation of Regional Dependency.* Toronto: University of Toronto Press.
The very Canadian problem of regional dependency is given sophisticated treatment here.

Global Source

Suzan Lewis, Dafna N. Izraeli, and Helen Hootsmans. 1992. *Dual-Earner Families: International Perspectives.* Newbury Park, CA: Sage.
This discussion highlights changing economic and family patterns in Hungary, Sweden, Singapore, Japan, India, and elsewhere.

CHAPTER 17 Politics and Government

CHAPTER OUTLINE

I. **Power and Authority**
   A. Traditional Authority
   B. Rational-Legal Authority
   C. Charismatic Authority
II. **Politics in Global Perspective**
   A. Monarchy
   B. Democracy
      1. Democracy and Freedom: Capitalist and Socialist Approaches
   C. Authoritarianism
   D. Totalitarianism
   E. A Global Political System?
III. **Politics in Canada**
   A. Culture, Economics, and Politics
   B. Political Parties
      1. Functions of Political Parties
      2. Parties and the Political Spectrum
   C. Voter Apathy
      1. Party Support
   D. Political Socialization
   E. Political Participation
      1. The Participation of Women
IV. **Theoretical Analysis of Power in Society**
   A. The Pluralist Model: The People Rule
   B. The Power Elite Model: A Few People Rule
   C. The Marxist Model: The System is Biased
V. **Power beyond the Rules**
   A. Revolution
   B. Terrorism
   C. War and Peace
      1. The Causes of War
      2. Is Terrorism a New Kind of War?
      3. The Costs and Causes of Militarism
      4. Nuclear Weapons
      5. Mass Media and War
      6. Pursuing Peace
VI. **Politics: Looking Ahead**
VII. **Making the Grade**
VIII **Key Points**
IX. **Key Concepts**
X. **Applications and Exercises**
XI. **MySocLab**

LEARNING OBJECTIVES

- To explain the difference between power and authority
- To distinguish among the three types of authority: traditional, rational-legal, and charismatic
- To compare and contrast the four principal kinds of political systems and to conceptualize a possible global system
- To explain the balance between individualism and communal responsibility in Canada
- To identify what a political party is and the functions political parties serve in Canadian society
- To understand political ideology and how the parties and their supporters fit on the ideological continuum
- To understand voter apathy in Canada
- To describe the nature of change in Aboriginal self-government
- To describe the ways in which people participate in the political system focusing on political socialization and political participation, including the participation of women
- To understand the impact of modern communications on politics
- To compare and contrast the pluralist model of political power, the power-elite model of political power, and the Marxist model of political economy
- To describe the types of political power that exceed, or seek to eradicate, established politics
- To identify the factors that are involved in creating conditions that increase the likelihood of war
- To recognize the historical pattern of militarism in the United States, Canada, and around the world
- To understand that September 11, 2001 had an impact upon our relationship with the U.S.
- To identify factors that can be used in the pursuit of peace
- To conceptualize what political systems will look like in the future

CHAPTER REVIEW

This chapter begins by looking at the 60% turnout of voters at the Iraq election in 2005, despite the dangers in doing so. That figure matched Canada's and exceeded that of the United States. ***Politics*** is the institutionalized system by which a society distributes power, sets the society's goals, and makes decisions.

POWER AND AUTHORITY

Max Weber defined ***power*** as the ability to achieve desired ends despite resistance from others and it is ***government***, a formal organization that directs the political life of a society, that exercises power. Few governments openly force their will, rather they govern through ***authority***, power that people perceive as legitimate rather than coercive. Weber identifies three sources of authority.

Traditional Authority

Traditional authority is defined as power legitimated by respect for long-established cultural patterns. This type of power is very common in pre-industrialized societies and it has a sacred character. As societies industrialize and become more diverse, traditional authority declines. Yet traditional authority is still expressed in Canadian society by parental dominance over children and the domination of women by men.

Rational-Legal Authority

Rational-legal, or bureaucratic authority, is defined as power legitimated by legally enacted rules and regulations. This type of authority resides in the position, not the person occupying it.

Charismatic Authority

Charismatic authority is defined as power legitimated through extraordinary personal abilities that inspire devotion and obedience. Martin Luther King, Jr. and Mahatma Gandhi are obvious examples, but so is the "Trudeaumania" of Canadian Prime Minister Pierre Trudeau. The impact of his charisma was released again in the outpouring of emotion at his death in 2000.

Charismatic movements are very dependent on their leader. The long-term persistence of such a movement requires ***routinization of charisma***, the transformation of charismatic authority into some combination of traditional and bureaucratic authority. Christianity is an example of this process, as Christ's charisma was routinized in the tradition and bureaucratic structure of the Roman Catholic Church.

POLITICS IN GLOBAL PERSPECTIVE

In hunting and gathering societies, leaders typically emerge as a result of having some unusual amount of strength, hunting skill, or charisma. In agrarian societies, traditional authority develops. As political organization grows, it leads to the formation of a ***political state***, and the advance of technology significantly increases its power.

During the last several centuries political organizations have evolved toward nation-states. At the present time 192 ***nation-states*** are recognized but four categories of political systems are seen to exist.

Monarchy

A ***monarchy*** is a type of political system where power is passed from generation to generation in a single family and is legitimated primarily through tradition. Absolute monarchies flourished in the mediaeval era but have been replaced today mostly with constitutional monarchies, where the monarchs are symbolic heads of state.

Democracy

Democracy refers to a political system in which power is exercised by the people as a whole. In large societies it is not possible for everyone to be directly involved in politics. Therefore, a representative democracy, which places authority in the hands of elected officials who are accountable to the people, develops. This type of system is most common in the relatively rich industrial societies of the world. This system is characterized by rational-legal patterns of authority and functions as a bureaucracy. In Canada large-scale bureaucracies, whose members are unelected, make decisions for the rest of us. If they listen to anyone, it is likely the rich. **Figure 17-1** (p. 435) indicates the huge amount of spending by these bureaucracies. Canada spends relatively little compared to some of the bureaucracies in other countries, but its expenditures are very large at 40% of Gross Domestic Product.

➢Democracy and Freedom: Capitalist and Socialist Approaches

While the capitalist and the socialist countries have had different political systems for most of this century, both claim to provide freedom for their people. In Canada, the U.S,. and Europe, political freedom means the freedom to vote for one's preferred leader and act in one's best financial interest. In the socialist nations, freedom was understood as "having basic needs met" within the context of heavy government control. While capitalism fosters great inequality, the socialist nations reduce inequality while restricting individual freedom. Globally, political freedom has increased substantially (**Global Map 17-1**, p. 436) in the past century. Now 44% of humanity is described as free.

Authoritarianism

Authoritarianism refers to denying popular participation in government. While to some degree this is true for all political systems, as used here, authoritarianism characterizes political systems that are indifferent to people's lives. Saudi Arabia and Ethiopia are current examples. The **Thinking Globally Box** (p. 438) provides a glimpse of "soft authoritarianism," which stifles dissent while providing security and prosperity.

Totalitarianism

A more restrictive political control characterizes ***totalitarianism***, a highly centralized political system that extensively regulates people's lives. Such systems have emerged only within this century as technological means have enabled such governments to rigidly regulate citizen's activities. They bridge the political continuum from the far right, like Nazi Germany, to the far left, like North Korea.

A Global Political System?

Although economic systems have become global, no similar development has taken place politically. The United Nations has played a very limited role in global politics. The very fact, however, that multinational corporations make economic decisions that cannot be controlled by individual nations suggests that these corporations represent a new political order. As well, international nongovernmental organizations, such as Greenpeace, have sought to advance universal principles.

POLITICS IN CANADA

While Americans opted for life, liberty, and the pursuit of happiness, Canadians chose peace, order, and good government. While the Americans revolted, Canada evolved with various of the parts coming together over time and quite reluctantly. **Table 17-1**, (p. 439) reveals the coming together between 1867 and 1999. The provinces have never had uniform relationships with the federal government and many important powers are in provincial hands. In addition one "French speaking" province adds a special dimension. Canada's constitutional review never seems to end.

Canadians are represented in Parliament by a non-elected Senate with 105 seats apportioned on a regional basis, and an elected House of Commons with 308 seats distributed roughly on the basis of population. Quebec and Ontario exert enormous power in the House of Commons, which troubles other regions of the country.

Culture, Economics, and Politics

While Canadians endorse individualism, they are concerned with the good of the collectivity, endorsing interventionist government. Some people think government at all levels should be even more involved in areas like child care and pay equity, for example, while others believe governments already do too much at too great an expense. These differences are in part a reflection of socioeconomic status and regional subcultures, and are represented in the policies of Canada's political parties. **Figure 17-1** (p. 435) indicates that Canada spends more than the U.S., but less than most European governments on programs. The Federal government's special relationship with Aboriginal peoples and the issue of self-government is addressed in the **Thinking About Diversity Box** (pp. 440-441).

Political Parties

Political parties are organizations operating within the political system that seek control of the government. Today's political parties (at least some of them) trace their origins to 1840 when Upper and Lower Canada came into being with the "Tory" (Conservative) and "Grit" (Liberal) factions proposing specific policies. A number of other minor parties came into existence after the World War I but only the CCF (now the NDP) has lasted. In recent years, close to twenty registered parties have sought election, but only the Progressive Conservative, Liberal, New Democratic Party, and Social Credit parties have elected M.P.s over an extended period. But recently the Bloc Québecois and the Reform (now Alliance) parties have "regionalized" politics in Canada. An attempt to merge the Alliance and Progressive Conservatives was successful and the new Conservative Party of Canada with Stephen Harper as its leader, formed a minority government in 2006.

➢Functions of Political Parties

Political parties persist by serving important functions, namely promoting political pluralism, increasing political involvement, selecting political candidates, forging political coalitions, and maintaining political stability.

➢Parties and the Political Spectrum

Political ideology is commonly viewed as a continuum from communism on the left to extreme conservatism on the right**.** **Figure 17-2** (p. 443) places Canadian political parties on that continuum. The old N.D.P. on the left, the Liberals in the middle, and Progressive Conservatives on the middle-right has shifted because of the merger of the Canadian Alliance with the Progressive Conservatives to form the new Conservative Party of Canada. This new Conservative Party has been holding in check its more extreme right members in order to appeal to a wider middle-of-the-road constituency.

Voter Apathy

Historically, Canadians voted in federal elections in very substantial numbers, between 70% and 90% of eligible voters. In the last four elections, the turnout was in the 60% range. Most of the low turnout has to do with indifference, the attitude that one vote makes very little difference to the election results.

➢Party Support

Although many Canadians consistently support one political party, there is considerable switching from election to election, with voting for one party at the provincial level and another at the federal level.

While there used to be some consistent patterns across the country, the 1993 election marked some dramatic changes. The Liberals were the only party with support across the country, while regional parties, the Bloc Québecois and the Reform party, drew heavy support in

Quebec and the West respectively. Although there were some shifts in support for the Conservatives and the N.D.P. (they lost support from 1997 to 2000), the overall results are not substantially changed. **Figure 17-3** (p. 445) shows the national shift in voting in the 1988, 1993, 1997, 2000, 2004, and 2006 elections. The political landscape shifts remarkably in 2004 with the merger of the Alliance and Progressive Conservative parties to form the new Conservative Party of Canada. Now there is no splitting of the vote on the right, and in 2006 a minority government was formed by the Conservative Party of Canada, with substantial breakthroughs in Ontario and Quebec. In the large metropolitan areas of Toronto, Montreal, and Vancouver, there is a real divide in the voting, with the Conservative Party of Canada getting support in ridings outside the urban areas but nothing in the strictly urban ridings. In smaller cities, there was no such divide. The new party is not being supported in the ethnically diverse major urban areas. **Figure 17-4** (p. 446) shows the support for political parties by province for the elections in 1988, 1993, 2000, and 2006.

Political Socialization

The family is the first agent of political socialization and children of politically involved and upper socioeconomic parents learn more. The educational institution and the mass media are also significant agents of socialization, with the media, especially television, playing a dominant role. Opinion polls are also a socializing agent and some concern exists whether they shape, rather than reflect, public opinion. Adult interest and occupational groups can also become involved in political socialization. The **Media Perspectives Box** (pp. 448-449) discusses the impact of media coverage on political outcomes.

Political Participation

Not everyone participates in politics, especially those who feel the system does not respond to their needs. The Spicer Commission, in fact, found in 1991 that Canadians have become cynical about politicians and the political process and more recently we have discovered a distrust of all elites. Research in 1966 characterized political participation at three levels: gladiator, transitional, and spectator. It would appear that recently in Canada more spectator-level participation takes place as the percentage of eligible voters who vote is now at the 60% level, rather than the above 70% level in the past.

➢The Participation of Women

Women acquired the right to vote in federal elections and most provincial elections by 1918. Since then, Agnes McPhail ran successfully for Parliament in 1921, a female cabinet member was named in 1957, Audrey McLaughlin became a party leader in 1989, and Kim Campbell became prime minister in 1993. Although women are still underrepresented in Parliament, they have moved from 5% of M.P.s in 1980 to 21% in 2006. Since Canada is such a large country, the barrier of distance for women with family responsibilities is considerable.

THEORETICAL ANALYSIS OF POWER IN SOCIETY

The Pluralist Model: The People Rule

This approach is linked to the structural-functional paradigm. The ***pluralist model*** is an analysis of politics that views power as dispersed among many competing interest groups.

In *The Vertical Mosaic*, John Porter identifies five competing elites, but notes that these elites are highly integrated and accommodate each other's interests.

The Power Elite Model: A Few People Rule

The ***power elite model*** is an analysis of politics that views power as concentrated among the rich. The term power elite was introduced by C. Wright Mills in 1956. He perceived American society, its economy, government, and military as being dominated by a coalition of the super rich.

Clement's examination of economic power in Canada concludes that Canada is ruled by an economic or corporate elite that is becoming increasingly powerful. Networks bind economic, political, and bureaucratic elites who have a vested interest in maintaining the capitalist system.

The Marxist Model: The System Is Biased

The Marxist political-economy model explains politics in terms of a society's economic system. The capitalist system shuts out politically those who do not exercise economic power.

The **Applying Theory Table** (p. 452) summarizes the three models of power. Research has supported the existence of all three models and probably no one theory matches the reality of the exercise of power in Canada.

POWER BEYOND THE RULES

Revolution

Political revolution is the overthrow of one political system in order to establish another. While reform involves change within a system, revolution means change of the system itself. No political system is immune from revolution. Several general patterns characterize revolutions. These include rising expectations, nonresponsiveness of the government, radical leadership by intellectuals, and establishing a new legitimacy. Canada recently experienced revolutionary potential when Quebec almost voted to begin a process to sovereignty.

Terrorism

Terrorism is the use of violence or the threat of violence by an individual or group as a political strategy. Four insights are offered about terrorism. First, it elevates violence to a legitimate political tactic. Second, it is especially compatible with totalitarian governments as a means of sustaining widespread fear and intimidation to reach what is called ***state terrorism***. Third, extensive civil liberties make democratic societies vulnerable to terrorism. Canada experienced terrorism in the 1960s at the hands of the FLQ and in 1970 when Prime Minister Pierre Trudeau suspended civil liberties to deal with the crisis. Four, one person's terrorist is another person's freedom fighter; definition is important.

Of course, the 9/11 hijacking of four commercial airliners that crashed into public buildings full of people changed North American way of life for the foreseeable future. Americans and Canadians have been traumatized and the civil rights of everyone, but especially visible minorities, have been challenged, as the U.S. and Canada try to coordinate a protective stance. The **Thinking Critically Box** (pp. 456-457) identifies the difficulty facing Canada as we try to manage our relationship with the United States. Eight-five percent of our exports go to the U.S., yet we often annoy them with social policies they abhor (at least many of them do). Although civil liberties are compromised, democratic governments have little choice but to act lest they encourage further terrorist acts.

War and Peace

War is defined as organized conflict among the people of two or more nations, directed by their governments. War is not extraordinary; it has been commonplace in the twentieth century. Canada lost over 100 000 troops in World Wars I and II and continues to lose lives in Afghanistan today.

➢The Causes of War

War, according to research, is not the result of some natural human aggressive tendency; it is a product of society. The following factors are identified by Quincy Wright as promoting war: perceived threats, social problems, political objectives, moral objectives, and the absence of alternatives.

➢Is Terrorism a New Kind of War?

Terrorism has been referred to as a new kind of war because it is asymmetrical: there is no easy way to identify who the enemy is. A small number of attackers can use terror and their own willingness to die in order to shatter public morale.

The Costs and Causes of Militarism

The cost of militarism runs far greater than actual war. To fund it, governments must divert resources away from social needs. Globally, $1 trillion is spent annually on militarism; in the U.S., 20 percent of federal government spending goes to the military and related activities.

Some argue that the U. S. economy has relied on militarism to generate corporate profits and suggests that the result is a ***military-industrial complex***, a close association between the federal government, the military, and defence industries. As well, regional conflicts have helped maintain militarism, along with the nuclear threat from North Korea and possibly Iran.

➢Nuclear Weapons

The destructive capability of the 20 000 nuclear weapons in existence today is incredible. As well, ***nuclear proliferation,*** the acquisition of nuclear weapons technology by more and more societies, continues to place us all at risk.

➢Mass Media and War

The media have the capacity to be quite selective in what they report to particular audiences and therefore have the capacity to influence the outcome of fighting.

➢Pursuing Peace

Several approaches can be used to reduce the danger of nuclear war. These include deterrence, high-technology defence, like the strategic defence initiative, diplomacy and disarmament, and resolving underlying conflict.

POLITICS: LOOKING AHEAD

Change in political systems is ongoing. One issue of concern in Canada is the low turnout at the polls. Is it because people are satisfied or that they believe the holding of political power is in the hands of the wealthy? The **Thinking It Through Box** (p. 459) offers some possible reforms of the voting system.

Global political and economic models are being rethought, but we are still threatened with the possibility of nuclear war from new superpowers.

KEY CONCEPTS

Define each of the following concepts on a separate sheet of paper. Check the accuracy of your answers by referring to the text, as well as by referring to italicized definitions located throughout the chapter.

authoritarianism
charismatic authority
government
military-industrial complex
nuclear proliferation
political economy
political revolution
power
rational-legal authority
state terrorism
totalitarianism
war
authority
democracy
marxist political economy model
monarchy
pluralist model
political parties
politics
power elite model
routinization of charisma
terrorism
traditional authority

STUDY QUESTIONS

True-False

1. T F In the first democratic Iraq election in decades, more people voted, percentage-wise, than was the case in the 2004 U.S. federal election.

2. T F Traditional authority is compelling only as long as everyone shares the same heritage and world view.

3. T F Any organization governed by rational-legal authority faces a crisis of survival upon the loss of its leader.

4. T F According to Freedom House, in 2005, 44% of the world's people were politically free.

5. T F Singapore forbids smoking in public and bans eating on its subways.

6. T F If the Charlottetown Accord had been approved, the inherent right to self-government by Aboriginal peoples would have been given constitutional recognition.

7. T F In 1993, Canadian politics shifted dramatically as the Bloc Québécois and the Reform party entered federal politics.

8. T F Candidates for the American presidency are more likely than candidates for Canadian prime minister to don the mantle of religiosity.

9. T F In the 2006 federal election in Canada, 50% of the successfully elected candidates were women.

10. T F Research by Wallace Clement supports the power elite model of how power is distributed in Canada.

Multiple Choice

1. Who defined power as the likelihood that a person can achieve personal ends in spite of possible resistance from others?

   (a) C. Wright Mills
   (b) Alexis de Tocqueville
   (c) Max Weber
   (d) Robert Lynd

2. Which of the following is ***not*** one of the ways that Weber suggested that governments transform raw power into more stable authority?

   (a) authoritarian
   (b) traditional
   (c) rational-legal
   (d) charismatic
   (d) all of the above were identified by Weber

3. The survival of a charismatic movement depends upon ________, according to Max Weber.

   (a) pluralism
   (b) political action
   (c) legality
   (d) routinization of charisma

4. A highly centralized political system that extensively regulates people's lives is called ______________.

   (a) democracy
   (b) state democracy
   (c) totalitarianism
   (d) authoritarianism
   (e) pluralism

5. Which Canadian province or territory joined Canadian Confederation in 1949?

   (a) Nunavut
   (b) Saskatchewan
   (c) Newfoundland
   (d) British Columbia
   (e) Yukon Territory

6. Which Canadian political party is on the far left of the left-right continuum?

   (a) Liberal
   (b) Communist
   (c) N.D.P.
   (d) Green
   (e) Christian Heritage

7. Which idea below does not represent the power elite model of power?

   (a) Power is highly concentrated.
   (b) Voting cannot create significant political changes.
   (c) The state and capitalists act as one.
   (d) Wealth, social prestige, and political office are rarely combined.

8. Which of the following is ***not*** one of the common traits of revolution?

   (a) rising expectations
   (b) unresponsive government
   (c) leadership from the masses
   (d) establishing a new legitimacy

9. Quincy Wright has identified which of the following circumstances as conditions that lead humans to go to war?

   (a) perceived threats
   (b) social problems
   (c) moral objectives
   (d) all of the above
   (e) a and b above

10. Which of the following are irritants in Canada's current relationship with the United States?

    (a) possible decriminalization of marijuana use
    (b) legalization of same-sex marriage
    (c) the sale of cheaper prescription drugs to Americans
    (d) all of the above
    (e) a and b above

11. The idea that there is a close association between the federal government, the military, and the defence industries in the United States is referred to as the ____________________.

    (a) nuclear club
    (b) pluralist model
    (c) power elite model
    (d) interactionist model
    (e) military-industrial complex

12. When the number of seats awarded to a party mirrors their portion of the popular vote the system is called ________________________.

    (a) first-past-the-post
    (b) triple E
    (c) democratic population
    (d) proportional representation
    (e) populist representation

Fill in the Blank

1. ____________ is the ability to achieve desired ends despite the resistance from others.

2. Power widely perceived as legitimate rather than coercive is referred to as ______________.

3. ________________ authority is power legitimized by legally enacted rules and regulations.

4. The transformation of charismatic authority into some combination of traditional and bureaucratic authority is called _______________.

5. ___________ is a political system in which a single family rules from generation to generation.

6. ______________________ is political control denying the majority participation in a

government that extensively regulates people's lives.

7. The triple concept of Triple E Senate stands for ___________ , _____________, and __________ .

8. Free-trade with the U.S. is not supported by the political __________ in Canada.

9. The first female to win federal political office in Canada was _____________.

10. The acquisition of nuclear weapons technology by more and more nations is referred to as _____________________________.

Definition and Short Answer

1. Differentiate between the concepts of power and authority.

2. Differentiate among Weber's three types of authority.

3. Four types of political systems are reviewed in the text. Identify and describe these systems.

4. How are politics different in Canada and the U.S.?

5. What are the functions served by political parties?

6. Why is there voter apathy in Canada and the U.S.?

7. How do people acquire political attitudes?

8. Differentiate between the pluralist, power elite, and Marxist models concerning the distribution of power in Canada.

9. How does the media affect political decision making?

10. What are the four general traits identified in the text concerning revolutions?

11. What are the five factors identified in the text as promoting war?

12. Several approaches to pursuing peace are addressed in the text. What are these approaches?

13. How will global politics operate in the future?

Answers to Study Questions

True-False

1. T (p. 433)
2. T (p. 433)
3. F (p. 434)
4. T (p. 436)
5. T (p. 438)
6. T (p. 440)
7. T (p. 442)
8. T (pp. 447-448)
9. F (p. 450)
10. T (p. 452)

Multiple Choice

1. c (p. 433)
2. a (p. 433)
3. d (p. 434)
4. c (p. 437)
5. c (p. 439)
6. b (p. 443)
7. d (pp. 451-452)
8. c (p. 453)
9. d (p. 455)
10. d (p. 457)
11. e (p. 457)
12. d (p. 459)

Fill in the Blank

1. power (p. 433)
2. authority (p. 433)
3. rational, legal (p. 433)
4. routinization of charisma (p. 434)
5. monarchy (p. 434)
6. totalitarianism (p. 437)
7. equal, effective, elected (p. 439)
8. left (p. 443)
9. Agnes Macphail (451)
10. nuclear proliferation (p. 458)

ANALYSIS AND COMMENT

Go back through the chapter and write down in the spaces below key points from each of the following boxes.

THINKING GLOBALLY

"'Soft' Authoritarianism or Planned Prosperity? A Report from Singapore"
Key Points:

THINKING ABOUT DIVERSITY

"Aboriginal Self-Government"
Key Points:

MEDIA PERSPECTIVES

"Who Decides? The Impacts of Modern Communications"
Key Points:

THINKING CRITICALLY

"After 9/11: Managing Our Relationship with the United States"
Key Points:

THINKING IT THROUGH

"Reforming Canada's Political System: Throwing out the Baby with the Bath Water"
Key Points:

SUGGESTED READINGS

Classic Sources

Alexis de Tocqueville. 1969; orig. 1834-40. *Democracy in America.* Garden City, NY: Doubleday-Anchor Books.
This classic analysis of politics and society is based on a journey through the United States made by a brilliant French aristocrat in the early 1830s. Many of de Tocqueville's insights remain as fresh and valuable today as when he wrote them.

Hannah Arendt. 1958. *The Origins of Totalitarianism.* Cleveland: Meridian Books.
This classic description of totalitarianism and its rise in the modern world is written by a woman deeply influenced by her captivity in a Nazi death camp during World War II.

Contemporary Sources

Lyman Tower Sargent, ed. 1995. *Extremism in America: A Reader.* New York: New York University Press.
This collection of essays probes radical political organizations that advocate violence, such as the Oklahoma City bombing.

Mary Ann Glendon. 1991. *Rights Talk: The Impoverishment of Political Discourse.* New York: The Free Press.
Among the questions posed by this provocative book: Should we claim more and more "rights"? What does this focus on the individual do to our sense of political responsibility for others?

John Porter. 1965. *The Vertical Mosaic: An Analysis of Social Class and Power in Canada.* Toronto: University of Toronto Press.
Wallace Clement. 1975. *The Canadian Corporate Elite: Economic Power in Canada.* Toronto: McClelland & Stewart.
The exercise of power by multiple or single elites is the topic of these two Canadian classics.

Canadian Sources

Raymond Breton. 1992. *Why Meech Failed: Lessons for Canadian Constitution Making.* Toronto: C.D. Howe Institute.
This thoughtfully analytical and easy-to-read book is a must for political sociologists.

Sylvia B. Bashevkin. 1993. *Toeing the Lines: Women and Party Politics in English Canada.* 2nd Ed. Toronto: Oxford University Press.
This book provides a comprehensive analysis of women's political participation in Canada.

J. Anthony Long and Menno Boldt, eds. 1998. *Governments in Conflict? Provinces and Indian Nations in Canada.* Toronto: University of Toronto Press.

This collection of articles deals with many aspects of Native policy, rights, land claims, and self-government.

Frederick J. Fletcher, ed. *Media and the Voters in Canadian Election Campaigns.* Vol. 18 of the Research Studies of the Royal Commission on Electoral Reform and Party Financing. Ottawa and Toronto: RCERPF/Dundurn.
A current debate concerns the effects of the media on our political system.

Global Sources

Patrick Garrity and Steven A. Maaranen, eds. 1992. *Nuclear Weapons in the Changing World: Perspectives from Europe, Asia, and North America.* New York: Plenum,
This collection of essays by experts examines nuclear-weapons issues from the points of view of nations in various regions of the world.

Cynthia Enloe. 1990. *Bananas, Beaches, and Bases: Making Feminist Sense of International Politics.* Berkeley, CA: University of California Press.
This feminist analysis of the world political scene maintains that gender is at the centre of global power structures.

CHAPTER 18

Family

CHAPTER OUTLINE

I. The Family: Basic Concepts

II. Families: Global Variations

- A. Marriage Patterns
- B. Residential Patterns
- C. Patterns of Descent
- D. Patterns of Authority

III. Theoretical Analysis of the Family

- A. Functions of the Family: Structural-Functional Analysis
- B. Inequality and the Family: Social-Conflict and Feminist Analysis
  - 1. Constructing Family Life: Micro-Level Analysis
- C. Symbolic Interaction Analysis
  - 1. Social-Exchange Analysis

IV. Stages of Family Life

- A. Courtship
  - 1. Romantic Love
- B. Settling In: Ideal and Real Marriage
- C. Child Rearing
- D. The Family in Later Life

V. Canadian Families: Class, Race, and Gender

- A. Social Class
- B. Ethnicity and Race
  - 1. Aboriginal Families in Canada
  - 2. Racial and Ethnic Minority Families
- C. Mixed Marriages
- D. Gender

VI. Transitions and Problems in Family Life

- A. Divorce
  - 1. Who Divorces?
  - 2. Divorce and Children
- B. Remarriage
- C. Family Violence
  - 1. Violence against Women
  - 2. Violence against Children
  - 3. Elder Abuse

VII. Alternative Family Forms

- A. One-Parent Families
- B. Cohabitation
- C. Gay and Lesbian Couples
- D. Singlehood

VIII. New Reproductive Technology and the Family

IX. The Family: Looking Ahead

X. Making the Grade

XI. Key Points

XII. Key Concepts

XIII. Applications and Exercises

XIV. MySocLab

LEARNING OBJECTIVES

- To define the basic concepts of kinship, family, and marriage
- To cross-culturally compare and contrast extended and nuclear families marriage patterns, residential patterns, patterns of descent, and patterns of authority
- To describe the four functions of the family from the structural-functional perspective
- To explain the link between family and social inequality using the social-conflict perspective
- To identify the contributions that symbolic-interaction analysis and social-exchange analysis have made to the sociological knowledge of the family
- To describe the life course of the average Canadian family
- To explain the impact of social class, race, ethnicity, and gender socialization on the family
- To describe the problems and transitions that seriously affect family life: divorce, remarriage, and violence
- To describe the composition and prevalence of alternative family forms: one-parent families, cohabitation, gay and lesbian couples, and singlehood
- To explain the impact, both technologically and ethically, of new reproductive techniques on the family
- To identify five sociological conclusions about the family as we look ahead

CHAPTER REVIEW

It is estimated that 20% to 30% of lesbian women are mothers. Though they often face difficulty in retaining custody of their children, definitions of family in Canada are changing quickly. As well, in Canada more divorce and increased numbers of children born to unmarried mothers means that fully half of children born today will live with a single parent at some point. As more women enter the workforce, Canadians are concerned about a decline in family life, but immense change has previously occurred and families did manage to adjust.

THE FAMILY: BASIC CONCEPTS

The ***family*** is a social institution that unites individuals into co-operative groups that care for each other, including any children, while ***kinship*** is a social bond based on common ancestry, marriage or adoption. Families form around ***marriage***, a legal relationship, usually involving economic co-operation, sexual activity, and child bearing. Certainly, however, children are born to single women and common-law couples and many married couples remain childless. As well, marriage can now unite people of the same sex.

FAMILIES: GLOBAL VARIATIONS

In pre-industrial societies, the ***extended*** or ***consanguine*** families included parents, children, and other kin, while in industrial societies the focus is upon the ***nuclear*** or ***conjugal family,*** composed of one or two parents and their children. While extended families are not irrelevant in Canada, the ***nuclear family*** is most important. The **Thinking About Diversity Box** (p. 468) describes a growing method of becoming parents—international adoption.

Marriage Patterns

Norms identify categories of people suitable for marriage for particular individuals. ***Endogamy*** refers to a normative pattern of marriage between people of the same social group or category. It is differentiated from the norm of ***exogamy***, or marriage between people of different social categories. ***Monogamy*** means marriage that joins two partners. Serial monogamy refers to a number of monogamous marriages over one's lifetime. ***Polygamy*** is defined as marriage that unites a person with two or more spouses. Polygamy takes one of two forms. One type is called ***polygyny***, by far the most common, referring to a marriage that joins one male with more than one female. The second type is called ***polyandry***, referring to marriage that joins one female with more than one male. **Global Map 18-1** (p. 467) looks at marital forms in global perspective.

Residential Patterns

Where people live after they are married also varies cross-culturally. ***Neolocality***, a residential pattern in which a married couple lives apart from the parents of both spouses, is the most common form in industrial societies. In pre-industrial societies residing with one set of parents is more typical. ***Patrilocality*** is a residential pattern in which a married couple lives with or near the husband's family. ***Matrilocality*** is a residential pattern in which a married couple lives with or near the wife's family.

Patterns of Descent

Descent refers to the system by which kinship is traced over generations. Industrial societies follow the ***bilateral descent*** system of tracing kinship through both males and females. Pre-industrial societies typically follow one of two patterns of unilineal descent. The more common, ***patrilineal descent,*** is a system tracing kinship through males. ***Matrilineal descent*** refers to a system of descent tracing kinship through females. Patrilineal systems are typical of pastoral or agrarian societies, while matrilineal systems are common in horticultural societies.

Patterns of Authority

The universal presence of patriarchy is reflected in the predominance of polygyny, patrilocality, and patrilineal descent. Canada is moving toward more egalitarian family patterns.

THEORETICAL ANALYSIS OF THE FAMILY

Functions of the Family: Structural-Functional Analysis

The structural-functionalists focus on several important social functions served by the family.

➢Socialization

The family serves as the primary agent in the socialization process. Children are typically socialized for different kinds of roles and learning never stops as adults learn from socializing their children.

➢Regulation of Sexual Activity

Some restrictions on sexual behaviour are characteristic of every culture. Every society has some type of ***incest taboo***, a cultural norm forbidding sexual relations and marriage between certain relatives. However, the specific members who are subject to the taboo varies greatly cross-culturally. The significance of the incest taboo is primarily social rather than biological. It minimizes sexual competition, helps integrate the larger society, and establishes specific linkages of rights and obligations between people.

➢Social Placement

Parental identities are passed on to their children in the family.

➢Material and Emotional Security

Families provide for the physical, emotional, and financial support of its members. People living in families tend to be healthier than those living alone.

Structural-functionalists tend to underemphasize problems in families, and underestimate the great diversity of family forms.

Inequality and the Family: Social-Conflict and Feminist Analysis

The focus of the social-conflict approach to the study of the family is how this institution perpetuates patterns of social inequality.

➢Property and Inheritance

Social class divisions are preserved by the inheritance of wealth.

➢Patriarchy

Patriarchal values maintain the sexual and economic subordination of women. Despite the fact that women have increased their participation in the paid labour force, they still do most of the housework and child rearing.

➢Race and Ethnicity

These continue to be strong endogamous characteristics of marriage.

Social-conflict theorists tend to ignore the important functions carried out by the family. The structural-functional and social-conflict paradigms provide a macro-level perspective from which to understand the institution of the family, while micro-level approaches explore how individuals shape their family life.

Symbolic-Interaction Analysis

This analysis examines how emotional bonds are created as family members share activities.

➢Social-Exchange Analysis

Social-exchange theory draws attention to the power of negotiation within families. People are seen as socially exchanging valued resources with each other. As gender roles are converging, so also is what males and females have to exchange.

While providing a meaningful counterbalance to the macro-level approaches, the micro-level is limited in its ability to allow us to see the social and cultural forces having an impact on the family.

The **Applying Theory Table** (p. 471) summarizes the three approaches to understanding the family.

STAGES OF FAMILY LIFE

Family life is viewed as dynamic, consisting of changing patterns over its life cycle.

Courtship

Pre-industrial societies typically are characterized by arranged marriages where the kinship group determines marriage partners. See **Thinking Globally Box (**p. 473) for a description of child marriage.

In industrial societies, personal choice in mate selection dominates, although arranged marriages are becoming more common in Canada.

➢Romantic Love

Romantic love is a less stable foundation for marriage than are social and economic considerations. Although most people like to think that contemporary marriages are purely a matter of individual choice, ***homogamy*** is a reality, where individuals marry those who are socially like themselves.

Settling In: Ideal and Real Marriage

Marriage and family tend to be idealized by most, with real life experiences never meeting expectations, including sexuality. Those who have the most fulfilling sexual relationships experience the most marital satisfaction. **Figure 18-1** (p. 472) shows the amount of sexual activity by marital status. Although most Canadians suggest ***infidelity***, sexual activity outside of marriage, is wrong, a substantial amount takes place.

Child Rearing

Child rearing creates major transitions for families, some of them problematic. Despite the demands children make of families, most Canadians still desire them, albeit at reduced numbers than the past. Children are certainly now a considerable economic liability compared to pre-industrial times. As well, women have entered the labour force and husbands resist accepting responsibility for household tasks. In response, women are having their children later in married life.

Because parents have less time for their children, issues such as "latchkey kids" have arisen. The **Media Perspectives Box** (pp. 486-487) discusses the child-care situation in Canada. Despite this concern, most children think their parents are doing a good job.

The Family in Later Life

With life expectancy increasing, the number of years a couple live together without children during what is known as the "empty nest" years is increasing. Many new challenges are faced by couples during these years. The departure of children and the maintenance of relationships with them, the increased value of companionship in marriage, and the death of one's spouse are major events in later life. An additional adjustment is required of "boomers" who may still be raising children while caring for elderly parents. The problem of this "sandwich generation" is often exacerbated by the return to the family nest of children who had previously left and even total care of their grandchildren

CANADIAN FAMILIES: CLASS, RACE, AND GENDER

Social Class

Social class has a major impact on the family, including determining a family's economic security, and range of opportunities. Further, research by Lillian Rubin illustrates how social class affects the relationship of spouses, with middle-class couples sharing their feelings and the housework. Differences in socialization patterns between classes also have an impact on children's achievement.

Ethnicity and Race

➢Aboriginal Families in Canada

There are many Aboriginal bands and Inuit and Métis settlements in Canada, with perhaps 50% of Aboriginal peoples living off reserve. To talk of family patterns of Aboriginal peoples is therefore problematic. What we do know, however, is that many of the family traditions of extended kin solidarity, family values, respect for elders, and welfare of children have been weakened by church and state attempts to Christianize and Canadianize Aboriginal children, to the point that Aboriginal culture is at risk. The federal government has recently apologized and offered financial compensation, but for many Aboriginals, life in big cities is a mixed success.

➢Racial and Ethnic Minority Families

Canada's racial and ethnic diversity brings many traditional values on religion, parenting, and marriage, for example, that are different from those held by the majority of Canadians. Intergenerational conflict is common as the children in these minority groups begin to accept the values of the majority.

Mixed Marriages

Racially mixed marriages are increasingly accepted in Canada (see **Table 18-1** (p. 476), but some resistance still exists, and the actual number is still quite small.

Gender

Jessie Bernard succinctly suggests that in reality there are two marriages: a female marriage and a male marriage. Even today, despite considerable change in female roles in society, men tend to dominate in marriages and experience health and happiness advantages, while women experience poorer mental health and lesser levels of happiness than single women do.

TRANSITION AND PROBLEMS IN FAMILY LIFE

Divorce

As **Figure 18-2,** (p. 478) indicates, the divorce rate in Canada has increased dramatically since 1968, when the *Divorce Act* was liberalized. The rates have now levelled off to where they were in the late 1970s. The societal factors that appear to have influenced the rate of divorce are emphasis on the individual, the subsiding of romantic love, the increasing independence of women, the stress of dual career marriages, and the social and legal ease of obtaining a divorce.

➢Who Divorces?

Divorce is more common among young couples, especially in the following cases: those whose marriage took place after an unexpected pregnancy, those whose parents were divorced, those with no strong religious values, and those where both partners have successful careers.

Canada Map 18-1 (p. 479) shows the varying rates by province. Once a person has divorced, they are more likely to divorce again.

➢Divorce and Children

Divorce has a negative impact upon children especially with respect to maintaining contact with both parents and self-blame. Another problem for children is the low rate of compliance with court-ordered support payments. Joint custody of children has been favoured by Canadian courts for the last twenty years and it can work well if parents put children's needs first. Too often, the children are caught in the middle of fights and recriminations.

Remarriage

About 80% of people who divorce in Canada remarry and remarriage rates are higher for men than for women. Remarriage often creates a ***blended family*** consisting of a biological parent and stepparent, along with children of their respective first marriages and any children of the blended marriage.

Family Violence

Many families are characterized by ***family violence***, or emotional, physical, or sexual abuse of one family member by another. The family has been characterized as one of the most violent institutions in our society.

➢Violence against Women

Violence transcends the boundaries of social class. One-fifth of all couples are estimated to have relationships characterized by at least some violence each year, and the seriousness of abuse is greater for wives than for husbands.

Traditionally, women have had few options and the violent marriage acts as a trap for many women. The traditional view of domestic violence as a private concern of families has also hindered the effectiveness of programs and policies, but more communities are establishing shelters and "stalker" legislation in Canada assists police in protecting women and their children. Some research indicates that men are at least as likely as women to be victims of violent assault in families, but no real effort exists to help men so victimized. The **Thinking It Through Box** (p. 481) discusses spousal violence in Canada.

➢Violence against Children

Perhaps 4% of children suffer abuse each year that can inflict both physical and emotional harm. Large numbers of children simply run from family abuse and these runaways are getting younger. Most abused children suffer guilt as they are sure they must be responsible for the abuse. Ninety percent of the abusers are estimated to be men and the majority were themselves abused as children.

➢**Elder Abuse**

The "sandwich generation" that is raising children and looking after aging parents, experiences stress that may lead to increased levels of abuse of their parents.

ALTERNATIVE FAMILY FORMS

One-Parent Families

Over the last forty years there has been a dramatic increase in single-parent families. **Figure 18-4**, (p. 482) indicates that in 2001, 15.6% of families were headed by single parents, most of them women. Almost 12% of children in Canada live in these families and many of them live in relative poverty, which probably accounts for their lower level of success. **Table 18-2** (p. 483) shows the impact of family structure on poverty.

Cohabitation

Cohabitation is the sharing of a household by an unmarried couple. **Figure 18-5,** (p. 483), shows the increase between 1981 and 2001 of common-law couples by province. The **Applying Sociology Box** (p. 484) indicates that although cohabitation is unstable, increasing portions of Canadians are choosing this structural alternative.

Gay and Lesbian Couples

Several countries, including Canada, now recognize same-sex marriage and the 2006 Census will give us data on how many same-sex marriages have taken place. Change is coming much more slowly in the U.S.

Singlehood

Historically, singlehood was seen as a transitory stage, but increasingly women and men are choosing to remain single**. Table 18-3** (p. 485) indicates dramatic differences in age cohorts. Much of singlehood is really delay in getting married in order to go to college or university and establish a career. Women who delay will confront a lack of available men, but many young women are simply choosing not to marry.

NEW REPRODUCTIVE TECHNOLOGY AND THE FAMILY

The impact of new reproductive technology on the family in recent years has been significant, with many benefits having been realized. However, the new technology has brought with it many difficult ethical problems.

In vitro fertilization is a process involving the union of the male sperm and the female ovum "in glass" rather than in the woman's body. The benefits are twofold. First, couples who otherwise could not conceive may be able to use this technique. Second, the genetic screening of sperm and eggs reduces the incidence of birth defects.

THE FAMILY: LOOKING AHEAD

Family life has changed dramatically and will continue to do so. Five changes are likely in the years ahead. First, divorce will be increasingly accepted. Second, family forms will be highly variable. Third, more children will grow up without ties to their fathers. Fourth, both parents will work. Fifth, new reproductive technology will continue to affect family life.

KEY CONCEPTS

Define each of the following concepts on a separate sheet of paper. Check the accuracy of your answers by referring to the text, as well as by referring to italicized definitions located throughout the chapter.

bilateral descent
cohabitation
descent
endogamy
exogamy
extended family
family
family violence
homogamy
incest taboo
infidelity
kinship
marriage
matrilineal descent
matrilocality
monogamy
neolocality
nuclear family
patrilineal descent
patrilocality
polyandry
polygamy
polygyny

STUDY QUESTIONS

True-False

1. T F By some estimates, 20% to 30% of lesbian women are mothers.

2. T F For the 2006 Canadian Census, a couple living common-law might be of the opposite sex or same sex.

3. T F Neolocality is a residential pattern most common in hunting and gathering societies.

4. T F Every known culture has some type of incest taboo.

5. T F Social exchange analysis describes courtship and marriage as forms of negotiation.

6. T F — The "crowded nest" is created when children who have left their parents' home return for various reasons.

7. T F — The involvement of church and state in Aboriginal lives tended to assist them to adjust to the Canadian culture.

8. T F — The highest rate of divorce in 2001 (percentage of population aged 15 and above) is found in Quebec.

9. T F — We have recently discovered in Canada that 50% of child abusers are women.

10. T F — Cohabitation rates are higher in Quebec than any other province.

11. T F — Same-sex marriage became legal in Canada in 2005.

12. T F — Test-tube babies are, technically speaking, the result of the process of *in vitro* fertilization.

Multiple-Choice

1. Exogamy and endogamy are cultural norms relating to ____________________.

   (a) marriage patterns
   (b) descent regulations
   (c) beliefs about romantic love
   (d) residence patterns
   (e) authority patterns

2. A form of marriage uniting one male and two or more females is called ___________.

   (a) nuclear
   (b) extended
   (c) endogamy
   (d) polyandry
   (e) polygyny

3. Which of the following is not a descent pattern?

   (a) matrilineal
   (b) patrilineal
   (c) bilateral
   (d) neolocal
   (e) all are descent patterns

4. Critiques of the structural-functional approach to studying the family suggest which of the following?

   (a) Problems of family life are minimized.
   (b) Diversity of family life is ignored.
   (c) The impact of socialization is ignored.
   (d) (a and b above)
   (e) (b and c above)

5. The type of sociological analysis of the family that holds that the family serves to perpetuate patriarchy is ______________________.

(a) social-exchange analysis
(b) social-conflict analysis
(c) structural-functional analysis
(d) symbolic-interaction analysis

6. The ______________ analysis explores how individuals shape and experience family life.

(a) macro-level
(b) micro-level
(c) felicitous
(d) mechanical
(e) multivariate

7. Marriage between people with the same social characteristics is called ________________.

(a) heterogamy
(b) homogamy
(c) connubial
(d) courtship
(e) mechanical solidarity

8. With respect to extramarital sexual relationships, Reginald Bibby found that __________ of adults viewed such behaviour as always wrong.

(a) one-quarter (b) one-half (c) three-quarters (d) almost all

9. Which of the following are accurate observations about Aboriginal Canadian families?

(a) The historical family forms of most Aboriginal peoples have been recently strengthened.
(b) The involvement of church and state in Aboriginal family life has been useful.
(c) Residential schools strengthened Aboriginal family life.
(d) About half now live off reserve.
(e) All of the above

10. Which of the following is ***not*** one of the reasons that divorce rates are so high in Canada?

(a) People in families do not work and play together often.
(b) Our culture bases marriage on romantic love.
(c) Women are not so financially dependent on men.
(d) Divorce still carries a powerful stigma.

11. Cohabitation is highest in the province of ______________.

(a) British Columbia
(b) Alberta
(c) Ontario
(d) Nova Scotia
(e) Quebec

Fill in the Blank

1. ____________ is a social bond based on common ancestry, marriage, or adoption.

2. The __________________ family is based on blood ties.

3. ______________ is the normative pattern referring to marriage between people of the same social group or category.

4. A system tracing kinship through both women and men is a ____________ descent pattern.

5. Social exchange analysis depicts courtship and marriage as forms of _______________ .

6. Many experts agree that couples with the most fulfilling _____________experience the greatest satisfaction in their marriage.

7. Baby boomers are often called the ________________ _________________ because they care for aging parents while still raising their children.

8. Only __________ % of cohabitation unions last for 15 years.

9. The divorce rate in the future is like to _______________ ________________.

10. Parents pay $_______________ per day for child care in Quebec.

Definition and Short Answer

1. What are the four basic functions of the family according to structural-functionalists?

2. Define and describe the three patterns of descent outlined in the text.

3. Why do families have fewer children now than in the past?

4. Why has the divorce rate increased in recent decades in Canada?

5. What are the four stages of the family life cycle that are outlined in the text? Describe the major events that occur during each stage.

6. Who is most likely to get divorced?

7. What impact does divorce have on children?

8. What are the controversies about child care in Canada?

9. What are the characteristics of cohabitation in Canada?

10. What are the five conclusions being made about marriage and family in the twenty-first century?

Answers to Study Questions

True-False

1. T (p. 464)
2. T (p. 465)
3. F (p. 466)
4. T (p. 469)
5. T (p. 470)
6. T (p. 474)
7. F (p. 475)
8. T (p. 479)
9. F (p. 482)
10. T (p. 483)
11. T (p. 484)
12. T (p. 485)

Multiple Choice

1. a (p. 465)
2. e (p. 466)
3. d (p. 466)
4. d (p. 469)
5. b (p. 470)
6. b (p. 470)
7. b (p. 472)
8. c (p. 472)
9. d (pp. 475-476)
10. d (pp. 477-478)
11. e (p. 483)

Fill in the Blank

1. kinship (p. 465)
2. consanguine (p. 465)
3. endogamy (p. 465)
4. bilateral (p. 467)
5. negotiation (p. 470)
6. sexual relationships (p. 472)
7. sandwich generation (p. 474)
8. 5 (p. 484)
9. remain high (p. 485)
10. 7 (p. 486)

ANALYSIS AND COMMENT

Go back through the chapter and write down in the spaces below key points from each of the following boxes.

THINKING ABOUT DIVERSITY

"International Adoption"
Key Points:

THINKING GLOBALLY

"Early to Wed: A Report from Rural India"
Key Points:

THINKING IT THROUGH

"Spousal Violence in Canada"
Key Points:

APPLYING SOCIOLOGY

"Cohabitation among Canadians"
Key Points:

MEDIA PERSPECTIVES

"The Controversy over Child Care"
Key Points:

SUGGESTED READINGS

Classic Source

Michael Young and Peter Willmott. 1992; orig. 1957. *Family and Kinship in East London.* Berkeley, CA: University of California Press.
One of the best studies of the working-class family, this account of the lives of "Eastenders" reveals the power of class to shape family life.

Contemporary Canadian Sources

Pat Armstrong and Hugh Armstrong. 1984. *The Double Ghetto: Canadian Women and Their Segregated Work.* Toronto: McClelland & Stewart.
This book describes and analyzes the gendered nature of the Canadian labour force.

Maureen Baker, ed. 1989. *Families: Changing Trends in Canada.* 2nd ed. Toronto: McGraw-Hill Ryerson.
Margrit Eichler. 1988. *Families in Canada Today: Recent Changes and Their Policy Consequences.* 2nd ed. Toronto: Gage.
Emily Nett. 1993. *Canadian Families Past and Present.* Toronto: Buterworths.
These three books provide various overviews of the nature and condition of the family in Canadian society. The first and third are general texts. The second focus on policies that affect the family and on feminist understandings of families.

Margrit Eichler. 1989. "Reflections on Motherhood, Apple Pie, the New Reproductive

Technologies, and the Role of Sociologists in Society." ***Society/Societé*** **13(1): 1-5.**
This article critiques some aspects of new reproductive technologies.

Patrick Johnston. 1983. ***Native Children and the Child Welfare System.*** **Toronto: Lorimer.**
Linda MacLeod. 1987. ***Battered But Not Beaten...Preventing Wife Abuse in Canada.*** **Ottawa: Canadian Advisory Council on the Status of Women.**
These books focus on "problems" within the Canadian family. The first examines Aboriginal children. The second discusses violence in the family. The third portrays the extent of poverty in Canada.

Global Sources

William J. Goode. ***World Changes in Divorce Patterns.*** **New Haven, CN: Yale University Press, 1993.**
This global survey explains how divorce is affected by economic patterns such as industrialization; it also explores variation in divorce by class.

Mark Mathabane. 1994. ***African Women: Three Generations.*** **New York: HarperCollins,**
This personal look at three women—a grandmother, a mother, and a sister--by a South African details the struggles common to women under a system of racial oppression.

CHAPTER 19

Religion

CHAPTER OUTLINE

I. **Religion: Basic Concepts**
   A. Religion and Sociology
II. **Theoretical Analysis of Religion**
   A. Functions of Religion: Structural-Functional Analysis
   B. Constructing the Sacred: Symbolic Interaction Analysis
   C. Inequality and Religion: Social Conflict Analysis
III. **Religion and Social Change**
   A. Max Weber: Protestantism and Capitalism
   B. Liberation Theology
IV. **Types of Religious Organization**
   A. Church
   B. Sect
   C. Cult
V. **Religion in History**
   A. Religion in Pre-industrial Societies
   B. Religion in Industrial Societies
VI. **World Religions**
   A. Christianity
   B. Islam
   C. Judaism
   D. Hinduism
   E. Buddhism
   F. Confucianism
   G. Religion: East and West
VII. **Religion in Canada**
   A. Religious Affiliation
   B. Religiosity
   C. Religion: Class and Ethnicity
      1. Social Class
      2. Ethnicity
VIII. **Religion in a Changing Society**
   A. Secularization
   B. Civil Religion
   C. "New Age" Seekers: Spirituality without Formal Religion
   D. Religious Revival: "Good Ole-time Religion"
   E. Religious Fundamentalism
   F. The Electronic Church
IX. **Looking Ahead: Religion in the Twenty-First Century**
X. **Making the Grade**
XI. **Key Points**
XII. **Key Concepts**
XIII. **Applications and Exercises**
XIV. **MySocLab**

LEARNING OBJECTIVES

- To define the basic concepts of religion, faith, profane, sacred, and ritual
- To explain the aspects of religion that sociology addresses
- To identify and describe the three functions of religion as developed by Emile Durkheim
- To identify and describe the view that religion is socially constructed
- To identify and describe the role religion plays in maintaining inequality
- To identify the relationship between religious values and economic development including political activism, which aims to right social inequality
- To compare and contrast the basic types of religious organizations: church (two types), sect, and cult
- To distinguish between pre-industrial and industrial societies in terms of religious beliefs and practices
- To identify and describe the size, location, and type of belief system of the major world religions: Christianity, Islam, Hinduism, Buddhism, Confucianism, and Judaism
- To explain religious affiliation, religiosity, and the correlates of religious affiliation in Canada
- To describe the pattern of secularization in Canadian society
- To identify and describe religious revival in North American society, especially religious fundamentalism
- To understand the relationship between science and religion

CHAPTER REVIEW

The chapter opens by describing a busy evangelical church in Ontario, a good beginning for the examination of the changing face of religion here and elsewhere.

RELIGION: BASIC CONCEPTS

Durkheim suggested human beings distinguish between the ***profane***, meaning ordinary elements of everyday life, and the ***sacred***, or that which is defined as extraordinary, inspiring a sense of awe and reverence. This differentiation, according to Durkheim, is the key to religious belief. ***Religion*** is therefore a system of beliefs and practices based upon a conception of the sacred. The sacred is approached through ***ritual,*** or formal ceremonial behaviour.

Religion and Sociology

Because religion transcends everyday experience, its truth cannot be tested by science. It is a matter of ***faith***, belief anchored in convictions, not scientific evidence. Sociology is concerned with the understanding of religious practices and the consequences of religious activity for social life.

THEORETICAL ANALYSIS OF RELIGION

Functions of Religion: Structural-Functional Analysis

Durkheim argued society has an existence of its own, beyond the lives of the people who create it. Society and the sacred are inseparable in Durkheim's view. He believed that the power of society was understood by people through their creation of sacred symbols. In technologically simple societies, a ***totem*** is an object within the natural world that is imbued with sacred qualities that can transform individuals into a collectivity. He saw religion as providing three major functions for society:

➢Social Cohesion

Religion unites members of a society through shared symbolism, values, and norms.

➢Social Control

Every society promotes some degree of social conformity. Cultural norms, for example, are justificd using rcligious doctrinc.

➢Providing Meaning and Purpose

Religion provides people with a sense of meaning and purpose by addressing the ultimate issues of life.

A weakness in the structural-functional view is that it downplays the dysfunctions of religion, particularly its role in producing destructive social conflict.

Constructing the Sacred: Symbolic-Interaction Analysis

Peter Berger, operating from the symbolic-interaction point of view, theorized that religion is a socially constructed reality much as the family and economy are. The sacred can provide permanence for society as long as society's members ignore the fact that the sacred is socially constructed.

Inequality and Religion: Social-Conflict Analysis

The social-conflict view of religion draws attention to the social ills perpetuated by religion through justifying inequality and suggesting that a better life will come. The **Thinking About Diversity Box** (p. 496), addresses the question of the extent to which religion favours males. The conflict perspective, however, ignores the extent to which religion can promote positive social change. The **Applying Theory Table** (p. 495) summarizes the three theoretical approaches.

RELIGION AND SOCIAL CHANGE

Max Weber: Protestantism and Capitalism

Max Weber contends that Calvinism was the engine of change for industrialization in Western Europe. The doctrine of predestination led Protestants to demonstrate that they possessed God's favour by working hard and becoming prosperous. But the fruits of the labour were to be reinvested by the thrifty Calvinists, providing the foundation for industrial capitalism.

Liberation Theology

Liberation theology is a combining of Christian principles with political activism, often marxist in character. This view originated in the 1960s, and asserts that social oppression is contrary to Christian morality, so the Church must help people liberate themselves from poverty. This approach is not supported by the official church.

TYPES OF RELIGIOUS ORGANIZATIONS

Church

A ***church*** is a type of religious organization that is well integrated into the larger society. Two types of church organization are the ***state church***, a church that is formally allied with the state, and a ***denomination***, or a church that is independent of the state and recognizes religious pluralism. The Catholic Church of the Roman Empire and the Anglican Church of England are examples of a state church. The Baptist, Methodist, and Catholic churches in Canada are examples of denominations.

Sect

A ***sect***, distinct from a church, is a type of religious organization that stands apart from the larger society. Sects tend to lack the formal organization of a church and they exalt the personal experience of divine power. Leaders are often those people who manifest ***charisma***, or extraordinary personal qualities that attract followers. Proselytizing is important to obtain new members through ***conversion***, a personal transformation or religious rebirth. Sects tend to reject the established society and sect members tend to be people of lower social standing than those in churches and those who feel like outsiders.

Cult

Cults are religious organizations substantially outside a society's cultural traditions. They offer messages that are seen as new and are often judged by outsiders as deviant. Many cults, like early Christianity, become more churchlike over time.

RELIGION IN HISTORY

Religion in Pre-industrial Societies

Among hunter/gatherer societies, religion typically takes the form of ***animism***, or the belief that natural objects are conscious forms of life that can affect humanity. Belief in a single divine power emerged in pastoral and horticultural societies and a specialized priesthood developed in agrarian societies.

Religion in Industrial Societies

With industrialization, science begins as a force that diminishes the scope of religious power and thinking. Yet science has not caused religion to be eliminated as it cannot answer certain fundamental questions about the reason for human existence.

WORLD RELIGIONS

Religion is found virtually everywhere in the world. Many of the thousands of religions are highly localized, but a few may be termed ***world religions*** because they have millions of followers and are known throughout the world.

Christianity

Christianity is the world's largest religion with 2 billion followers. Christianity is based on ***monotheism***, or religious beliefs recognizing a single divine power. When this view first emerged, it challenged the Roman Empire's tradition of ***polytheism***, or religious beliefs recognizing many gods. Eventually Christianity became the official religion of the Roman empire, but over the centuries there have been several divisions within Christianity**. Global Map 19-1** (p. 500) shows us Christianity in a global perspective.

Islam

Islam is the world's second largest religion with about 1.2 billion followers called Muslims. This religion is based on the life of Muhammad, born in Mecca in 570. He is seen as a prophet, not a divine being. Islam means "submission and peace." While divisions exist, there are five pillars of Islam: recognition of Allah as the one true God and Muhammed as God's messenger, ritual prayer, giving alms to the poor, regular fasting, and making at least one pilgrimage to Mecca. Muslims are obligated to defend their faith occasionally, justifying holy wars. As in most religions, women's lives are dominated by men, but most Muslim women accept the mandates of their religion**. Global Map 19-2** (p. 500) shows the global distribution of followers.

Judaism

A small religion with only 15 million adherents, Judaism, nonetheless, has a special relationship with North America where 6 million Jews reside. Judaism has a long history and is animist in origin. After Moses led the exodus from Egypt, Judaism became monotheistic, recognizing one all-powerful God. A belief in the "covenant" suggests to Jews they have a special relationship with God. Their teachings emphasize moral behaviour in the world rather than the personal salvation of Christianity. There are divisions of Judaism based upon greater or lesser adherence to traditional practices but all Jews share an awareness of rejection, which more recently is expressed through anti-Semitism. Also in Canada, Jews have experienced discrimination in the occupational and educational institutions. The University of Toronto has recently added two chairs in Jewish studies since Jewish culture is so important to an understanding of the development of Western civilization. There is concern about the maintenance of culture since many are not taught Jewish culture and more than half marry non-Jews.

Hinduism

Hinduism is probably the oldest religion, coming into existence about 4500 years ago. It has about 800 million followers. Hinduism and Indian society are closely fused, so unlike Islam and Christianity, it has not diffused widely to other nations. Since it is not linked to the life of one person, beliefs and practices vary greatly. All Hindus generally believe that a force termed dharma confronts all people with moral responsibility. Karma, a belief in the spiritual progress of a person's soul and involving reincarnation, is also a fundamental aspect of this religion. Hinduism is neither monotheistic nor polytheistic. Many recent migrants to Canada from India are Hindus. **Global Map 19-3** (p. 503) shows the global distribution of followers.

Buddhism

Buddhism emerged in India about 2500 years ago and currently has 350 million adherents. Siddhartha Gautama was its founder. After years of travel and meditation, he reached "*bodhi*," or enlightenment. Followers began spreading his teachings, called the ***dhamma***. Buddhists see existence as suffering and reject the idea of wealth as a solution to human problems. Reincarnation is also a belief in this religion. The answer to the world problems lies in personal transformation toward a spiritual existence and ***nirvana***, a state of enlightenment and peace. **Global Map 19-4** (p. 503) shows the global distribution of adherents.

Confucianism

Confucianism was the official religion of China from 200 BCE until the revolution in 1949. This religion was shaped by Kung-Fu-Tzu (Confucius) who lived in the 6th and 5th centuries BCE. This religion is based on the concept of the *jen*, humaneness. Lacking a clear concept of the sacred, it is more a disciplined way of life than a religion.

Religion: East and West

Although all religions have a conception of a higher moral force or purpose, Western religions (Christianity, Islam, Judaism) have a clear focus on God and celebrate their faith in congregations, while Eastern religions (Hinduism, Buddhism, Confucianism) focus on ethical codes and celebrate their faith in society itself.

RELIGION IN CANADA

Although religious service attendance has declined, religion still seems to be important to Canadians.

Religious Affiliation

A clear majority of Canadians identify with a religion, but a growing number report "no religion." **Canada Map 19-1** (p. 505) shows the distribution of those reporting no religion across Canada. **Table 19-1** (p. 504) shows religious affiliation for Canadians with Roman Catholics the largest at 43.2%.

Religiosity

Religiosity is the importance of religion in a person's life. The majority of Canadians (84%) claim to believe in God. However, fully 16.6 % claim no religion at all (see **Canada Map 19-1**, p. 505) and church attendance figures continue to drop. See the **Applying Sociology Box** (p. 506) for a picture of a possible renaissance of religiosity in Canada.

Religion: Class and Ethnicity

➢Social Class

Protestants tend to have somewhat higher social positions than Catholics, and Jews, despite being fairly recent immigrants, have a high social standing, probably as a result of commitment to education and achievement. **Table 19-2** (p. 507) demonstrates that religious stratification can be measured by average income levels.

➢Ethnicity

Religion is strongly linked with ethnicity worldwide and some of those identities are continued in Canada. However, nearly all ethnic groups in Canada display some religious diversity.

RELIGION IN A CHANGING SOCIETY

Secularization

A pattern of social change in Canada and elsewhere is ***secularization,*** a historical trend away from the supernatural and the sacred. As scientific explanation has been accepted, religious explanation has declined. The Quiet Revolution in Quebec is a perfect example of the loss of influence of the Catholic Church. Some dimensions of religiosity are in decline, such as attendance at services, but affiliation with a religious perspective may be increasing. While conservatives decry the loss of faith, progressives hail the loss of stifling beliefs such as the inferior position of women. As the **Applying Sociology Box** (p. 506) suggests, future attendance may increase.

Civil Religion

There remains in industrial societies "civil religion," a quasi-religious loyalty binding individuals in essentially secular societies. Various patriotic symbols evoke religious feelings, such as the belief that life in Canada is the best in the world. As well, the flag, the national anthem, and social programs infuse most Canadians with a sense of collective identity.

"New Age" Seekers: Spirituality without Formal Religion

An increasing number of people are seeking spiritual development outside established religious organizations. It is about personal "transcendence," rather than accepting a particular doctrine. Meditation and prayer are often the avenues taken to achieve the transcendence.

Religious Revival: "Good Ole-Time Religion"

As mainline churches lose membership, sectlike organizations grow.

Religious Fundamentalism

Religious fundamentalism is a conservative religious doctrine that opposes intellectualism and worldly accommodation in favour of restoring a traditional other-worldly focus. Fundamentalism has spread rapidly in the U.S. and it is often assumed in Canada as well. However, as Bibby suggests, fundamentalist church membership made up 8% of our population in 1871, 1951, and 2001.

Five characteristics identify fundamentalists: a literal interpretation of scripture, less tolerance for religious diversity, an emphasis on the personal experience of God's presence, an adversity to secularisation, and an endorsement of conservative political goals.

➢The Electronic Church

Fundamentalist churches have made substantial use of the mass media. The **Media Perspectives Box** (p. 511) examines the more recent practice of finding God online.

LOOKING AHEAD: RELIGION IN THE TWENTY-FIRST CENTURY

Secularization is not squeezing out religion from our society. If anything, processes of change appear to be creating more need for religious faith. The **Thinking It Through Box** (p. 512) examines the tension between religion and science.

KEY CONCEPTS

Define each of the following concepts on a separate sheet of paper. Check the accuracy of your answers by referring to the text, as well as by referring to italicized definitions located throughout the chapter.

animism
charisma
church
civil religion
cult
denomination
faith
fundamentalism
liberation theology
monotheism
polytheism
profane
religion
religiosity
ritual
sacred
sect
secularization
state church
totem

STUDY QUESTIONS

True-False

1. T F Faith is belief anchored in conviction rather than scientific evidence.

2. T F Marx suggested religion was the opium of the people.

3. T F According to Weber, Calvinism was a key factor in the development of capitalism in Western Europe.

4. T F In organizational terms sects are more formal than churches.

5. T F Christianity is an example of polytheism.

6. T F In Arabic, the word *Islam* means both "submission" and "peace."

7. T F Canada, unlike most of the Western democracies, has never been guilty of anti-

Semitism.

8. T F — Eastern religions tend to make less clearcut distinctions between the sacred and the secular.

9. T F — The province in Canada with the highest report of "no religion" is Quebec.

10. T F — Canadian politicians make frequent references to God, while American politicians almost never do.

11. T F — A quasi-religious loyalty binding individuals with a basically secular society is called civil religion.

Multiple Choice

1. ___________, according to Durkheim, is that which is defined as extraordinary, inspiring a sense of awe and reverence.

   (a) The sacred
   (b) The profane
   (c) Religion
   (d) *Jen*

2. A totem—an object imbued with sacred qualities—is characteristically found within which of the following societies?

   (a) technologically simple
   (b) advanced modern
   (c) heathen
   (d) agrarian

3. Liberation theology, developed in the late 1960s, advocates a blending of religion with ______________.

   (a) family
   (b) education
   (c) economy
   (d) politics

4. Which of the following is true of sects?

   (a) They are not different from churches in their social composition.
   (b) They typically attract people of high social standing.
   (c) They do not appeal to people who perceive themselves as outsiders.
   (d) They discount the beliefs of others.
   (e) They do not promise personal fulfilment as the church might.

5. The religious view that elements of the natural world are conscious life forms that affect humanity is called ___________.

(a) religion
(b) ecclesia
(c) animism
(d) charisma
(e) proselytization

6. Because of the high birth rates of its followers, it could become the largest major religion by the end of this century. It is ______________.

(a) Christianity
(b) Islam
(c) Buddhism
(d) Hinduism
(e) Judaism

7. Buddha's teachings were called _______________.

(a) *dharma*
(b) *nirvana*
(c) *moksha*
(d) *dhamma*
(e) *jen*

8. Confucianism still influences the _______________ way of life.

(a) Indian
(b) Chinese
(c) Pakistani
(d) Egyptian
(e) Mesopotamian

9. Which of the following churches in Canada has the largest number of adherents?

(a) Jehovah's Witnesses
(b) Presbyterian
(c) Lutheran
(d) Anglican
(e) United Church

10. Frank Jones has found that ___________of Canada's children attend religious services weekly.

(a) 11% (b) 18% (c) 23% (d) 35% (e) 56%

11. An increasing number of people are seeking spiritual development outside established religious organizations. This has led some analysts to say: "Are we becoming a _________________ society?"

(a) quasi-religious
(b) secularized
(c) non-religious
(d) fundamentalist
(e) postdenomination

Fill in the Blank

1. Durkheim labelled the ordinary elements of everyday life the ________________.

2. Karl Marx claimed that religion serves ____________ by legitimizing the status quo.

3. John Calvin advanced the doctrine of ______________.

4. A______________ is a church, independent of the state, that accepts religious pluralism.

5. A belief in many Gods is referred to as _________________.

6. Most Christians live in ______________ or the ___________.

7. ______ is the second largest religion in the world, with 1.2 billion followers who are called ____________.

8. ______________ differs from most other religions by not being linked to the life of any single person.

9. A historical trend away from the supernatural and the sacred is referred to as ___________________.

10. In 1951 and in 2001 _________ churches made up 8% of our population.

11. In 1992, the Catholic Church conceded that the church had erred in silencing __________.

Definition and Short Answers

1. Is sociology a threat to religious institutions?

2. What are the three major theoretical sociological perspectives on the role of religion in society?

3. What does Max Weber say about the development of capitalism in Western Europe?

4. What is the major difference between sects and cults?

5. Identify the major characteristics of the world religions.

6. What is the position of religion in contemporary society?

7. How does the development of "civil religion" or "new age seekers" relate to the secularization process?

8. What will religiosity look like in the Canada of 2010?

9. What is the likelihood of the development of a cyber-church?

Answers to Study Questions

True-False

1. T (p. 493)
2. T (p. 494)
3. T (p. 495)
4. F (p. 497)
5. F (p. 499)
6. T (p. 499)
7. F (p. 502)
8. T (p. 504)
9. F (p. 505)
10. F (p. 505)
11. T (p. 508)

Multiple Choice

1. a (p. 492)
2. a (p. 493)
3. d (p. 495)
4. d (p. 497)
5. c (p. 498)
6. b (p. 499)
7. d (p. 502)
8. b (p. 503)
9. e (p. 504)
10. c (p. 506)
11. e (p. 508)

Fill in the Blank

1. profane (p. 492)
2. ruling elites (p.494)
3. predestination (p. 495)
4. denomination (p. 497)
5. polytheism (p. 499)
6. Europe, Americas (p. 499)
7. Islam, Muslims (p. 499)
8. Hinduism (p. 502)
9. secularization (p. 507)
10. evangelical (p. 509)
11. Galileo (p. 512)

ANALYSIS AND COMMENT

Go back through the chapter and write down in the spaces below key points from each of the following boxes.

THINKING ABOUT DIVERSITY

"Religion and Patriarchy: Does God Favour Males?"
Key Points:

APPLYING SOCIOLOGY

"Religion in Canada: Decline or Renaissance?"
Key Points:

MEDIA PERSPECTIVES

"Check the Media: Religion is Hot!"
Key Points:

THINKING IT THROUGH

"Does Science Threaten Religion?"
Key Points:

SUGGESTED READINGS

Classic Source

Max Weber. 1958. *The Protestant Ethic and the Spirit of Capitalism.* New York: Charles Scribner's Sons.
This is the classic account of the power of religion to effect sweeping social change.

W.E. Mann. 1955. *Sect, Cult and Church in Alberta.* Toronto: University of Toronto Press.
This is the first sociological study of religion in Canada. It focuses on the growth of various religious groups in Alberta between the 1920s and 1940s.

Contemporary Sources

Helen Rose Ebaugh. 1993. *Women in the Vanishing Cloister: Organizational Decline in Catholic Religious Orders in the United States.* New Brunswick, N.J.: Rutgers University Press.
This account, written by a nun-turned-sociologist, explores the drop in the number of women in Catholic religious orders since the 1960s.

Wade Clark Roof. 1992. *A Generation of Seekers: The Spiritual Journeys of the Baby Boom Generation.* New York: HarperCollins.
Mounting evidence points to a return to religion for many members of the generation of young people who came of age in the 1960s.

Canadian Sources

Tom Harpur. 1994. *The Uncommon Touch: An Investigation of Spiritual Healing.* Toronto: McClelland & Stewart.
This is a review of spiritual healing from a historical and cross-cultural perspective.

Reginald W. Bibby. 1987. *Fragmented Gods: The Poverty and Potential of Religion in Canada.* Toronto: Irwin.
This is a comprehensive analysis of religion in Canada based on three national surveys conducted in 1975, 1980, and 1985.

George A. Mori. 1990. *Religious Affiliation in Canada: Canadian Social Trends.* Ottawa: Statistics Canada.
This is a government publication that provides a demographic review of religion in Canada.

John R. Williams, ed. 1984. *Canadian Churches and Social Justice.* Toronto: Lorimer.
This book examines views on social justice of a variety of religious groups in Canada.

Reginald W. Bibby. 1993. *Unknown Gods.* Toronto: Stoddart.
This book explains why Canadian churches are in a state of decline and makes some future predictions.

Global Sources

Richard W. Bulliet. 1994. *Islam: The View From the Edge.* New York: Columbia University Press.
Although the heart of Islam lies in the Middle East, Muslims live in North America and around the world. This book examines how Islam differs in its central and peripheral settings.

Christian Smith. 1991. *The Emergence of Liberation Theology: Radical Religion and Social Movement Theory.* Chicago: University of Chicago Press.
This account of liberation theology among politically active Catholics during the 1960s assesses the movement's successes and failures.

CHAPTER 20

Education

CHAPTER OUTLINE

I. **Education: A Global Survey**
   - A. Schooling and Economic Development
   - B. Schooling in India
   - C. Schooling in Japan
   - D. Schooling in the United Kingdom
   - E. Schooling in Canada

II. **The Functions of Schooling**
   - A. Socialization
   - B. Cultural Innovation
   - C. Social Integration
   - D. Social Placement
   - E. Latent Functions of Schooling

III. **Schooling and Social Interaction**
   - A. The Self-Fulfilling Prophecy

IV. **Schooling and Social Inequality**
   - A. Social Control
   - B. Standardized Testing
   - C. Streaming and Social Inequality
   - D. Access to Higher Education
   - E. Privilege and Personal Merit

V. **Problems in Schools**
   - A. School Discipline
   - B. Dropping Out
   - C. Academic Standards
   - D. Home Schooling
   - E. Education and the World of Work

VI. **Education: Looking Ahead**

VII. **Making the Grade**

VIII. **Key Points**

IX. **Key Concepts**

X. **Applications and Exercises**

XI. **MySocLab**

LEARNING OBJECTIVES

- To understand how the role of education changes in response to economic development
- To compare and contrast schooling in the United Kingdom, Japan, India, and Canada
- To identify and describe the functions of schooling
- To understand how school is affected by social interaction
- To explain how education supports social inequality through social control, standardized testing, and streaming
- To describe the problems associated with unequal access to higher education
- To identify and analyze the problems facing Canadian education today: discipline, dropout rates, academic standards, home schooling, and the relationship between education and the world of work
- To describe the changes in society that the educational system will have to face, namely an increasingly diverse population, a revolution in technology, and a global political and economic restructuring

CHAPTER REVIEW

We are introduced to the possibility that Aboriginal Canadians, who receive their education on reserves, will not be successful in the modern Canadian economy. On the other hand, urban Aboriginal people who finish high school fare well in education and occupational opportunities.

This chapter focuses upon ***education***, the social institution through which society provides its members with important knowledge, including basic facts, job skills, and cultural norms and values. This is accomplished through ***schooling***, formal instruction under the direction of specially trained teachers.

EDUCATION: A GLOBAL SURVEY

Schooling and Economic Development

In low- and middle-income countries, families teach young people important knowledge. Formal schooling is available to few. As a result about one-third of the world's people cannot read or write. **Global Map 20-1** (p. 520) shows the extent of illiteracy around the world.

Schooling in India

Although India has recently become a middle-income country, less than half of its population go on to secondary school. There is also a gender differential with 30% of the girls and 45% of the boys reaching the secondary grades. Therefore most of the children working in factories are girls.

Schooling in Japan

Mandatory education laws began in 1872. The cultural values of tradition and family are stressed in the early grades. In their early teens, students begin to face the rigorous and competitive exams of the Japanese system. Test scores determine whether a person will go to university or college, rich and poor alike. Some 96% of Japanese students graduate from high school, a much higher rate than Canada. However, only 50% go on to the postsecondary level, compared to 55% in Canada. There is tremendous pressure on students to be successful in exams for postsecondary attendance, but Japanese students outperform students in every other high-income country.

Schooling in the United Kingdom

Schooling in Great Britain has long been associated with the elite. Traditional social distinctions still exist, with many children from wealthy families attending public schools, the equivalent of our private boarding schools. Expansion of the university system has allowed all children to compete for Britain's government-funded university system. However, graduates of the elite schools of Oxford and Cambridge have considerable economic and political power in Britain. Quite clearly, the examples from India, Japan, and Great Britain indicate how social and cultural patterns help shape educational participation.

Schooling in Canada

In Canada, church-controlled schools were started in the early French settlements and by 1636, the Jesuits started a college which became Laval University. Gradually other universities were added in English Canada and boarding schools became the first step in a secondary school system. Prior to Confederation, both Catholic and Protestant school systems were in place and by 1920, compulsory education to 16 years of age was adopted. Mass education was, in part, a response to the requirements for a skilled and literate workforce.

But, official literacy and functional literacy are not the same. While absolute illiteracy has been minimized in industrial societies, ***functional illiteracy***, a lack of reading and writing skills needed for everyday living, is a reality for some. The **Thinking It Through Box** (p. 522) deals with this issue. Even so, educational attainment has grown tremendously. Between 1961 and 1986 the proportion of Canadians between 25 and 44 years of age with some postsecondary education has moved from 8% to 55% and in 2001, 15.2% of Canadians had completed university degrees.

In the 1800s in Canada, education was seen as a precondition to economic growth and widespread participation was the goal. Full public funding for elementary and secondary education has gradually been established in both the public and Catholic systems. Although government support has declined, 30% of funding for colleges and universities is still supplied by government.

Canada ranks only behind Sweden in public expenditures for education, however, Canada is behind both the U.S. and the Netherlands in proportion of citizens with university degrees. See **Figure 20-1** (p. 521) for this information.

Canada has long valued a ***practical*** education. The educational philosophy of John Dewey played a role in this development. Despite this, Canada is lagging behind many other nations in number of engineering degrees awarded. There is some recent change as engineering, mathematics, and science degrees increase while social sciences and humanities degrees decline.

THE FUNCTIONS OF SCHOOLING

Structural-functional analysis focuses our attention on the functions that educational systems satisfy for society.

Socialization

As societies become more technologically advanced, social institutions must emerge beyond the family to help socialize members of the society to become functioning adults. Important lessons on cultural values and norms are learned in schools at all levels, along with basic mathematical and language skills. As compared to the United States, the Canadian classroom focuses on co-operative activities and the celebration of diversity.

Cultural Innovation

Education is not merely a transmission of culture; it is also a factor in the creation of culture through critical inquiry and research. Marshall McLuhan foresaw the use of the electronic media to create classrooms without walls.

Social Integration

Through the teaching of certain cultural values and norms, people become more unified. This is a particularly critical function in culturally diverse societies.

This social integration has met with mixed success, however, in Canada and elsewhere. What is recognized is that education is necessary for success, and while cultural traditions can be protected, certain linguistic and other skills must be learned in order to survive in the larger society. In a bilingual society, French is a useful occupational tool, and the response has been an increase in French immersion programs, but enrolments are quite low.

Social Placement

Schooling operates as a screening device to place people in the society according to their aptitudes and abilities. Ideally the "brightest and best" take the challenging tasks.

Latent Functions of Schooling

Schools serve as babysitters for younger children, and by occupying the time of teenagers keeps them from engaging in higher rates of socially disruptive behaviours. Lasting relationships are also established in school.

The structural-functionalists stress the ways in which education supports the operation of the industrial economy. One weakness of this approach, however, is that it fails to focus on how the quality of education varies greatly for different groups of people.

SCHOOLING AND SOCIAL INTERACTION

Stereotypes can shape what goes on in the classroom.

The Self-Fulfilling Prophecy

If you are told often enough that you are inferior, you may come to believe it and your performance in school may well deteriorate.

A problem with this approach is that a person or persons may not accept the definition of inferiority.

SCHOOLING AND SOCIAL INEQUALITY

Social-conflict analysis views schooling as a perpetuation of social stratification in Canada. It is clear that gender, race, and ethnicity have been good predictors of participation rates and subjects studied. There has, however, been a real effort in recent years to rid curriculum and textbooks of gender bias and negative racial or ethnic stereotypes. Certainly women have increased their participation rates at the postsecondary level. Social class is linked to educational aspirations and the opportunity to use computers in the home.

Regional variations in educational attainment are outlined in **Canada Map 20-1**, p. 527.

Social Control

Social-conflict analysis views social control as an outcome of schooling because youth are socialized to accept the status quo. The term ***hidden curriculum*** refers to the content of schooling that subtly espouses certain ideas. Compliance, punctuality, and discipline are part of the hidden curriculum, which are seen to support the capitalist system.

Standardized Testing

Standardized tests have traditionally been used for streaming and placement purposes. These tests, however, are weighted in favour of those students from middle- and upper-class backgrounds.

Streaming and Social Inequality

Streaming is the assignment of students to different types of educational programs. The idea is to provide education appropriate to a student's aspirations and aptitudes. Critics suggest that streaming simply replicates the stratification system, students from affluent families expect to be in university-bound streams and those from modest backgrounds expect to learn a trade. Many schools are now more cautious about streaming, but there is some concern among the parents of university-bound children who feel the de-streamed classroom will result in lower quality education.

Access to Higher Education

In Canada and other industrial societies, higher education is regarded as the path to occupational achievement. **Figure 20-2** (p. 528) shows the number of years of education beyond the age of 15 for selected OECD countries. **Figure 20-3** (p. 528) indicates a dramatic upturn in university enrolment in Canada since the year 1993.

The reasons young people do not attend include finding a job after high school, the expense involved in living in a university city, or being convinced that they cannot be successful. The barriers against women appear to have disappeared since female enrolment is now higher than for males. The **Applying Sociology Box** (p. 534) discusses various factors that have an impact on educational attainment. **Figure 20-4** (p. 529) demonstrates that the highest levels of educational attainment are achieved by Japanese and Chinese people in Canada, while the lowest levels are for Aboriginal peoples. The **Thinking About Diversity Box** (pp. 532-533) addresses this issue.

Clearly, educational attainment is positively related to both employment success and average yearly income as illustrated in **Figure 20-5** and **Table 20-1** on page 530.

Privilege and Personal Merit

An important theme of social-conflict analysis is that schooling turns social privilege into personal merit. University is seen as a rite of passage for children of wealthier families, while children from modest beginnings must struggle to overcome the lack of resources. The **Applying Sociology Box** (p. 534) demonstrates that family structure and parents' educational achievement are strong predictors of educational attainment.

The social-conflict approach focuses on education in terms of social inequality. However, it ignores the social mobility provided by education and the challenge to the system offered in educational curricula. The **Applying Theory Table** (p. 531) summarizes the three theoretical approaches to understanding education.

PROBLEMS IN SCHOOLS

Canadians are increasingly concerned with the quality of education their children are receiving.

School Discipline

There is a concern with discipline in Canadian schools. Assaults upon students and teachers are common, but the largest concern is with the lack of respect shown to teachers whose major task is often a matter of maintaining control.

Dropping Out

The dropout rate in Canada has declined considerably in the last few years. It is currently at 9.8%. Since employers are unlikely to hire high school dropouts, we can expect to see the rate drop further. The rates vary by province, but all are headed downward.

Academic Standards

There has been a growing concern in the United States and Canada about a decline in educational standards. Few students write or think in complex ways and many high school graduates are functionally illiterate. (See the **Thinking It Through Box**, p. 522.) Canadians fare poorly on international tests, but many countries have only their elite students take such tests. Nonetheless, the feeling persists that Canadian standards of academic excellence have declined in recent years.

Home Schooling

Home schooling in the past was practised primarily by parents who wanted their children to experience a strongly religious upbringing. Increasingly, it is practised by parents who believe the schools are not doing a good job. These are mostly affluent parents who will pool their academic resources with other parents so each specializes in what he or she knows best. Home-schooled children outperform those who learn in school. The **Media Perspectives Box** (p. 536) shows the development in online learning, which has implications for home schooling.

Education and the World of Work

While its clear that the educational system must develop technical skills in students, what seems to be missing is the development of skills to integrate and use information, adapt to change, take reasonable risks, and conceptualize the future.

EDUCATION: LOOKING AHEAD

In a society characterized by diversity, in the midst of a technological revolution and competing in a global economy, the educational institution must be a catalyst, an adaptive mechanism, and a force for maintaining continuity in a period of change. While computers and the internet can improve the overall quality of learning, they are not a panacea nor a replacement for a plan to provide quality universal schooling. Look at the **Thinking Critically Box** (p. 537) for another view on educational open-mindedness being challenged by political correctness.

KEY CONCEPTS

Define each of the following concepts on a separate sheet of paper. Check the accuracy of your answer by referring to the text, as well as by referring to italicized definitions located throughout the chapter.

education
functional illiteracy
hidden curriculum
schooling
streaming

STUDY QUESTIONS

True-False

1. T F In the poorest nations of the world, just half of all children attend secondary school.

2. T F In mathematics and science, Japanese students outperform students in every other high-income country.

3. T F By 2001, 22.5% of Canadians possessed university degrees.

4. T F Although Canada produces few engineers compared to societies like Japan and Germany, there is a clear shift toward engineering, math, and science degrees.

5. T F In Canadian schools as opposed to American schools, there is less emphasis on a unified cultural identity, and more on respect for the many cultures that make up the Canadian mosaic.

6. T F When students and teachers in a school system come to believe that one race is academically superior to another, the ensuing behaviour is likely to be a self-fulfilling prophecy.

7. T F Hidden curriculum refers to categorically assigning students to different types of education programs.

8. T F Women are now more likely than men to attend university.

9. T F Aboriginal children are now as likely to finish university as English and French children.

10. T F Average earnings in 2001 were highest in Alberta.

11. T F The dropout rate from high school is higher in urban areas of Canada.

12. T F Parents with university degrees are much more likely to read to their children.

Multiple Choice

1. Which of the following countries has the highest level of public expenditures on education?

   (a) U.S.A.
   (b) Canada
   (c) Australia
   (d) Sweden
   (e) Portugal

2. About ______________ % of Canadians have difficulty recognizing familiar words or doing simple addition and subtraction.

   (a) 5 (b) 7 (c) 10 (d) 15 (e) 25

3. John Dewey endorsed ______________, which reflected people's changing concerns and needs.

   (a) functional education
   (b) private schools
   (c) progressive education
   (d) cultural integration
   (e) affiliative education

4. Which of the following functions of formal education help to forge a population into a single, unified society?

   (a) socialization
   (b) social integration
   (c) social placement
   (d) cultural innovation

5. In which province or territory is the highest university completion level?

   (a) Quebec
   (b) Ontario
   (c) Alberta
   (d) British Columbia
   (e) Northwest Territories

6. The subtle presentation of political or cultural ideas in the classroom is called _______________.

   (a) the hidden curriculum
   (b) streaming
   (c) social placement
   (d) cultural innovation
   (e) persuasion

7. Enrolment at Canadian universities recorded its strongest increase in twenty-eight years in 2003-2004. Which of the following are reasons for that increase?

   (a) A rise in the number of students aged 18-24
   (b) Ontario's double cohort
   (c) An increased number of students from other countries
   (d) All of the above
   (e) None of the above

8. Which of the following groups in Canada has the highest level of university degree completion?

   (a) English
   (b) French
   (c) Black
   (d) Japanese
   (e) Aboriginal

9. Which Canadian province offered to pay for educational upgrading if employers found the skills of a high school graduate wanting?

   (a) Ontario
   (b) Alberta
   (c) New Brunswick
   (d) Prince Edward Island
   (e) Nova Scotia

10. The skills most in demand and shortest in supply in Canadian university students going to the job market are _______________.

   (a) using a computer
   (b) the ability to integrate and use information
   (c) the capacity to adapt to change
   (d) (a and b above)
   (e) (b and c above)

Fill in the Blank

1. In India, only about ____________ of the people are literate.

2. Many wealthy families in England send their children to what the British call ____________________, the equivalent to Canadian private boarding schools.

3. Canada ranks second to ________________ in the proportion of 20-24 year olds enrolled in postsecondary education.

4. The __________ and __________ communities have higher levels of educational attainment than the English or the French.

5. ____________________ schools are now seen as a significant factor in the oppression of Aboriginal children.

6. Children from families with _______________ are the most likely to complete high school.

7. The __________ people experience a 45% dropout rate from school.

8. Students who learn at ________ , outperform those who learn in ___________.

9. For years, the top-achieving students in the Toronto public school system have been ___________.

10. Many think that the open-mindedness of universities is being compromised by _________________________.

Definition and Short Answer

1. Describe the four basic functions of education as reviewed in the text.

2. What are the latent functions of schooling?

3. Describe the three theoretical approaches to understanding education.

4. What are the relationships between level of schooling and employment?

5. What are the major problems in the school system?

6. How must education change in order to fit more readily with the world of work?

7. Compare the educational systems of Canada, Japan, Great Britain, and India.

8. How have Aboriginal peoples been disadvantaged by the educational system in Canada?

Answers to Study Questions

True-False

1. T (p. 519)
2. T (p. 519)
3. F (p. 521)
4. T (p. 523)
5. T (p. 523)
6. T (p. 526)
7. F (p. 527)
8. T (p. 529)
9. F (p. 529)
10. F (p. 530)
11. F (p. 533)
12. T (p. 534)

Multiple Choice

1. d (p. 521)
2. d (p. 522)
3. c (p. 523)
4. b (p. 524)
5. b (p. 527)
6. a (p. 527)
7. d (pp. 528-529)
8. d (p. 529)
9. c (p. 536)
10. e (p. 537)

Fill in the Blank

1. 39% (p. 519)
2. public schools (p. 520)
3. United States (521)
4. Chinese, Japanese (p. 529)
5. residential (pp. 532-533)
6. Both biological parents (p. 534)
7. Aboriginal (p. 533)
8. home, school (p. 535)
9. Asian (p. 534)
10. political correctness (p. 537)

ANALYSIS AND COMMENT

Go back through the chapter and write down in the space below key points from each of the following boxes.

THINKING IT THROUGH

"Functional Illiteracy: Must We Rethink Education?"
Key Points:

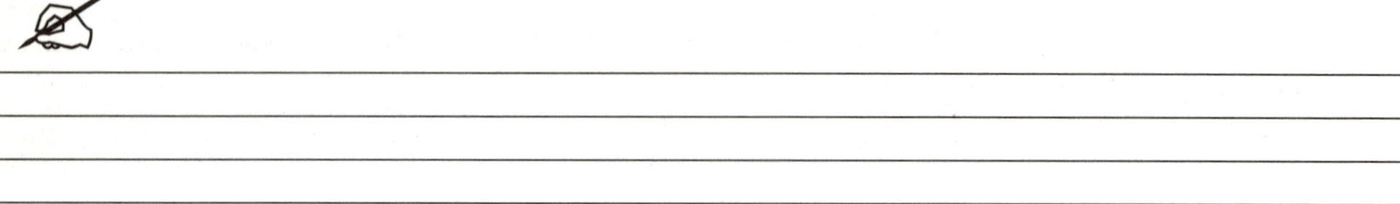

THINKING ABOUT DIVERSITY

"Aboriginal Education: The Legacy of Canada's Residential Schools"
Key Points:

APPLYING SOCIOLOGY

"Explaining Educational Attainment"
Key Points:

MEDIA PERSPECTIVES

"Welcome to Cyber-School"
Key Points:

THINKING CRITICALLY

"Is Political Correctness Undermining Education?"
Key Points:

SUGGESTED READINGS

Classic Source

John Dewey. 1963; orig. 1938. *Experience and Education.* New York: Collier.
In this short book—originally presented as a series of lectures—Dewey sketches his vision of progressive education.

Contemporary Sources

Allan Bloom. 1987. *The Closing of the American Mind: How Higher Education Has Failed Democracy and Impoverished the Souls of Today's Students.* New York: Simon & Schuster.
Dinesh D'Souza. 1991. *Illiberal Education: The Politics of Race and Sex on Campus.* New York: The Free Press.
The first of these books is a best-seller that helped launch the current debate over "political correctness" on the university campus. The second echoes these conservative sentiments, indicting "PC" for undermining higher education.

Dorothy C. Holland and Margaret A. Eisenhart. 1990. *Educated in Romance: Women, Achievement, and College Culture.* Chicago: University of Chicago Press.
These researchers investigate how a "culture of romance" erodes the career aspirations of women on university campuses.

Canadian Sources

Ratna Ghosh and Douglas Ray, eds. 1991. *Social Change and Education in Canada.* Toronto: Harcourt Brace Jovanovich.
This is an excellent reader for detailed and concise explorations of current educational issues.

John Porter, Marion Porter, and Bernard R. Blishen. 1982. *Stations and Callings.* Toronto: Methuen.
This report of a large-scale cross-sectional study argues that Canada' s meritocratic educational system does not benefit the majority of working-class children.

Terry Wotherspoon, ed. 1987. *The Political Economy of Canadian Schooling.* Toronto: Methuen.
This collection of articles approaches the sociology of education from a critical perspective, showing how schools perpetuate inequalities.

Sid Gilbert, Lynn Barr, Warren Clark, Mathew Blue, and Deborah Sunter. 1993. *Leaving School.* Ottawa: Government of Canada.
A national survey comparing school leavers and high school graduates on a wide range of variables is the basis of this provocative publication.

Global Source

Nelly P. Stromquist, ed. 1992. *Women and Education in Latin America: Knowledge, Power and Change.* Boulder, CO: Lynne Rienner.
This book is a collection of thirteen essays that focus on the educational opportunities for women in this important world region.

CHAPTER 21

Health and Medicine

CHAPTER OUTLINE

I. **What is Health?**
  - A. Health and Society

II. **Health: A Global Survey**
  - A. Health in History
  - B. Health in Low-Income Countries
  - C. Health in High-Income Countries

III. **Health in Canada**
  - A. Who is Healthy? Age, Gender, Class, and Race
  - B. Age and Gender
  - C. Social Class and Race
  - D. Cigarette Smoking
  - E. Eating Disorders
  - F. Obesity
  - G. Sexually Transmitted Diseases
    1. Gonorrhea and Syphilis
    2. Genital Herpes
    3. Acquired Immune Deficiency Syndrome (AIDS)
  - H. Ethical Issues Surrounding Death
    1. When Does Death Occur?
    2. Do People Have a Right to Die?
    3. What about Mercy Killing?

IV. **The Medical Establishment**
  - A. The Rise of Scientific Medicine
  - B. Holistic Medicine
  - C. Paying for Medical Care: A Global Survey
  - D. Medicine in Socialist Nations
  - E. Medicine in Capitalist Nations
  - F. Medicine in Canada
  - G. The Shortage of Nurses
  - H. Canadian Women in Medicine

V. **Theoretical Analysis of Health and Medicine**
  - A. Structural-Functional Analysis: Role Theory
    1. The Sick Role
    2. The Physician's Role
  - B. Symbolic-Interaction Analysis: The Meaning of Health
    1. The Social Construction of Illness
    2. The Social Construction of Treatment
  - C. Social-Conflict Analysis: Health and Inequality
    1. Access to Care
    2. The Profit Motive
    3. Medicine as Politics

LEARNING OBJECTIVES

- To understand the ways in which the health of a population is shaped by society's cultural patterns, its technology and social resources, and its social inequality
- To know the ways that health differs historically and in low- and high-income countries today
- To explain how age, gender, race, and social class affect the level of health of individuals in our society
- To identify and describe the issues of eating disorders, obesity, cigarette smoking, and sexually transmitted diseases to world health today and very recently the issues of SARS, West Nile and mad cow
- To explain the ethical issues related to dying and death
- To compare and contrast scientific medicine with holistic medicine
- To compare and contrast medical care in socialist and capitalist societies
- To understand the characteristics of Canada's health care system, including the increasing number of female physicians
- To describe, compare, and contrast the three sociological paradigms and their contributions to understanding health and medicine

CHAPTER REVIEW

The chapter opens with a description of a contemporary health crisis, obesity. The long-term impact upon the health of individuals and the health care system because of the high consumption of large quantities of high-fat food will be immense.

WHAT IS HEALTH?

Health is defined as a state of complete physical, mental, and social well-being. Therefore, it is viewed as much a ***social*** as a ***biological*** issue.

Health and Society

Health is shaped by several factors in a society: its cultural patterns, such as standards of health and ideas of moral goodness, its technological development, and level of inequality Canada has universal medical coverage, where costs are covered by the state, but the rich have better physical and mental health than the poor. A cultural emphasis on masculinity may lead to illness in Canada. See the **Applying Sociology Box** (p. 543).

HEALTH: A GLOBAL SURVEY

Health in History

Health as a social issue is demonstrated by the significant increase in well-being over the course of history. The simple technology of hunting and gathering societies made it difficult to maintain a healthful environment. As many as one-half of the people in such societies died by age twenty, and few lived passed the age of forty.

The agricultural revolution increased surpluses, but also inequality, so only the elite enjoyed better health. Urbanization during mediaeval times created horrible health problems.

Health in Low-Income Countries

Abject poverty leads to poor nutrition and is linked to poor sanitation, contaminated drinking water, and infectious diseases. Combined with a lack of trained medical personnel, health is poor and life expectancy low for most residents of low-income countries. In some countries, half the children never reach adulthood. When medical technologies are introduced to these countries and infectious diseases are reduced, the population often soars, bringing on yet more poverty.

Health in High-Income Countries

Early industrialization was characterized by crowded, filthy cities where disease was rampant. By the late 1800s, medical advances reduced the impact of infectious diseases and sewer systems were separated from drinking water. In the longer term industrialization has delayed death considerably; although the diseases of affluence, cancer and heart disease, are very much with us.

HEALTH IN CANADA

Canada enjoys good health by international standards, but look at the **Thinking It Through Box** (p. 545) for some discussion of recent health crises in Canada.

Who Is Healthy? Age, Gender, Class, and Race

Social epidemiology is the study of how health and disease are distributed throughout a society's population. The links among health and physical and social environments are examined.

Age and Gender

Death is rare among young Canadians, but we have seen an increase in accidental deaths and death from AIDS. Many children today have poor diets and exercise patterns that will likely make them heart patients in the future. An increasing portion of adults see their health as good. See **Table 21-1** (p. 546).

Social Class and Race

The richest children in Canada enjoy very good health but the poorest, especially Aboriginal children, are as vulnerable as the children in low-income countries. **Table 21-2** (p. 546) shows that death rates and infant mortality rates are much higher for Aboriginal peoples than other Canadians. As well, affluent Canadians and immigrants enjoy better health than other Canadians.

Cigarette Smoking

Cigarette smoking is the leading preventable cause of illness and death in Canada and is increasingly seen as deviant behaviour. The percentage of smokers has declined from 45% in 1960 to 21.5% in 2001. (See **Canada Map 21-1**, p. 547 for provincial smoking rates.)

Smoking is estimated to be responsible for one-quarter of the deaths of men and women between 35 and 84 years of age. Lung cancer rates for women are almost as high as the rates for breast cancer and pregnant women who smoke put their fetus at risk. Tobacco companies have conceded that smoking is harmful to health but they continue to market tobacco products in other countries. Sponsorship of sporting events by tobacco companies has ended in Canada and smoke-free environments are increasingly supported by legislation in some provinces.

Eating Disorders

These disorders involve intense forms of weight control in order to become very thin. Ninety-five percent are women and most are White and middle class. The cultural ideal of thinness for women is espoused by affluent families and the mass media, who provide unrealistic standards of beauty.

Obesity

Obesity rates for children and adults in Canada have been rising rapidly such that 8% of children and 23% of adults are now obese. Once people are overweight, few manage to take it off and they are at increased risk of heart disease, stroke, and diabetes. The causes of this problem are fairly obvious; lack of exercise, high fat and salt diets, and larger serving portions.

Sexually Transmitted Diseases

Increased concern about sexually transmitted diseases occurred during the 1960s at the beginning of the "sexual revolution." They are viewed by many as not just an illness, but also a mark of immorality.

Sexually transmitted diseases (STDs) represent an exception to the general decline in infectious diseases during this century.

➢Gonorrhea and Syphilis

These are among the oldest diseases and are almost always transmitted by sexual contact. Gonorrhea can cause sterility and syphilis can damage major organs. Both diseases were on the decline in Canada, but both are on the increase in the last five years.

➢Genital Herpes

This virus infects large numbers of Canadians. Although not as serious as gonorrhea, there is currently no cure available.

➢Acquired Immune Deficiency Syndrome (AIDS)

The most serious sexually transmitted disease is AIDS. It is incurable and almost always fatal, although new drug treatments are extending lives. The first case in Canada was discovered in 1982. By December, 2002, there were 12,674 deaths, 19, 213 people diagnosed with AIDS, and 52,640 diagnosed with HIV, the virus responsible for the weakening of the immune system. There has been some decline since then, probably because of an educational program that promotes safer sex practices such as the use of a latex condom.

Figure 21-1a (p. 550) compares infection routes from the past and the present and there are decreases in homosexual contact and increases in heterosexual contact.

Figure 21-1b (p. 550) shows that acquisition groups have changed greatly. There are large reductions in Whites and large increases for Asians, Blacks, and especially Aboriginal peoples. There is also an increase in cases for women and children.

Globally, some 40 million people have been infected and 8,700 people die each day. In some sub-Saharan African societies, 15 year olds face a 50/50 chance of becoming infected.

HIV is transferred from person to person through blood, semen, or breast milk, so the use of condoms and not sharing needles cuts the level of risk, however abstinence or an exclusive sexual relationship with an uninfected person are the only sure way of avoiding infection.

Ethical Issues Surrounding Death

➢When Does Death Occur?

Medical and legal experts presently define death as an irreversible state involving no response to stimulation, no movement or breathing, no reflexes, and no indication of brain activity.

➢Do People Have a Right to Die?

The Sue Rodriguez case in B.C. goes to the heart of the issue of whether people have a right to die. The current Criminal Code retains a prohibition against assisting a suicide, but Rodriguez, who had Lou Gehrig's disease and little time to live, wished for a physician-assisted death when she neared the end. The Supreme Court of Canada ruled against her request. In the end an anonymous physician helped her to die.

➢What about Mercy Killing?

Euthanasia, assisting in the death of a person suffering from an incurable disease, is a contentious issue in Canada. Support for passive euthanasia is growing but active euthanasia provokes controversy, as the Robert Latimer case indicates. He is now serving a ten-year prison term for murdering his daughter.

THE MEDICAL ESTABLISHMENT

Medicine is a social institution for combating disease and improving health. For most of human history, the individual and family were responsible for health care. In pre-industrial societies, traditional healers, from herbalists to acupuncturists, provided for the health needs of their society's members. Medicine emerges within technologically complex societies as people fill specialized roles as healers.

The Rise of Scientific Medicine

Scientific medicine dominates health care in Canada, meaning the logic of science is applied to research and treatment of disease and injury.

In colonial Canada, medicine was the domain of herbalists, druggists, midwives, and ministers. These medical people knew little by today's standards and the surgeons of the time probably killed as many as they saved.

Gradually specialists came to know more about anatomy, physiology, and biochemistry, and medicine came under self-regulating medical societies. Doctors established the General Council of Medical Education and Registration in Upper Canada in 1865 and the Canadian Medical Association in 1867. By these activities they won control of the certification process and relegated other health practitioners, such as naturopaths to fringe roles.

Medicine became a male, higher social level background preserve. Even in 1992, more than 80% of physicians were men and 97% of nurses were women.

Holistic Medicine

Holistic medicine is an approach to health care that emphasizes prevention of illness and takes account of the whole person within a physical and social environment. The following are major concerns of the holistic approach: patients are people, individual responsibility for health is stressed instead of dependency on medicine, a personal treatment environment is sought, and the goal of holistic medicine is optimum health for all by concentrating on health rather than disease.

Medicine in Socialist Nations

In societies like the People's Republic of China and the former Soviet Union, government directly controls medical care. Medical costs are paid for by public funds, and medical care is distributed equally among all.

The People's Republic of China is still a relatively poor agrarian society that is just beginning to industrialize. With over 1 billion people, reaching everyone within one system is difficult. Barefoot doctors, equivalent to paramedics in America, bring modern methods to millions of rural residents in China, but traditional healing arts remain strong.

The former Soviet Union is struggling to formulate a new medical care system within the switch from a state-dominated economy to a market system. Currently people receive their care at a local government health facility. Physicians, mainly women, are poorly paid and the health care system is in crisis, providing standardized, impersonal care.

Medicine in Capitalist Nations

In capitalist societies citizens provide for health care with their own resources with varying levels of government assistance.

In Sweden there is a socialized medical system where the system and the facilities are owned and operated by the government and most physicians are salaried employees.

Britain has a dual system where everyone is eligible for care provided by the National Health Service, but where private care can be purchased.

Japan has a private system where most of the costs are covered by government or privately run plans. (See **Figure 21-2**, p. 556 for the extent of "socialized medicine" in various countries.)

For the most part, medicine in the United States is a private, profit-making industry where more money brings better care. It is called a ***direct-fee system*** where patients pay directly for the services of physicians and hospitals. The poor in the US fare badly compared to their counterparts in Europe and Canada, accounting for the relatively high death rates among both infants and adults. It is the most expensive medical care system in the world, yet leaves 16% of Americans with no medical insurance at all.

Medicine in Canada

The governments pay doctors and hospitals, which operate privately, for the services they provide according to a schedule of fees set annually after consultation with professional medical associations. See the **Media Perspectives Box** (pp. 558-559) for a discussion of multiple payers and the possibility of a two-tier system developing.

In 1961 the Hall Commission on Health Service recommended a health scheme with universality, portability, comprehensive coverage, and administered on a non-profit basis. This plan was adopted across Canada in 1972.

The Canadian system has the advantage of providing care to everyone at a societal cost less than that which exists in the U.S.

The Shortage of Nurses

There is a shortage of nurses in North America and Canadian nurses are actively recruited by the United States, exacerbating the problem here. Enrolments in nursing programmes have dropped because women have expanded occupational opportunities more and many nurses leave the profession because of difficult working conditions and lack of recognition from physicians and hospital managers.

Canadian Women in Medicine

While in 1992 more than 80% of physicians were men, now 30.4% of physicians are female and in the youngest cohort (under 35 years) 50.9% are female. See **Table 21-3** (p. 557).

THEORETICAL ANALYSIS OF HEALTH AND MEDICINE

Structural-Functional Analysis: Role Theory

Structural-functionalism provides a view of illness as dysfunctional for society.

➢The Sick Role

The key concept in structural-functionalist analysis of illness is the ***sick role***, or patterns of behaviour that are defined as appropriate for those who are ill. As explained by Talcott Parsons, the sick role has three characteristics: (1) a sick person is exempted from routine responsibilities, (2) a sick person must want to be well, and (3) a sick person must seek competent help.

➢The Physician's Role

Physicians evaluate claims of sickness and use their specialized knowledge to restore patients to normal routines.

Critics suggest that Parson's model does not deal with a more prevention-oriented approach to health and applies to acute rather than chronic illnesses.

Symbolic-Interaction Analysis: The Meaning of Health

Health and medical care are seen as social constructions.

➢The Social Construction of Illness

The health of any person must be put into the context of the general health of the society. The definition of health and healthy lifestyles varies cross-culturally and historically. Further, definitions of illness are negotiated within particular social situations. What may be illness to a person in one situation, may be seen as a mere inconvenience in another..

➢The Social Construction of Treatment

Research by Joan Emerson involving gynaecological exams is used to illustrate how physicians "craft" their physical surroundings to make specific impressions on others.

A problem with the symbolic-interaction approach is that it minimizes an objective sense of health and illness.

Social-Conflict Analysis: Health and Inequality

➢ Access to Care

Social-conflict analysis suggests that capitalist systems allocate health care resources in an unequal fashion. This problem is most obvious in the U.S. where 46 million Americans lack medical coverage.

➢The Profit Motive

It is argued that the profit motive encourages unsafe medical practices, needless tests, unnecessary surgery, and the overprescribing of drugs, rather than focusing on improvement in people's lifestyles.

➢Medicine as Politics

Medicine has not been as politically neutral as it claims when it opposes government-supported health programs, ignores the impact of inequality on health, practises racial and sexual discrimination, and focuses on biological rather than social causes of illness. Clearly, however, gains in health through medicine have happened. The **Applying Theory Table** (p. 561) summarizes the three approaches to health.

HEALTH AND MEDICINE: LOOKING AHEAD

Health and health care are improving, especially in the industrialized world, and people recognize that they can personally influence their health through quitting smoking, eating sensibly, and exercising regularly.

The major problem to be tackled is inequality within societies and between societies as the poor receive less adequate medical care.

Life expectancy in the world as a whole has been improving and the U.S. and Canada have pledged significant amounts for AIDS treatment and research.

Challenges still exist as poor health conditions remain in many poor societies and the possibility of a flu pandemic continues.

The **Thinking Critically Box** (p. 563) looks at the possibility of genetic manipulation to deal with medical challenges.

KEY CONCEPTS

Define each of the following concepts on a separate sheet of paper. Check the accuracy of your answers by referring to the text, as well as by referring to italicized definitions located throughout the chapter.

direct-fee system
eating disorder
health
holistic medicine
medicine
sick role
social epidemiology
socialized medicine
universal medical coverage

STUDY QUESTIONS

True-False

1. T F The health of any population is dependent upon the surrounding societal structures.

2. T F One in six people suffer from serious illness because of poverty in the world.

3. T F Infant mortality is much higher in Aboriginal peoples than in all Canadians.

4. T F Smoking is highest in the province of British Columbia.

5. T F HIV/AIDS infection is increasing in Canada among women, children, and Aboriginal peoples.

6. T F The incidence of HIV infection in predominantly Muslim nations is extremely low.

7. T F In Russia, 70% of physicians are women.

8. T F Health expenditures in Canada have dropped between 1993 and 2000 as measured by percentage of GNP.

9. T F The "social construction of treatment" of illness is a product of the structural-functional theory.

10. T F AIDS in Canada increasingly afflicts the poor.

Multiple Choice

1. Which of the following is ***not*** one of the ways in which society shapes health as outlined in your text?

   (a) People judge their health as compared to others.
   (b) People pronounce as "healthy" what they hold to be morally good.
   (c) Cultural standards of health change over time.
   (d) Health relates to a society's technology.
   (e) Health relates to a society's religious values.

2. A system in which the costs of essential medical services are covered by the state is called ____________.

(a) socialized medicine
(b) a direct-fee system
(c) universal medical coverage
(d) comprehensive medicine
(e) government driven

3. Death in Canada among young people is rare except for ________________.

(a) the mentally retarded.
(b) accidents
(c) AIDS
(d) (all of the above)
(e) (b and c above)

4. Which of the following statements is (are) accurate with respect to cigarette smoking in Canada?

(a) Quitting is difficult because nicotine is highly addictive.
(b) Smoking rates are higher in Ontario than Quebec.
(c) By 1994, only 40% of Canadians were smokers.
(d) Worldwide, more than 3 billion adults smoke.
(e) All of the above are accurate.

5. With respect to obesity in North America, which of the following statements is ***not*** accurate?

(a) In 2004, obesity rates among children rose to 8% in Canada.
(b) Women, younger men, and the poor were most likely to be obese.
(c) Fortunately, being overweight does not limit physical activity.
(d) 5.5 million adult Canadians are obese.
(e) All of the above are accurate.

6. The institutionalization of scientific medicine by the CMA resulted in ____________.

(a) expensive medical education
(b) domination of medicine by males
(c) an inadequate supply of physicians in rural areas
(d) (all of the above)
(e) (a and b only)

7. Which of the following is ***not*** among the foundations of holistic health care?

(a) an emphasis on the environment in which the person lives
(b) an emphasis on providing a professional setting for appropriate treatment
(c) an emphasis on patient responsibility
(d) an emphasis on an active approach to health rather than a reactive approach to illness

8. Which country has the highest amount of "socialized medicine"?

   (a) Canada
   (b) Japan
   (c) Sweden
   (d) United States
   (e) Belgium

9. Which of the following is ***not*** one of the basic characteristics of the recommendations of the Hall Commission that became law in Canada in 1972?

   (a) universality
   (b) partial coverage of most procedures
   (c) portability
   (d) non-profit administration

10. In 2003 in Canada, __________ % of physicians under the age of 35 were women.

    (a) 12.2
    (b) 35.6
    (c) 50.9
    (d) 62.4
    (e) 75.7

11. Which of the following theoretical paradigms in sociology utilizes concepts like "sick role" and "physician's role" to explain health behaviour?

    (a) social-conflict
    (b) symbolic-interaction
    (c) structural-functionalist
    (d) exchange
    (e) materialism

Fill in the Blank

1. Patterns of well-being and illness are rooted in the __________ __________ _________.

2. Canadians today tend to die of chronic illnesses, such as _________ and _____________.

3. ____________________________ is the study of the distribution of health and disease through a society's population.

4. Ninety-five percent of people who suffer from anorexia nervosa or bulimia are _____________ .

5. _________________are an exception to the general decline in infectious diseases during the past century.

6. _______________ medicine is an approach to health care that emphasizes prevention of illness and takes account of the whole person within the physical and social environments.

7. When patients pay directly for physicians services it is called a _______________.

8. One limitation of the sick-role concept is that it applies to acute conditions better than it does to ______________illness.

9. As long as there is a single ____________, there cannot be a two-tier health care system created.

10. Life expectancy for the world as a whole has been ____________.

Definition and Short Answer

1. It is pointed out in the text that the health of any population is shaped by important characteristics of the society as a whole. What are the four characteristics identified? Provide an example of each.

2. How have the causes of death changed in Canada over the last century in terms of which ones account for most deaths?

3. Compare the health care conditions of low-income and high-income countries.

4. What is social epidemiology? Provide two illustrations of patterns of health found using this approach.

5. How are cigarette smoking, eating disorders, obesity, and sexually transmitted diseases socially explained?

6. What are the two types of euthanasia? Discuss the Rodriguez and Latimer cases to illustrate. Relate these cases to the "ethical issues confronting death" as reviewed in the chapter.

7. What is meant by the "sick role"?

8. Describe the characteristics of holistic medicine. How do they differ from those of scientific medicine?

9. How do health care systems operate in socialist societies? Provide specific examples.

10. In what ways does the health care system of the United States differ from health care systems in other capitalist societies?

11. What are social-conflict analysts' arguments about the health care systems in the United States and Canada?

12. Discuss how symbolic-interactionists help us understand our health system and our sense of health and illness.

13. How might a two-tier health system be created in Canada?

14. What are some of the concerns associated with manipulation of DNA?

Answers to Study Questions

True-False

1. T (pp. 542-543)
2. T (p. 544)
3. T (p. 546)
4. F (p. 547)
5. T (pp. 549-550)
6. T (p. 551)
7. T (p. 555)
8. T (p. 557)
9. F (p. 560)
10. T (p. 562)

Multiple Choice

1. e (pp. 542-543)
2. c (p. 543)
3. e (p. 544)
4. a (p. 547)
5. c (p. 548)
6. d (p. 554)
7. b (p. 554)
8. c (p. 556)
9. b (p. 557)
10. c (p. 557)
11. c (pp. 558-559))

Fill in the Blank

1. organization of society (p. 542)
2. cancer and heart disease (p. 544)
3. social epidemiology (p. 544)
4. women (p.548)
5. STDs (p. 549)
6. holistic (p. 554)
7. direct-fee system (p. 556)
8. chronic (p. 559)
9. payer (p. 559)
10. rising (p. 562)

ANALYSIS AND COMMENT

Go back through the chapter and write down in the space below key points from each of the following boxes.

APPLYING SOCIOLOGY

"Masculinity: A Threat to Health?"
Key Points:

THINKING IT THROUGH

"SARS, West Nile, Mad Cow, and Bird Flu"
Key Points:

MEDIA PERSPECTIVES

"Two-Tiered Health Care: Threat, Fact, or Fiction?"
Key Points:

THINKING CRITICALLY

"The Genetic Crystal Ball: Do We Really Want to Look?"
Key Points:

____

____

____

____

____

____

SUGGESTED READINGS

Classic Sources

Elisabeth Kübler-Ross. 1969. *On Death and Dying.* New York: Macmillan.
This study of the orderly process of dying illustrates how social research can assist terminally ill patients.

Michel Foucault. 1975. *The Birth of the Clinic: An Archaeology of Medical Perception.* New York: Vintage Books.
This history of medicine emphasizes not scientific developments but the cultural forces that gradually changed how people thought about illness and health care.

Contemporary Sources

Clyde B. McCoy and James A. Inciardi. 1995. *Sex, Drugs, and the Continuing Spread of AIDS.* Los Angeles, CA: Roxbury.
The "second wave" of the AIDS epidemic is placing poor people at risk, according to this book.

Susan Sherwin. 1992. *No Longer Patient: Feminist Ethics and Health Care.* Philadelphia: Temple University Press.
This author argues that ethical issues in medicine should be resolved in a feminist context.

Peter E. S. Freund and Meredith B. McGuire. 1991. *Health, Illness, and the Social Body.* Englewood Cliffs, NJ: Prentice Hall.
This book probes many of the issues raised in this chapter

Canadian Sources

B. Singh Bolaria and Harley D. Dickenson, eds. 1994. *Sociology of Health Care in Canada.* 2nd ed. Toronto: Harcourt Brace.
This is a reader with extensive coverage of a wide variety of issues related to the Canadian medical care system. For the most part the writers are from a variety of social science disciplines

Joel Lexchin. 1984. *The Real Pushers: A Critical Analysis of the Canadian Drug Industry.* Vancouver: New Star Books.
This is a critical study of the pharmaceutical industry in Canada.

Juanne Nancarrow Clarke. 1985. *It's Cancer: The Personal Experiences of Women Who Have Received a Cancer Diagnosis.* Toronto: IPI Publishing.
This is based on qualitative interviews with women about the impact of cancer on their lives.

Juanne Nancarrow Clarke. 1996. *Health, Illness, and Medicine in Canada.* Toronto: Oxford University Press.
This is an overview of medical sociology and the sociology of health and illness from a paradigmatic perspective.

Global Sources

Kaja Finkler. 1994. *Women in Pain: Gender and Morbidity in Mexico.* Philadelphia: University of Pennsylvania Press.
Women in low-income countries face especially serious threats to health.

Bruce Kapferer. 1990. *A Celebration of Demons.* New York: Berg.
Describing rituals of exorcism in Sri Lanka, the book above explores forms of healing that defy understanding in Western terms

CHAPTER 22

Population, Urbanization, and the Environment

CHAPTER OUTLINE

I. **Demography: The Study of Population**
   - A. Fertility
   - B. Mortality
   - C. Migration
   - D. Population Growth
   - E. Population Composition

II. **History and Theory of Population Growth**
   - A. Malthusian Theory
   - B. Demographic Transition Theory
   - C. Global Population Today: A Brief Survey
     1. The Low-Growth North
     2. The High-Growth South

III. **Urbanization: The Growth of Cities**
   - A. The Evolution of Cities
     1. The First Cities
     2. Pre-industrial European Cities
     3. Industrial European Cities
   - B. The Growth of North American Cities
     1. Settlement in North America to 1850
     2. Urban Expansion
     3. The Metropolitan Era
   - C. Suburbs and Central Cities

IV. **Urbanism as a Way of Life**
   - A. Ferdinand Tönnies: *Gemeinschaft* and *Gesellschaft*
   - B. Emile Durkheim: Mechanical and Organic Solidarity
   - C. Georg Simmel: The Blasé Urbanite
   - D. The Chicago School: Robert Park and Louis Wirth
   - E. Urban Ecology
   - F. Urban Political Economy

V. **Urbanization in Poor Nations**

VI. **Environment and Society**
   - A. The Global Dimension
   - B. Technology and the Environmental Deficit
   - C. Culture: Growth and Limits
     1. The Logic of Growth
     2. The Limits to Growth
   - D. Solid Waste: The Disposable Society
   - E. Water and Air
     1. Water Supply
     2. Water Pollution

3. Air Pollution

F. Rain Forests

1. Global Warming

G. Declining Biodiversity

H. Environmental Racism

VII. Looking Ahead: Towards A Sustainable Society and World

VIII. Making the Grade

IX. Key Points

X. Key Concepts

X. Applications and Exercises

XI. MySocLab

LEARNING OBJECTIVES

- To learn the basic concepts used by demographers to study population: fertility, mortality, and migration
- To describe, compare, and contrast the Malthusian theory and the demographic transition theory
- To explain how populations differ in industrialized societies and less developed societies
- To compare and contrast the first cities of the world, pre-industrial cities in Europe, and industrial-capitalist cities in Europe
- To trace the transformation of North America into an urban civilization, from early settlement through urban expansion and the metropolitan era to urban decentralization
- To understand the relationship between suburbs and central cities
- To compare and contrast the characteristics of rural and urban life by explaining the theoretical views of Tönnies, Durkheim, Simmel, and the Chicago school
- To describe the key ideas of urban ecology and the related models of city structure
- To understand the causes of urbanization in low-income countries and the future prospects of cities in those countries
- To understand the nature of ecology and the natural environment
- To describe the impact of technology on the environment
- To comprehend the limits of growth
- To understand the impact of industrial growth on water and air

- To recognize the relationship between rain forests and global warming
- To recognize the ways of creating a sustainable world

CHAPTER REVIEW

As population increases and the urban population becomes ever more dependent on "intensive livestock operations," the environment is compromised and water pollution becomes an increasing reality.

DEMOGRAPHY: THE STUDY OF POPULATION

Demography is the study of human population, investigating the size, age, sex composition, and migration patterns of given populations. Several basic concepts central to demographic analysis are discussed in the following sections.

Fertility

Fertility is the incidence of child bearing in a society's population. A female's child-bearing years last from the beginning of menstruation to menopause. But, ***fecundity***, or potential child bearing, is greatly reduced by health and financial constraints, cultural norms, and personal choice.

A typical measurement used for fertility is the ***crude birth rate***, or the number of live births in a given year for every 1000 people in a population. In 2002-2003, 331 552 live births occurred in Canada (population 31.6 million) for a crude birth rate of 10.5. **Canada Map 22-1**, (p. 569) shows birth rates across Canada. The term "crude" relates to the fact that comparing such rates can be misleading because it doesn't focus on women of child-bearing age, and doesn't consider varying rates between racial, ethnic, and religious groups. It is, however, easy to calculate and provides a measure of a society's overall fertility. **Figure 22-1a**, (p. 570) shows that crude birth rates in industrial societies are low in the global context. In Ontario many babies who die shortly after birth are not recorded, perhaps because of the cost to purchase a birth certificate.

Mortality

Mortality is the incidence of death in a society's population. The ***crude death rate*** refers to the number of deaths in a given year for every 1000 people in a population. In 2001, Canada's crude death rate was 7.5, low by world standards.

The ***infant mortality rate*** refers to the number of deaths within the first year of life for each 1000 live births in a given year. The infant mortality rate in Canada in 2001 was 5.0. **Figure 22-1b** (p. 570) compares infant mortality rates for countries around the world. Significant differences exist between industrialized and less developed nations.

Life expectancy, or the average life span of a society's population, is negatively correlated with a society's infant mortality rate. For males born in Canada in 2001, life expectancy is 77 years of age and for females 82 years. See **Figure 22-1c** (p. 570) for global comparisons.

Migration

Migration is defined as the movement of people into and out of a specified territory. Some is involuntary, such as the historical existence of slave trading, while most is voluntary and based on various "push-pull" factors like dissatisfaction and attraction.

Movement into a territory is termed ***in-migration,*** and is measured by the number of people entering an area for every 1000 people in the total population. Movement out of an area, termed ***out-migration***, is measured by using the number of people leaving an area for every 1000 people in the population. The difference between the two figures is termed ***net-migration rate.***

Population Growth

Migration, fertility, and mortality each affect a society's population size. ***The natural growth rate*** of a society is determined by subtracting the crude death rate from the crude birth rate. This figure for Canada in 2002-2003 was 3.3 per thousand, or 0.33% annually. The rates for different world regions are presented in **Global Map 22-1** (p. 572). Industrialized regions, Europe, North America, and Oceania have very low rates, while the low-income regions—Asia, Africa and Latin America—have relatively high rates. An annual growth rate of 2.0% (as found in some Latin America countries) doubles a population in 33 years. In some parts of Africa, the growth rate is 3.0%, which doubles the population in 23 years. This calculation is called "doubling time."

Population Composition

The ***sex ratio*** refers to the number of males for every 100 females in a given population. In Canada in 2001 the sex ratio was 98.1. A more complicated descriptive device is the ***age-sex pyramid,*** which is a graphic representation of the age and sex composition of a population. **Figure 22-2**, (p. 573) presents the age-sex pyramids for Canada for the years 1971-2001. For Canada the ***baby boom*** and ***baby bust*** birth cohorts lead to a bulge gradually moving up the pyramid from 1971-1981 and 2001.

HISTORY AND THEORY OF POPULATION GROWTH

Until relatively recently in human history, societies desired high birth rates as they were needed to offset high death rates.

A critical point in world population growth occurred in about 1750 as the earth's population turned upward. By 1900 the world population was 1 billion and by 1930, 2 billion. Currently there are more than 6 billion people on earth. By 2050 the world's population is projected to reach 8 to 9 billion as it gains 74 million people each year.

Malthusian Theory

In the late eighteenth century, Thomas Malthus developed a theory of population growth in which he warned of disaster. He predicted population would increase according to a geometric progression, while food production would only increase in arithmetic progression.

Birth control he felt was immoral and abstinence unlikely.

For several reasons his projections have not been realized. First, the birth rate in Europe began to drop in the nineteenth century as children became less of an economic asset. He also underestimated human ingenuity, specifically in terms of technological applications in solving food production and population-related problems.

But his warnings still need to be taken seriously. Technology has caused problems for the environment, and population growth in the low-income nations remains very high. Even if population growth rate is reduced, any rate of increase in the long term can be dangerous.

Demographic Transition Theory

Demographic transition theory has now replaced Malthusian theory and is the thesis that population patterns are linked to a society's level of technological development**. Figure 22-3** (p. 574) illustrates four stages of technological change, and the related birth and death rates. Stage 1 is represented by the pre-industrial agrarian society with high birth rates and high death rates. Stage 2, represented by industrialization, marks the beginning of the demographic transition, with high birth rates continuing, but death rates dropping significantly. In stage 3, the fully industrialized society, birth rates begin to drop significantly and death rates remain stable and low. In Stage 4, the post-industrial economy, birth rates continue to drop and death rates remain steady.

The lower birth rate in the third stage is related to a higher standard of living, resulting in children being a greater economic burden. Smaller families are also more functional, as a higher percentage of women work outside the home. In the post-industrial society population may actually decrease.

This view provides far more optimism than Malthusian theory. It has been incorporated into modernization theory. Dependency theorists have therefore been critical of this view, as they predict continued poverty in the pre-industrial world and continued high birth rates, leaving the industrialized as "haves" and the non-industrialized as "have-nots."

Global Population Today: A Brief Survey

➢The Low-Growth North

Shortly after industrialization began, the population growth in Europe and North America peaked at 3% annually. It has been generally declining since, and since 1970 has not been above 1%. The Canadian birth rate is now below 2.1 children per woman, a point that is called ***zero population growth***, a level of reproduction that maintains population at a steady state. Nations like Canada face an underpopulation problem because we are not replacing ourselves.

➢The High-Growth South

Most of the poor societies of the southern hemisphere have reached Stage 2 of the demographic transition theory. Birth rates remain high, but mortality rates are falling dramatically because of the importation of medical technology from the industrialized nations. Part of the answer is provided in the **Thinking Globally Box** on p. 575 where declining fertility is seen as attached to elevated standing for women. Some progress on declining fertility is observable but mortality continues to decline as well.

URBANIZATION: THE GROWTH OF CITIES

For most of human history people have lived in small, nomadic groups. Urbanization, the concentration of humanity into cities, can be traced to three urban revolutions.

The Evolution of Cities

The first urban revolution occurred about 12 000 years ago with the emergence of permanent settlements.

➢The First Cities

The enabling factor for the growth of cities was a material surplus produced by advancing technology.

The first city is argued to have been Jericho, just north of the Dead Sea, coming into existence about 10 000 years ago. By 3000 B.C.E. there were several cities within the Fertile Crescent in present-day Iraq and along the Nile in Egypt, as well as China.

➢Pre-industrial European Cities

Urbanization began in Europe about 5000 years ago in Greece and later Rome. The "Dark Ages" followed the fall of Rome but by the eleventh century, cities flourished again.

➢Industrial European Cities

Increasing commerce in the Middle Ages created an affluent urban middle class or "**bourgeoisie,**" as it came to be known, which rivaled the power of the nobility. The second urban revolution was under way by about 1750. Industrial productivity caused cities to grow rapidly.

Besides population changes, the physical layouts of cities were transformed. Broad boulevards for transportation dominated the urban landscape.

Urban social life began to change as well, as crowding, impersonality, inequality, and crime became more and more characteristic of cities.

The Growth of North American Cities

Over tens of thousands of years indigenous peoples established few permanent settlements. Cities were first established by the Spanish at St. Augustine in Florida in 1565, by the English at Jamestown, Virginia in 1607, and by Champlain at Quebec in 1608. Many others were established over the next 150 years as trade expanded and more settlers arrived in the new world. By 2000 both the U.S. and Canada have more than 75% of their population living in urban areas.

➢Settlement in North America to 1850.

The quiet villages of northeastern U.S. were transformed during the seventeenth century. They became thriving towns with wide streets.

Canadian growth was later in this period. **Figure 22-4**, (p. 578) shows a map of York (Toronto) in 1793.

The first U.S. census in 1790 counted a population of 4 million, but by the time of Confederation in Canada (1867), the American population was 40 million and 20% urban, while Canada's population was 3 million, with 18% urban. **Table 22-1**, (p. 578) shows Canada's population growth and levels of urbanization from 1871 to 2001.

➢Urban Expansion

Transportation development encouraged the growth of towns and cities. B.C. joined Confederation at the promise of a transcontinental railway. By 1931, 50% of Canadians were living in cities.

➢The Metropolitan Era

As the Industrial Revolution picked up momentum, cities grew rapidly. **Table 22-2**, (p. 580) describes the growth of cities in Canada. This early growth marked the coming of the ***metropolis***, a large city that socially and economically dominates the surrounding area. Canada now has 25 CMAs (Census Metropolitan Areas), which have populations of at least 100 000 spread out among one or more municipalities with economic and commuting ties.

Suburbs and Central Cities

Since about 194,0 ***suburbs***, urban areas beyond the political boundaries of a city, have been flourishing. People began moving out from the central core to seek space to have families beyond the commotion of the city. Suburbanites tend to spend their dollars in suburban shopping malls rather than "main street" of the city.

In Canada the decay of the central core has not been so obvious, partly because of the creation of metropolitan areas where some political functions and tax dollars are shared between municipalities. In 1997, six municipalities merged to create the new city of Toronto.

When several metropolitan areas bump into each other they form a ***megalopolis***, a vast urban region containing a number of cities and their surrounding suburbs. The Boston to Washington area is an example, as is the "Golden Horseshoe" in Canada stretching from Oshawa through Toronto to St. Catharines, an area that contains one-third of Canada's population.

URBANISM AS A WAY OF LIFE

Ferdinand Tönnies: *Gemeinschaft* and *Gesellschaft*

This German sociologist of the late nineteenth century differentiated between two types of social organization. The first, ***gemeinschaft,*** refers to a type of social organization with strong solidarity based on tradition and personal relationships. It describes social settings dominated by primary groups and small villages. Its meaning is similar to Durkheim's mechanical solidarity. In contrast, ***gesellschaft*** is a type of social organization with weak social ties and individual self-interest. This represents city dwellers, and is similar to Durkheim's concept of organic solidarity.

Emile Durkheim: Mechanical and Organic Solidarity

Durkheim analyzed what held people together and he drew different conclusions than Tönnies, as he saw the bonds of interdependent specialization in a positive light, whereas Tönnies saw *gesellschaft* relationships as inferior.

Georg Simmel: The Blasé Urbanite

This German sociologist used a micro-level analysis to show how urban life shaped the behaviour and attitudes of people. He argued that city dwellers needed to be selective in what they responded to because of the social intensity of such a life. They develop then a blasé attitude out of necessity.

The Chicago School: Robert Park and Louis Wirth

The first major sociology program in the U.S. at the Chicago School saw the city as a focus for sociological interpretation of urban life. While relationships among people who occupied specialized positions might be pleasant, self-interest rather than friendship was the reason for the interaction. The differences among people in urban areas also makes them more tolerant than rural villagers. But class, race, and gender can still make a difference to people's lives. See the **Thinking About Diversity Box** (p. 583).

Urban Ecology

Urban ecology is the study of the link between the physical and social dimensions of cities. One important issue is why cities are located where they are. Another issue concerns the physical design of cities. Several models explaining urban forms exist, including the concentric zone model, the multicentred model, social area analysis, and integrated analysis.

Urban Political Economy

Urban political economy is a conflict model that suggests that the powerful make decisions about city life including moving it from the Maritime provinces to Montreal and now to Toronto.

Jane Jacobs, who lived in Toronto, suggests that sustaining economic development is not as simple as the availability of capital and political will. She felt cities should be built for people.

URBANIZATION IN POOR SOCIETIES

A third major urban revolution began in 1950 when about 25% of poor societies were urbanized. Most of the future growth will take place in less economically developed societies, where conditions in cities may not support positive lives.

ENVIRONMENT AND SOCIETY

The human species has prospered but only by placing increasing demands on the earth. ***Ecology*** is the study of the interaction of living organisms and the natural environment. Often we have compromised the natural environment, all the elements needed to sustain life, in order to meet our own interests and desires.

The Global Dimension

The ***ecosystem*** is composed of the interaction of all living organisms and their natural environment. What happens in Brazil has an impact on Canada.

Technology and the Environmental Deficit

Increasingly industrial technology has had an impact o the environment such that we are running up an ***environmental deficit***, profound and negative long-term harm to the natural environment caused by human focus on short-term material affluence. We make social decisions that have environmental effects. Presumably we can make social decisions to undo those effects.

Culture: Growth and Limits

➢The Logic of Growth

This is an optimistic view of the future where technology improves our lives. Critics of this optimism suggest that improving our lives uses up finite resources.

➢The Limits to Growth

This is a thesis that suggests that we are quickly consuming the earth's finite resources and the future holds starvation and industrial decline. Either we change the way we live, or calamity will force change upon us.

Solid Waste: The Disposable Society

North Americans generate 0.7 billion kilograms of solid waste each day. We consume a disproportionate share of the planet's natural resources, and we throw huge portions away. More efficient use and systematic recycling is in order. **Figure 22-6** (p. 588) shows the composition of household trash. More recycling is taking place but much remains to be done.

Water and Air

➢Water Supply

Water is the lifeblood of the global ecosystem, but soaring population and complex technology has reduced our global ready supply of water. Water consumption needs to be curbed.

➢Water Pollution

Not only must water be protected but also the ***quality*** of that water is a concern. Pollution, such as acid rain, can devastate forests and lakes.

➢Air Pollution

The deadly mix of automobile exhaust and coal-fired plants can plague the environment. Rich nations have reduced noxious outputs but poorer nations, relying on dirty fuels, will increasingly pollute the air. The **Media Perspectives Box** (p. 591) indicates that Canada, while on the face of it, is environmentally friendly, in reality is not.

Rain Forests

These regions of dense forestation help to cleanse the atmosphere of carbon dioxide that, we think, leads to global warming. We are, however, losing rain forests at an accelerating rate, suggesting that both global warming and declining biodiversity will compromise our future life on this planet.

Environmental Racism

It is often the poorest in a society who bear the brunt of environmental pollution.

LOOKING AHEAD: TOWARDS A SUSTAINABLE WORLD

Population growth and unabated urbanization in poorer countries leads to massive urban problems. The environmental deficit mortgages our future. The answer, perhaps, is to formulate an ***ecologically sustainable culture***, a way of life that meets the needs of the present generation without threatening the environmental legacy of future generations. This can be accomplished by controlling the world's population growth, conserving finite resources, and reducing waste. The **Thinking It Through Box** (p. 594) suggests that the task is substantial but manageable.

KEY CONCEPTS

Define each of the following concepts on a separate sheet of paper. Check the accuracy of your answers by referring to the text, as well as by referring to italicized definitions located throughout the chapter.

age-sex pyramid
crude birth rate
crude death rate
demographic transition theory
demography
ecology
ecologically sustainable culture
ecosystem
environmental deficit
environmental racism
fertility
gemeinschaft
gesellschaft
global warming
infant mortality rate
life expectancy
megalopolis
metropolis
migration
mortality
natural environment
rainforest
sex ratio
suburbs
urbanization
urban ecology
zero population growth

STUDY QUESTIONS

True-False

1. T F The infant mortality rate is the number of deaths in the first year of life for each thousand live births in a given year.

2. T F The net result of in-migration and out-migration is known as the total migration rate.

3. T F According to demographic transition theory, population growth patterns are linked to a society's level of technological development.

4. T F The 1994 Cairo Conference on Population and Development suggested that giving women more choices tends to reduce the fertility rate.

5. T F Today, more than 80% of Canadians live in urban areas.

6. T F There are now ten Census Metropolitan Areas in Canada.

7. T F A metropolis is a vast urban area containing a number of cities and their surrounding suburbs.

8. T F Ecology is the study of resources necessary to sustain life.

9. T F According to the limits of growth thesis, we are quickly consuming the earth's finite resources.

10. T F Rain forests have been found to be irrelevant to maintaining good air quality.

11. T F So lax are environmental regulations in Canada that Ontario ranks fourth among North America's polluters.

Multiple Choice

1. The incidence of childbearing in a society's population is called ____________________.

   (a) demography
   (b) fecundity
   (c) crude growth
   (d) fertility
   (e) infant occurrences

2. The first city to have ever existed is argued to be _______________.

   (a) Athens
   (b) Tikal
   (c) Rome
   (d) Cairo
   (c) Jericho

3. A vast urban region containing a number of cities and their surrounding suburbs is call a(n) ______________.

   (a) metropolis
   (b) megalopolis
   (c) census metropolitan area
   (d) borghetto
   (e) urban spread

4. The largest Census Metropolitan Area in Canada in 2001 was ______________.

   (a) Montreal
   (b) Toronto
   (c) Vancouver
   (d) Edmonton
   (e) Calgary

5. Durkheim observed that in urbanized societies, social organization was based upon __________.

   (a) sameness
   (b) *gemeinschaft*
   (c) difference.
   (d) *gesellschaft*
   (e) ritual

6. The study of the link between the physical and social dimensions of cities is called ________________.

   (a) technology
   (b) ecology
   (c) environment
   (d) growth
   (e) urban ecology

7. The logic of growth suggests ____________________.

   (a) a belief in progress
   (b) science will make our lives more rewarding
   (c) new discoveries will make life better
   (d) (all of the above)
   (e) (b and c above)

8. The average North American consumes about ________ litres of water in a lifetime.

   (a) five million
   (b) twelve million
   (c) seventeen million
   (d) twenty-six million
   (e) thirty-eight million

9. The pattern by which environmental hazards are greatest for poor people, especially minorities, is called __________________.

   (a) pattern prejudice
   (b) limited biodiversity
   (c) racism
   (d) environmental racism
   (e) sustainable culture

10. An ecologically sustainable culture depends on which of the following strategies?

   (a) controlling the world's population
   (b) development of new resources
   (c) reducing waste
   (d) a and b above
   (e) a and c above

Fill in the Blank

1. ________________ is the potential for child bearing.

2. Canadian females born in 2001 expect to live _____________ years.

3. In stage 2 of the demographic transition, ____________ rates fall dramatically.

4. A large city that socially and economically dominates the surrounding area is called a _______________.

5. The __________________ model argues that city life is defined primarily by people with power.

6. An ___________ is a system composed of interaction of all living organisms and their natural environment.

7. A profound and negative long-term harm to the natural environment caused by a focus on short-term material affluence is called ____________.

8. A rise in the earth's average temperatures due to an increasing concentration of carbon dioxide in the atmosphere is called _________________.

9. The world's population increases by _____________ annually.

10. A way of life that meets the needs of the present generation without threatening the environmental legacy of future generations is called a(n) _____________________.

Definition and Short Answer

1. What are the three basic factors that determine the size and growth rate of a population? Define each of the three concepts.

2. Differentiate between Malthusian theory and demographic transition theory as perspectives on population growth.

3. Describe the population trends in low-growth and high-growth countries.

4. Differentiate between the concepts of metropolis and megalopolis.

5. Differentiate between the population theories of the Chicago School and George Simmel.

6. What will the major urbanization patterns in the future look like?

7. What is meant by the "environmental deficit"?

8. How environmentally friendly is Canada?

9. What can be done to form an ecologically sustainable future?

Answers to Study Questions

True-False

1. T (p. 570)
2. F (p. 570)
3. T (p. 573)
4. T (p. 575)
5. T (p. 578)
6. F (p. 579)
7. F (p. 580)
8. F (p. 585)
9. T (p. 587)
10. F (p. 590)
11. T (p. 591)

Multiple Choice

1. d (p. 569)
2. e (p. 576)
3. b (p. 580)
4. b (p. 581)
5. c (p. 581)
6. e (p. 584)
7. d (pp. 587-588)
8. e (p. 589)
9. d (p. 592)
10. e (p. 593)

Fill in the Blank

1. fecundity (p. 569)
2. 82 (p. 570)
3. death (p. 574)
4. metropolis (p. 579)
5. urban political economy (p. 584)
6. ecosystem (pp. 585-586)
7. environmental deficit (p. 586)
8. global warming (p. 590)
9. 74 million (p. 593)
10. ecologically sustainable culture (p. 593)

ANALYSIS AND COMMENT

Go back through the chapter and write down in the spaces below key points from each of the following boxes.

THINKING GLOBALLY

"Empowering Women: The Key to Controlling Population Growth"
Key Points:

THINKING ABOUT DIVERSITY

"Census 2001: Minorities a Major Presence in Canada's Largest Metropolitan Areas"
Key Points:

MEDIA PERSPECTIVES

"Environmentally Friendly Canada, Eh!"
Key Points:

THINKING IT THROUGH

"Apocalypse: Will People Overwhelm the Planet?"
Key Points:

SUGGESTED READINGS

Classic Sources

Ehrlich, Paul R. 1968. *The Population Bomb.* New York: Ballantine Books.
This brief book, its reputation tarnished by some predictions that did not come to pass, nevertheless was crucial in igniting the contemporary debate over increasing global population.

Ferdinand Tönnies. 1963; orig. 1887. *Community and Society. (Gemeinschaft und Gesellschaft).* New York: Harper & Row.
This classic comparison of rural and urban social organization—widely cited but rarely read—introduced many of the themes that have shaped urban sociology ever since.

Contemporary Sources

Anthony Downs. 1994. *New Visions for Metropolitan America.* Washington, DC: Brookings Institute.
This analysis examines the core cultural and political values that underlie U.S. cities and urges us to rethink our ideas about how cities should work.

Stephanie Golden. 1992. *The Women Outside: Meaning and Myths of Homelessness.* Berkeley: University of California Press.
The author argues that our understanding of the urban problem of homelessness—especially when it involves women—is distorted by a pejorative cultural mythology about the poor.

Canadian Sources

Michael Goldberg and John Mercer. 1986. *The Myth of the North American City.* Vancouver: University of British Columbia Press.
This book provides a wide-ranging comparison of urban development in Canada and the United States.

Peter McGahan. 1982. *Urban Sociology in Canada.* Toronto: Butterworths.
This overview of research on urban communities in Canada covers a broad range of topics.

S. Dasgupta. 1987. *Rural Canada.* Toronto: Mellon.
This book examines rural social structures and change.

David K. Foot. 1996. *Boom, Bust & Echo: How to Profit From the Coming Demographic Shift.* Macfarlane, Walter & Ross.
Professor Foot asks us to consider the impact of the baby boom and bust cycles on education, real estate, the corporate world, retail sales, and leisure activities.

Global Sources

Belgin Tekce, Linda Oldham, and Frederic Shorter. 1994. *A Place to Live: Families and Health Care in a Cairo Neighbourhood.* Cairo, Egypt: American University in Cairo.
This study of an "unofficial" settlement of more than 60 000 immigrants to Cairo conveys the challenge of regulating urban growth in a poor country.

David Hakken with Barbara Andrews. 1993. *Computing Myths, Class Realities: An Ethnography of Technology and Working People in Sheffield, England.* Boulder, CO: Westview Press.
This community study examines changes within an English manufacturing city during a time of economic decline.

CHAPTER 23

Collective Behaviour and Social Movements

CHAPTER OUTLINE

I. **Studying Collective Behaviour**
II. **Localized Collectivities: Crowds**
   A. Mobs and Riots
   B. Crowds, Mobs, and Social Change
   C. Explaining Crowd Behaviour
      1. Contagion Theory
      2. Convergence Theory
   D. Emergent Norm Theory
III. **Dispersed Collectivities: Mass Behaviour**
   A. Rumour and Gossip
   B. Public Opinion and Propaganda
   C. Fashions and Fads
   D. Panic and Mass Hysteria
   E. Disasters
IV. **Social Movements**
   A. Types of Social Movements
   B. Claims Making
   C. Explaining Social Movements
      1. Deprivation Theory
      2. Mass Society Theory
      3. Structural Strain Theory
      4. Resource Mobilization Theory
      5. Culture Theory
      6. Political Economy Theory
      7. New Social Movements Theory
   D. Stages in Social Movements
   E. Social Movements and Social Change
V. **Social Movements: Looking Ahead**
VI. **Making the Grade**
VII. **Key Points**
VIII. **Key Concepts**
IX. **Applications and Exercises**
X. **MySocLab**

LEARNING OBJECTIVES

- To identify the problems associated with studying collective behaviour from a sociological perspective
- To explain the general characteristics of collectivities that distinguish them from social groups
- To distinguish among the concepts of crowds, mobs, and riots
- To describe, compare, and contrast contagion theory, convergence theory, and emergent norm theory in terms of how each orients researchers in the study of collective behaviour
- To describe, compare, and contrast the various dispersed collectivities: rumour, gossip, public opinion, propaganda, fashion, fads, panic, mass hysteria, and disasters
- To understand how crowds and mobs relate to social change
- To identify and describe the four sources of social movements in Canada
- To understand the process of making claims about the importance of a social issue
- To compare and contrast the seven theories of social movements: deprivation theory, mass society theory, structural strain theory, resource mobilization theory, culture theory, political economy theory, and new social movements theory
- To describe the four stages of a social movement
- To explain the relationship between social movements and social change

CHAPTER REVIEW

This chapter opens with a description of Elijah Harper's blockage of the ratification of the Meech Lake Accord and the confrontation of Aboriginal peoples, the Quebec police, and the Canadian Army. It is argued that a social movement was galvanized by these events.

A major focus of this chapter is ***social movements***, or organized activity that encourages or discourages social change. Social movements are one of the most important types of ***collective behaviour***, referring to activity involving a large number of people, often spontaneous, and typically in violation of established norms.

STUDYING COLLECTIVE BEHAVIOUR

Studying collective behaviour is difficult for several reasons, including its diverse nature, its complexity, and the fact that it is often ***transitory***. It is pointed out that this is perhaps true for all issues studied by sociologists, and advances in understanding have been made.

A ***collectivity*** is a large number of people who interact little if at all in the absence of well-defined and conventional norms. Two types of collectivities are (1) localized collectivities, referring to people in physical proximity to one another, and (2) dispersed collectivities, meaning people influencing one another, often from great distances.

These collectivities are distinguished from social groups on the basis of three characteristics, including limited social interaction, unclear social boundaries, and weak or unconventional norms.

LOCALIZED COLLECTIVITIES: CROWDS

A ***crowd*** is a temporary gathering of people who share a common focus of attention and whose members influence one another.

Herbert Blumer identifies four types of crowds, based in part on their level of emotional intensity. These include the ***casual*** crowd, or a loose collection of people who have little interaction; the ***conventional*** crowd, resulting from deliberate planning of an event and conforming to norms appropriate to the situation; the ***expressive*** crowd, which forms around an event that has emotional appeal; and an ***acting*** crowd, which is a crowd energetically doing something. Crowds can change from one type to another. A fifth type, or ***protest*** crowd, not identified by Blumer, is a crowd that has some political goal, like the anti-Iraq War protest crowds.

Mobs and Riots

When an acting crowd becomes violent it is classified as a ***mob***, a highly emotional crowd that pursues some violent or destructive goal. Lynching is a notorious example in the history of the United States. The freeing of the slaves, which provided Blacks with political rights and economic opportunities, was perceived by Whites as a threat. A violent crowd with no specific goal is termed a ***riot***, or a social eruption that is highly emotional, violent, and undirected. Throughout history riots have resulted from a collective expression against social injustice. In 1907, as a response to steady Chinese immigration and a sudden influx of Japanese, a riot broke out in Vancouver against Japanese individuals and their businesses. Sometimes riots can result from positive feelings, as they did in Montreal after the "Canadiens" won the Stanley Cup in 1993.

Crowds, Mobs, and Social Change

Although crowds and mobs can be seen as a threat to those in power, not all call for social change; some resist it.

Explaining Crowd Behaviour

➢Contagion Theory

One of the first social scientists to try and explain such behaviour was Gustave Le Bon, who developed ***contagion theory.*** This theory maintains that a crowd can exert a hypnotic effect on its members. Anonymity of a crowd creates a condition in which people lose their identity and personal responsibility.

Critics claim that many crowds do not take on a life of their own separate from the thoughts and actions of their members. Rather, specific structural features may be found to be responsible for the behaviour.

➢Convergence Theory

This theory leads researchers to see the motives that drive collective action as emerging prior to the formation of a crowd. The argument is that people of like-minds come together for a particular purpose and form a crowd. As opposed to contagion theory, which focuses our attention on irrational forces, this perspective provides a view of rational processes creating a crowd.

Emergent Norm Theory

Ralph Turner and Lewis Killian developed this theory and argue that, like convergence theorists, crowds are not merely irrational collectivities. However, they further suggest that patterns of behaviour emerge within the crowds themselves. Crowd behaviour is seen, in part, as a response to its members' motives, but norms emerge and guide behaviour within the development of the crowd itself.

DISPERSED COLLECTIVITIES: MASS BEHAVIOUR

Mass behaviour refers to collective behaviour among people dispersed over a wide geographic area

Rumour and Gossip

Rumour, or unsubstantiated information spread informally, often by word of mouth, is one example. Rumour has three essential characteristics, including thriving on a climate of uncertainty, being unstable, and being difficult to stop. The **Thinking Critically Box**, (p. 606) illustrates how the rumour of the death of a famous person can be self-sustaining.

Closely related to rumour is ***gossip***, or rumour about the personal affairs of others. Gossip is referred to as being more localized than rumour. It can be an effective means of social control.

Public Opinion and Propaganda

Another highly dispersed collective behaviour is ***public opinion***, widespread attitudes about controversial issues.

A public can grow larger and smaller over time as interest in a particular issue changes. The women's movement is used as an illustration. Certain categories of people are argued to have more social influence than others when it comes to shaping public opinion.

Propaganda is defined as information presented with the intention of shaping public opinion. It can be accurate or false, positive or negative. Various forms exist from politics to advertising to university lectures. **Figure 23-1** (p. 607) indicates that efforts to gauge public opinion can be influenced by the nature of the questions used to determine it.

Fashions and Fads

Fashion is defined as a social pattern favoured for a time by a large number of people. Fashions are transitory, as people like to try new lifestyles and demonstrate to others that they can monetarily afford to change. American sociologist Thorstein Veblen originated the term ***conspicuous consumption***, referring to the practice of spending money with the intention of displaying one's wealth to others.

A ***fad*** is an unconventional social pattern that is enthusiastically embraced by a large number of people for a short time. Fads are sometimes referred to as crazes. While fads are truly "passing fancies," fashions tend to reflect fundamental human values and social patterns that evolve over time.

Panic and Mass Hysteria

A ***panic*** is a form of localized collective behaviour in which people react to some stimulus with emotional, irrational, and often self-destructive behaviour. Generally, some threat provokes a panic, as in the case of a fire in a crowded theatre.

Mass hysteria is a form of dispersed collective behaviour in which people respond to a real or imagined event with irrational, frantic behaviour. The 1938 CBS radio broadcast of a dramatization of the novel *War of the Worlds*, is an example that illustrates how mass hysteria can emerge. The mass media continue to play a role as they dramatize various scenes such as the "bird flu pandemic."

Disasters

A disaster is an event, generally unexpected, that causes extensive harm to people and damage to property. Three types exist: a natural disaster such as a hurricane, a technological disaster such as the Chernobyl nuclear plant explosion, and intentional disasters, such as terrorist attacks. Disasters have an immediate effect of harm to persons and property, but also have long-term effects, especially on poorer people, such as residual toxic substances and the loss of trust in humans to care for one another. The **Applying Sociology Box** (p. 610) provides an excellent example.

SOCIAL MOVEMENTS

Social movements are a common phenomenon in the high level of diversity of industrial societies. In Canada, social movements often spring from four sources: the fact of Quebec, the disparate regions, Aboriginal peoples and their struggle for self-government, and the ethnic and racial minorities in an officially multicultural society.

The incorporation of the Charter of Rights and Freedoms into the 1982 constitution has given impetus to several movements to guarantee the rights of, for example, refugees, Immigrants, and gays who wish to marry.

Types of Social Movements

Social movements are classified by who is changed and by how much.

Four types of social movements are identified based on these dimensions. **Figure 23-2** (p. 612) presents a model of the different types identified along two dimensions. These types include ***alternative social movements***, which pursue limited change for certain individuals (planned parenthood being an example); ***redemptive social movements***, which focus on a limited number of individuals, but seek to change them radically (Alcoholics Anonymous is an example); ***reformative social movements***, which seek limited social change for the entire society (proponents and opponents of abortion are an example); and ***revolutionary social movements***, which seek basic transformations of the entire society (the Quebec separatists are an example).

Claims Making

Claims making is the process of trying to convince the public and public officials of the importance of joining a social movement to address a particular issue. It often starts with a small number of people who gradually convince others of the importance of the issue, which gradually leads to social change. The AIDS issue was identified and ultimately led to widespread research to find a cure. The issue of cellphone use in cars is addressed in the **Media Perspectives Box** (p. 613).

Explaining Social Movements

➢Deprivation Theory

Deprivation theory holds that social movements arise as people react to feeling deprived of things they consider necessary or believe they deserve.

Relative deprivation is a perceived disadvantage based on some comparison. In the middle of the nineteenth century, Alexis de Tocqueville studied the question as to why a revolution occurred in France and not in Germany in the late 1790s. What puzzled him was that social conditions in Germany were far worse than they were in France. His answer to this apparent paradox was that German peasants had known nothing but feudal servitude and thus had no basis for feeling deprived. Improving social conditions in France had raised the expectations of its people during the latter part of the eighteenth century.

Weaknesses with this perspective include its inability to explain why social movements emerge among some categories of people and not others, and the apparent circular reasoning involved in this approach. This latter point refers to the fact that deprivation is identified as a condition only if a social movement emerges. As well, the theory tells us little about what happens after the emergence of the movement.

➢Mass Society Theory

This approach, first developed by William Kornhauser, suggests people who feel isolated and insignificant within society are attracted to social movements. Using this perspective, involvement in social movements is viewed as being more personal than political.

Research provides inconsistent support for this approach and it should be recognized that it focuses heavily on psychological origins, and ignores issues of social justice.

➢Structural Strain Theory

This perspective was developed by Neil Smelser in the early 1960s. In this theory, six social conditions are identified as fostering social movements. These include (1) structural conduciveness, (2) structural strain, (3) growth and spread of an explanation, (4) precipitating factors, (5) mobilization for action, and (6) lack of social control. Each of these conditions is explained in the text, especially with respect to the pro-democracy movement in Eastern Europe.

This approach is identified as being distinctly social, rather than psychological. This theory, however, contains the same circularity of argument as found in the relative deprivation theory Further, it fails to incorporate the important variable of resources, such as the mass media, into a formula for explaining social movements and their relative success or failure.

➢Resource Mobilization Theory

Resource mobilization theory argues that social movements are unlikely to emerge, and if they do, are unlikely to succeed without necessary resources.

This theory's dual focus on discontent and available resources for the success of a social movement provides critical insight for researchers. However, critics argue that powerless segments of the population can promote successful social movements if they organize effectively and have strongly committed leaders. The Black Civil Rights movement of the 1950s and 1960s was primarily the result of Black people drawing on their skills and resources.

➢Culture Theory

This theory emphasizes the importance of cultural symbols. People begin to mobilize as they develop shared understanding. It does not yet explain how the symbols turn people against the system that creates the symbols.

➢Political Economy Theory

Social movements are seen to arise because the capitalist system fails to meet the needs of many. This explanation deals well with economic issues, but not all social movements are economically based.

➢New Social Movements Theory

This approach attempts to explain the distinctive features of more recent social movements that deal with global ecology and Aboriginal rights among others. These movements focus upon non-economic issues. The focus is national or international in scope and primarily middle-class adherents are involved. The **Summing Up Table** (p. 617) summarizes the seven theories.

Stages in Social Movements

While recognizing each social movement is unique, four stages are identified that most move through. These stages include ***emergence, coalescence, bureaucratization***, and ***decline***. **Figure 23-3** (p. 619) illustrates the stages.

A social movement declines for several reasons, including the accomplishment of its goals, poor political leadership, inability to counteract forces from the status quo, repression by officials of the society, and finally, some social movements may eventually become an accepted part of the system.

Social Movements and Social Change

Social movements either encourage or resist social change. Social change is both a cause and a consequence of social movements. Many past social movements, though taken for granted by most people today, did much to affect our social lives.

SOCIAL MOVEMENTS: LOOKING AHEAD

Social movements have always been a part of our society and are likely to continue to shape our lives. Excluded categories of people will continue to find their voice and information technology can spread that voice dramatically. As well, as suggested in the **Thinking It Through Box** (p. 620), taking a stand can make a difference. McLuhan's "global village" is upon us. Social movements can indeed become international in scope.

KEY CONCEPTS

Define each of the following concepts on a separate sheet of paper. Check the accuracy of your answers by referring to the text, as well as by referring to italicized definitions located throughout the chapter.

claims making
collective behaviour
collectivity
crowd
disaster
fad
fashion
gossip
mass behaviour
mass hysteria
mob
panic
propaganda
public opinion
relative deprivation
riot
rumour
social movement

STUDY QUESTIONS

True-False

1. T F Much collective behaviour is transitory.

2. T F A conventional crowd results from deliberate planning.

3. T F Crowds share no single political cast; some call for change and some resist it.

4. T F Rumour thrives in a climate of uncertainty.

5. T F Public opinion is solidly entrenched in society. Differences in questions to gauge it have no impact on the results.

6. T F The interesting thing about disasters is that they strike everyone in the same way, rich or poor.

7. T F According to structural-strain theory, people form social movements because of a shared concern about the inability of society to operate as they believe it should.

8. T F Political economy theory focuses on non-economic issues.

9. T F Some social movements are so successful in reaching their goals that they become part of the societal establishment.

10. T F New information technology tends to separate people from each other and reduce the possibility of joint global action.

Multiple Choice

1. Which of the following is not identified as a difficulty in researching collective behaviour using the sociological perspective?

   (a) The concept of collective behaviour is broad.
   (b) Collective behaviour is hard to explain.
   (c) Collective behaviour is often transitory.
   (d) All are identified as difficulties.

2. Herbert Blumer identified several types of crowds based on their level of emotional intensity. Which of the following is not a type of crowd identified by Blumer?

(a) casual
(b) conventional
(c) expressive
(d) acting
(e) emergent

3. A theory of crowds that claims the motives that drive collective action do not originate within a crowd, but rather precede its formation, is called _____________ theory.

(a) contagion
(b) reactive
(c) convergence
(d) subversive

4. Collective behaviour among people spread over a wide geographic area is called ___________.

(a) public opinion
(b) mass behaviour
(c) gossip
(d) frontier
(e) propaganda

5. The essential characteristics of rumour include which of the following?

(a) It thrives in a climate of uncertainty.
(b) It is unstable.
(c) It is easy to stop.
(d) (a and b above)
(e) (b and c above)

6. An unconventional social pattern that people embrace briefly but enthusiastically is called a _______________.

(a) rumour
(b) fashion
(c) fad
(d) panic
(e) (all of the above)

7. What type of social movement seeks limited social change for the entire society?

(a) revolutionary
(b) redemptive
(c) deprivation
(d) alternative
(e) reformative

8. A perceived disadvantage arising from some specific comparison is called _______________.

(a) fashion
(b) fad
(c) deprivation
(d) relative deprivation
(e) reformative

9. Which of the following is not identified as a stage in the evolution of a social movement?

(a) emergence
(b) coalescence
(c) decline
(d) realignment
(e) bureaucratization

10. Which of the following are reasons for the scope of social movements to increase?

(d) Women and other excluded categories of people gain greater political voice.
(e) Information technology spreads information quickly.
(f) Globalization unites people throughout the world.
(g) All of the above
(h) a and b above

Fill in the Blank

1. Riots, crowds, fashions, fads, panics, mass hysteria, public opinion, and social movements are all examples of __________ __________________.

2. A ______________________ is a large number of people who interact little, if at all, in the absence of well-defined and conventional norms.

3. A (n) ___________________ crowd forms around an event with emotional appeal.

4. _______________ was responsible for the belief by many in 1969 that Paul McCartney was dead.

5. Thorstein Veblen defined _____________________ ________________ as the practice of spending money with the intention of displaying one's wealth to others.

6. Running naked in public in the mid-1970s was called ______________.

7. Prior to 1980, the three major dynamic sources of social change in Canada were _____________, _______________ and _____________.

8. Using mass\society theory, social movements are viewed as _________________ as well as _________________.

9. Resource mobilization theory points out that no social movement is likely to succeed without substantial ___________.

10. According to a 1995 survey by Bibby, _________% of Canadians feel that the financial lot of the average person is getting worse.

Definition and Short Answer

1. What are three basic characteristics that distinguish collectivities from social groups?
2. Differentiate among the four types of crowds identified by Herbert Blumer.
3. Differentiate among contagion theory, convergence theory, and emergent-norm theory in terms of how each explains crowd behaviour.
4. Differentiate between the concepts rumour and gossip.
5. Describe four types of social movement.
6. Using structural strain theory, Smelser identifies six social conditions that help foster social movements. What are these social conditions?
7. What are the seven theories of social movements? Compare and contrast each of these in terms of how they help us explain social movements.
8. What are the four stages of social movements?
9. What is the relationship between social change and social movements?

Answers to Study Questions

True-False

1. T (p. 601)
2. T (p. 601)
3. T (p. 603)
4. T (p. 605)
5. F (p. 607)
6. F (p. 609)
7. T (p. 614)
8. F (p. 616)
9. T (p. 619)
10. F (p. 621)

Multiple Choice

1. d (p. 601)
2. e (pp. 601-602)
3. c (p. 604)
4. b (p. 605)
5. d (p. 605)
6. c (p. 608)
7. e (p. 611)
8. d (p. 612)
9. d (p. 618)
10. d (pp. 619-620)

Fill in the Blank

1. collective behaviour (p.600)
2. collectivity (p. 601)
3. expressive (p. 601)
4. rumour (p. 606)
5. conspicuous consumption (p. 607)
6. streaking (p. 608)
7. class relations, regional identity, bilingual/multiculturalism (p. 611)
8. personal, political (p. 614)
9. resources (p. 615)
10. 70 (p. 620)

ANALYSIS AND COMMENT

Go back through the chapter and write down in the spaces below key points from each of the following boxes.

THINKING CRIICALLY

"The Rumour Mill: Paul is Dead!"
Key Points:

APPLYING SOCIOLOGY

"A Never-Ending Disaster"
Key Points:

MEDIA PERSPECTIVES

"Car Phone Danger Too Great to Ignore"
Key Points

THINKING IT THROUGH

"Are You Willing to Take a Stand?"
Key Points

SUGGESTED READINGS

Classic Sources

Gustave Le Bon. 1960; orig. 1895. *The Crowd: A Study of the Popular Mind.* New York: Viking Press.
One of the first studies of crowd behaviour, this classic stimulated the investigation of collective behaviour and sparked debates that persist even today.

Jo Freeman, ed. 1983. *Social Movements of the Sixties and Seventies.* New York: Longman.
This collection of essays, with a useful introductory essay by the editor, investigates social movements in terms of four processes: mobilization, organization, strategy, and decline.

Contemporary Sources

Clark McPhail. 1994. *Acting Together: The Social Organization of Crowds.* Hawthorne, NY: Aldine de Gruyter.
A review of the research about crowds, this book also critiques various theoretical approaches.

James M. Jasper and Dorothy Nelkin. 1992. *The Animal Rights Crusade: The Growth of a Moral Protest.* New York: The Free Press.
Here is a survey of the organizations and politics that make up the animal protection crusade, one example of a new social movement.

Canadian Sources

S. D. Clark, J. Paul Grayson, and Linda M. Grayson. 1975. *Prophecy and Protest: Social Movements in Twentieth-Century Canada.* Toronto: Gage.
This collection of articles deals with the development of Social Gospel movements: Social Credit, the Co-operative Commonwealth Federation (CCF), unions, and Quebec nationalism.

Stanley R. Barrett. 1987. *Is God a Racist? The Right Wing in Canada.* Toronto: University of Toronto Press.
This book takes a close look at the people involved in several right-wing organizations in Canada. Based on interviews, it gives a real sense of the beliefs and commitments behind organizations such as the Western Guard and the Ku Klux Klan.

Global Sources

Hanspeter Kriesi. 1993. *Political Mobilization and Social Change: The Dutch Case in Contemporary Perspective.* Brookfield, VT: Avebury.
Many social movements have swept across Western Europe in recent decades; this book assesses what has changed and what has not.

Gao Yuan. 1987. *Born Red: A Chronicle of the Cultural Revolution.* Stanford, CA: Stanford University Press.
This personal account of one teenager's experiences during the Cultural Revolution in China between 1966 and 1969 explores the causes and consequences of a mass movement that spun out of control.

CHAPTER 24

Social Change: Traditional, Modern, and Postmodern Societies

CHAPTER OUTLINE

I. **What is Social Change?**

II. **Causes of Social Change**
- A. Culture and Change
- B. Conflict and Change
- C. Ideas and Change
- D. Demographic Change

III. **Modernity**
- A. Ferdinand Tönnies: The Loss of Community
- B. Emile Durkheim: The Division of Labour
- C. Max Weber: Rationalization
- D. Karl Marx: Capitalism

IV. **Theoretical Analysis of Modernity**
- A. Structural-Functional Theory: Modernity as Mass Society
  1. The Mass Scale of Modern Life
  2. The Ever-Expanding State
- B. Social Conflict Theory: Modernity as Class Society
  1. Capitalism
  2. Persistent Inequality
- C. Modernity and the Individual
  1. Mass Society: Problems of Identity
  2. Class Society: Problems of Powerlessness
- D. Modernity and Progress
- E. Modernity: Global Variation

V. **Postmodernity**

VI. **Looking Ahead: Modernization and our Global Future**

VII. **Making the Grade**

VIII. **Key Points**

IX. **Key Concepts**

X. **Applications And Exercises**

XI. **MySocLab**

LEARNING OBJECTIVES

- To know the four general characteristics of social change
- To explain the four sources of social change
- To understand the four general characteristics of modernization
- To compare and contrast the explanations of modernization offered by Tönnies, Durkheim, Weber, and Marx.
- To explain modernization through the structural-functional and conflict theories
- To understand how mass society and class society explanations account for social change
- To explain the relationship between modernity and progress
- To comprehend the social patterns of postmodernity in post-industrial societies
- To understand the differences between the modernization and dependency theories

CHAPTER REVIEW

The transformation of the Kaiapo culture in Brazil's Amazon rainforest and the Inuit in Northern Canada are discussed with reference to the impact of external culture through the medium of television. The Inuit people now have their own network, which can be seen by many non-Aboriginal Canadians. How, one might ask, is culture changed, and are the consequences positive or negative?

WHAT IS SOCIAL CHANGE?

Social change is the transformation of culture and social institutions over time. Four general characteristics represent the process of social change:

1. Social change happens all the time, but the rate of change varies between societies.
2. Social change is both intentional and often unplanned.
3. Social change is often controversial.
4. Social change has important and unimportant consequences.

CAUSES OF SOCIAL CHANGE

It can be argued that the causes of social change are found both inside and outside of a given society.

Culture and Change

Cultural change results from three basic processes: ***invention***, ***discovery***, and ***diffusion***.

Conflict and Change

Tension and conflict within a society can be a source of social change. Marx saw that inequality would cause conflict and lead to change.

Ideas and Change

Max Weber's thesis concerning the influence of the Protestant work ethic on industrialization in Europe reflects the influence of ideas on social change.

Demographic Change

Demographic factors are related to how societies change. Changing fertility and mortality rates along with migration can dramatically affect the nature of life in a society or globally. By 2031, for example, almost one-quarter of the Canadian population will be seniors.

MODERNITY

Modernity refers to patterns of social life linked to industrialization. ***Modernization*** is therefore the process of social change initiated by industrialization. Peter Berger has identified four general characteristics of modernization:

1. The decline of small, traditional communities,
2. The expansion of personal choice,
3. Increasing social diversity, and,
4. Future orientation and growing awareness of time.

Sociology itself began as an effort to comprehend the process of modernization.

Ferdinand Tönnies: The Loss of Community

Ferdinand Tönnies' classic book *Gemeinschaft and Gesellschaft* focuses on the process of modernization. Essentially, the Industrial Revolution weakened the fabric of community tradition and led people to associate mostly on the basis of self-interest.

One feature of *gesellschaft* is geographical mobility of a society's population. **Table 24-1**

(p. 631) shows that the rate of moving in Canada is high up to the 30-34 year category and drops thereafter.

While synthesizing various dimensions of social change, he ignored the persistence of close relationships in urban areas.

Emile Durkheim: The Division of Labour

Central to Durkheim's analysis of modernity is his view of the increasing division of labour in society. Durkheim did not see modernization as the loss of community, but rather as a change in the basis of community from ***mechanical solidarity***, or shared sentiments and likeness, to ***organic solidarity***, or community based on specialization and interdependence. These two types of solidarity are similar in meaning to Tönnies' concepts of *gemeinschaft* and *gesellschaft*.

Durkheim was more optimistic than Tönnies about the effects of modernity, yet he still feared anomie (little moral guidance) could result given the increasing internal diversity of society. The increasing rates of suicide in Canada fits with Durkheim's expectations.

Max Weber: Rationalization

For Weber, modernity meant increased rationality and a corresponding decline in tradition. In this process, bureaucracy increased as well. Compared to Tönnies and Durkheim, Weber was pessimistic and critical about the effects of modernity. He was concerned that rationalization would erode the human spirit.

Karl Marx: Capitalism

While other theorists were concentrating on social stability, Marx focused on social conflict. He agreed with Tönnies' analysis of the changing nature of community. He was concerned with Durkheim's sense of the increase in the division of labour. His position also supported Weber's view about increasing rationality and declining tradition. However, for Marx, these processes were all changes that supported the growth of capitalism, and of this he was very critical. Such changes, he suggested, would eventually lead to social revolution where egalitarian socialism would allow technology to enrich the many instead of the few. Marx, however, apparently underestimated the significant impact of centralized bureaucracy in socialist, as well as capitalist states.

THEORETICAL ANALYSIS OF MODERNITY

Modernity is a complex process involving many factors. The **Summing Up Table** (p. 634) summarizes the characteristics of traditional and modern societies along the dimensions of cultural patterns, social structure, social institutions, and social change. Seventeen different variables are used to compare the two types of societies.

Structural-Functional Theory: Modernity as Mass Society

One approach to the study of social change views modernization as a process that creates mass societies. A ***mass society*** is a society in which industrialization proceeds and bureaucracy expands while traditional social ties grow weaker. Two points are stressed. First, the expanding scale of social life leads to impersonality and cultural diversity, which overwhelms most individual's attachment to community. Second, the expanding role of the government dominates the regulation of people's lives through a complicated and impersonal bureaucratic structure. Critics suggest that the theory romanticizes the past and ignores inequality.

Social Conflict Theory: Modernity as Class Society

This approach is largely derived from Karl Marx's analysis of society. A ***class society*** is a capitalist society with pronounced social stratification.

For Marx, it was the growth of capitalism, not the Industrial Revolution that caused the growing scale of social life. He saw the profit motive promoting self-interest and greed, which broke down social ties that bound small-scale communities.

Marx saw science not only as a source for greater productivity, but also a justification for the status quo.

While many theorists argue that modernization began to break down rigid categorical distinctions, proponents of the theory of class society see a greater concentration of power and wealth occurring. Statistics Canada data, for example, has shown that the top 20% of individual earners get 46.5% of all income in Canada.

A criticism of this approach, however, is that it tends to underestimate the ways in which egalitarianism has increased in modern societies. The mass society theory and the class society theory are summarized in the **Summing Up Table** on page 637.

Modernity and the Individual

While mass society theory and the theory of class society have been discussed to this point as perspectives focusing on macro-level issues concerning patterns of change, they also offer micro-level insights into how modernity affects individuals.

➢Mass Society: Problems of Identity

According to this view, establishing an identity becomes more difficult with the social diversity, isolation, and rapid social change that modernization brings about. As Lipset suggests, identity is the quintessential Canadian issue.

David Riesman developed the term ***social character*** to mean personality patterns common to members of a society. He views pre-industrial societies as promoting ***tradition-directedness***, or rigid conformity to time-honoured ways of living. This would be associated with Tönnies' *gemeinschaft* and Durkheim's mechanical solidarity. In culturally diverse and rapidly changing industrial societies, another type of social character emerges. This type, called ***other-directedness***, refers to a receptiveness to the latest trends and fashions among people likely to imitate the behaviour of others.

➢Class Society: Problems of Powerlessness

According to this view, individual freedom is undermined by the persistence of social inequality. Herbert Marcuse, using this perspective, challenges Weber's contention that modern society is rational. For Marcuse, because society is failing to meet the basic needs of many people, it is actually irrational.

Modernity and Progress

Generally, people view modernity as progress, but this conception ignores the complexity of social change. The Kaiapo of Brazil, highlighted earlier in this chapter, illustrates this point.

While basic human rights have been advanced, the issue of individual choice and freedom versus duties and obligations towards one another is not resolved. The **Media Perspectives Box** (pp. 638-639) looks at the transformation of Canadian Society through the Information Revolution.

Modernity: Global Variation

Most societies are not either traditional or modern; they maintain characteristics of both types of society.

POSTMODERNITY

Postmodernity refers to social patterns characteristic of post-industrial societies. Postmodern theorists suggest that:

1. Modernity has failed.
2. "Progress" is fading.
3. Science does not hold the answers.
4. Cultural debates are intensifying.
5. Social institutions are changing.

Modernity has generally increased the quality of life. Is it better in Canada than elsewhere? Look at the **Thinking Critically Box** (pp. 642-643).

LOOKING AHEAD: MODERNIZATION AND OUR GLOBAL FUTURE

Modernization theory and dependency theory, discussed in great detail in Chapter 12, are seen as relevant. Modernization theorists see modernity as increasing the standard of living among the people of a society.

Dependency theory, on the other hand, suggests that social change brought on by modernization victimizes the poorer nations while further enriching the wealthy of the rich countries.

Whatever theory one supports the study of Canadian society cannot be isolated from the interconnections of global relationships since interactions between countries are technically more feasible today than discussions between neighbouring towns a century ago.

The problems of the world can be confronted with imagination, compassion, and determination.

KEY CONCEPTS

Define each of the following concepts on a separate sheet of paper. Check the accuracy of your answers by referring to the text, as well as by referring to italicized definitions located throughout the chapter.

class society
mass society
modernity
modernization
other-directedness
postmodernity
social change
social character
tradition-directedness

STUDY QUESTIONS

True-False

1. T F In any given society, all cultural elements change at the same speed.

2. T F Max Weber argued that technology and conflict are more important than ideas in transforming society.

3. T F By the year 2031, it is estimated that almost 25% of the Canadian population will be seniors.

4. T F According to Peter Berger, a characteristic of modernization is the expansion of individual choice.

5. T F According to our authors, Durkheim's view of modernity is both more complex and more positive than that of Tönnies.

6. T F Weber saw the Industrial Revolution as primarily a capitalist revolution.

7. T F According to mass society theory, geographical mobility, mass communications, and exposure to diverse ways of life erode traditional values.

8. T F Class society theory suggests that elites have essentially disappeared from capitalist societies.

9. T F Marcuse labels modern society irrational because it fails to meet the needs of so many people.

10. T F Peter C. Newman suggests that deference to authority is no longer an appropriate characterization of Canadians.

Multiple Choice

1. Which of the following are key characteristics of social change?

   (a) The rate of change varies from place to place.
   (b) Social change is always intentional.
   (c) Some social change is of only passing significance.
   (d) a and b above
   (e) a and c above

2. Canada's urban population grew from __________ % of the total population in 1871, to __________ % by 2001.

   (a) 40, 75
   (b) 22, 90
   (c) 18, 80
   (d) 10, 90
   (e) 30, 60

3. The process of social change initiated by industrialization is called __________________.

   (a) individualization
   (b) alienation
   (c) rationalization
   (d) *gesellschaft* organization
   (e) modernization

4. Critics of Tönnies' conception of modernization suggest that __________________.

   (a) he ignores the personal relationships that are maintained in modern societies
   (b) he romanticizes traditional societies
   (c) his cause-and-effect linkages are overstated
   (d) (all of the above)
   (e) (a and b above)

5. Which of the following is most accurate?

   (a) Durkheim's concept of organic solidarity refers to social bonds of mutual dependency based on specialization.
   (b) Tönnies saw societies as changing from social organization based on *gesellschaft* to social organization based on *gemeinschaft.*
   (c) Peter Berger argued that modern society offers less autonomy than is found in pre-industrial societies.
   (d) Durkheim's concept of mechanical solidarity is very similar in meaning to Tönnies' concept of *gesellschaft*.

6. Durkheim's concepts of mechanical and organic solidarity are similar to the notions of ______________________________.

(a) mass-society and class-society
(b) tradition-directedness and other directedness
(c) anomie and progress
(d) *gemeinschaft* and *gesellschaft*
(e) (none of the above)

7. Factors driven by the Industrial Revolution, such as __________, changed the relationships between individuals and how they came to know one another.

(a) a surge in population
(b) the growth of cities
(c) specialized economic activity
(d) (a and b above)
(e) (all of the above)

8. Class society theory suggests that _______________________________________.

(a) power rests primarily in the hands of those with wealth
(b) there is a persistence of inequality in capitalist societies
(c) discrimination is disappearing because of the intervention by the state
(d) (a and b above)
(e) (b and c above)

9. Mass society theory suggests that social diversity, isolation, and rapid social change make it difficult for many people to establish a coherent ___________.

(a) identity
(b) social character
(c) receptiveness
(d) modernity
(e) deference pattern

10. _______ ________ theory explains global poverty as the product of economic domination by rich, capitalist societies.

(a) modernization
(b) rationalization
(c) mass society
(d) alienation
(e) dependency

Fill in the Blank

1. ____________________ refers to the transformation of culture and social institutions over time.

2. _______________traced the roots of most social change to ideas.

3. As the power of tradition weakens, Berger says a process called __________ takes place where people have an unending series of options.

4. Despite Durkheim's optimistic view of the future, he feared that societies might become so internally diverse that they would collapse into ______.

5. Weber feared that ____________, especially in bureaucracies, would erode the human spirit.

6. In traditional societies, formal schooling is limited to _____________.

7. ______________________ is a society in which capitalism has generated pronounced social stratification.

8. A rigid conformity to time-honoured ways of living is what Riesman calls ______________.

9. ___________ refers to social patterns characteristic of post-industrial societies.

10. According to dependency theory, poor countries continuing ties with rich countries perpetuate patterns of _____________ __________.

11. Despite our improving economy, ____________% of Canadian families fall below the poverty line.

Definition and Short Answer

1. What are the four general characteristics of social change?

2. Four general domains that are involved in causing social change are identified and discussed in the text. List these and provide an example for each.

3. Peter Berger identifies four general characteristics of modern societies. What are these characteristics?

4. Differentiate among Tönnies', Durkheim's, Weber's, and Marx's perspectives of modernization.

5. What factors of modernization do theorists operating from the mass society theory focus on?

6. What factors of modernization do theorists operating from the theory of class society focus on?

7. What are the two types of social character identified by David Reisman?

8. Discuss the Information Revolution and postmodernity.

9. Evaluate our global future using the theories of modernization and dependency.

Answers to Study Guide Questions

True-False

1. F (p.627)
2. F (pp.628)
3. T (p. 628)
4. T (p. 629)
5. T (p. 631)
6. F (p. 632)
7. T (p. 633)
8. F (p. 635)
9. T (p. 638)
10. T (p. 638)

Multiple Choice

1. e (p. 627)
2. c (p.629)
3. e (p. 629)
4. e (p. 630)
5. a (pp. 629-631)
6. d (p. 631)
7. e (p. 633)
8. d (pp. 635-636)
9. a (p. 636)
10. e (p. 642)

Fill in the Blank

1. social change (p. 627)
2. Max Weber (p. 628)
3. individualization (p. 629)
4. anomie (p. 631)
5. rationalization (p. 631)
6. elites (p. 634)
7. class society (p. 635)
8. tradition directedness (p. 637)
9. postmodernity (p. 641)
10. global inequality (p. 642)
11. 15 (p. 643)

ANALYSIS AND COMMENT

Go back through the chapter and write down in the spaces below key points from each of the following boxes.

MEDIA PERSPECTIVES

"The Canadian Revolution through the Information Revolution: The Point of No Return"
Key Points:

THINKING CRITICALLY

"We're Different, Eh?"
Key Points:

SUGGESTED READINGS

Classic Sources

Emile Durkheim. 1964; orig. 1895. *The Division of Labour in Society.* New York: The Free Press.
This is the classic account of social change by one of the founders of sociology.

Derek Sayer. 1991. *Capitalism and Modernity: An Excursus on Marx and Weber.* New York: Routledge.
This recent book examines the limits of modernity and assesses the prospects for postmodernity through a review of the ideas of two seminal sociologists.

Contemporary Sources

Amitai Etzioni. 1993. *The Spirit of Community: Rights, Responsibilities, and the Communitarian Agenda.* New York: Crown Publishers.
In what might be called the "handbook of the communitarian movement," Etzioni suggests ways to fuse individual rights with collective responsibility.

Peter Berger, Brigitte Berger, and Hansfried Kellner. 1974. *The Homeless Mind: Modernization and Consciousness.* New York: Vintage Books.
Peter Berger. 1977. *Facing Up to Modernity: Excursions in Society, Politics, and Religion.* New York: Basic Books.
Highly readable, these books are filled with interesting insights about the modern world.

Canadian Sources

David Taras, Beverly Rasporich, and Eli Mandel, eds. 1993. *A Passion for Identity: An Introduction to Canadian Studies.* Scarborough, ON: Nelson.
This collection of articles by an unusually wide range of authors takes a fascinating look at the question of Canadian identity from national and regional perspectives.

Wallace Clement. 1990. "Comparative Class Analysis: Locating Canada in a North American and Nordic Context." *Canadian Review of Sociology and Anthropology* 27 (4).
This article looks at class formation in Canada in comparison with the U.S., Sweden, Norway, and Finland, taking gender into account.

S. D. Clark. 1978. *The New Urban Poor.* Toronto: McGraw-Hill Ryerson.
This very readable study deals with the experience of people, long caught in impoverished rural areas, who are finally forced to migrate to urban areas to seek a livelihood.

Ralph Matthews. 1978. *There's No Better Place Than Here: Social Change in Three Newfoundland Communities.* Toronto: Peter Martin Associates.
This book is about those "other Canadians who refuse to accept the urban dream and goal" and are left behind in the retreat from rural areas.

Global Sources

Joyce Gelb and Marian Lief Palley, eds. 1994. *Women of Japan and Korea: Continuity and Change.* Philadelphia: Temple University Press.
This collection of essays surveys the link between women's social standing and economic development in two rapidly changing Asian nations.

Wendy Griswold. 1994. *Cultures and Societies in a Changing World.* Thousand Oaks, CA: Pine Forge Press.
Close-up examinations of various countries, including Nigeria and China, illuminate this discussion of culture change.

NOTES